Academic Freedom and the Japanese Imperial University, 1868–1939

Academic Freedom and the Japanese Imperial University, 1868–1939

Byron K. Marshall

UNIVERSITY OF CALIFORNIA PRESS

Berkeley / Los Angeles / Oxford

University of California Press
Berkeley and Los Angeles, California

University of California Press, Ltd.
Oxford, England

Library of Congress Cataloging-in-Publication Data

Marshall, Byron K.
   Academic freedom and the Japanese imperial university,
1868–1939 / Byron K. Marshall.
       p.   cm.
   Includes bibliographical references and index.
   ISBN 0-520-07821-7 (cloth : alk. paper)
   1. Academic freedom—Japan—History. 2. Universities
and colleges—Japan—History. I. Title.
LC72.5.J3M37   1992
378.1′21—dc20   91-47093

Printed in the United States of America
9 8 7 6 5 4 3 2 1

The paper used in this publication meets the minimum re-
quirements of American National Standard for Information
Sciences—Permanence of Paper for Printed Library Materials,
ANSI Z39.48-1984. ∞

To the children and Vera,
by way of public apology

Contents

Tables and Figures

TABLES

FIGURES

A Note on Japanese
Names and Terms

Diacritics signifying long vowels are essential in romanizing Japanese and are indicated here with $\bar{O}$, $\bar{o}$, and $\bar{u}$, though the diacritics are dropped in well-known place names. The usage followed is usually that in the *Kenkyūsha New Japanese-English Dictionary*. Terms other than proper nouns or words in common use in English are italicized. Names of Japanese individuals are usually given in the Japanese order—family names first. See the Glossary and Biographical Notes for other potential confusions.

Acknowledgments

I wish to acknowledge at the outset how heavily this book has depended on the work and kindness of others. The most important emotional debts are stated in the dedication. Many, if not all, of the intellectual debts can be seen by a glance at the notes and List of Works Consulted. I want also to make mention here of several groups and individuals: the Joint Committee on Japanese Studies of the American Council of Learned Societies and the Social Science Research Council, the Fulbright-Hays Commission, and the Graduate School and the College of Liberal Arts of the University of Minnesota—each of which provided indispensable funding at critical times; Waseda University and Meiji University—which provided me with library privileges, study space, and other support at crucial junctures; the editors of the *Journal of Japanese Studies, History of Education Quarterly,* and *Modern Asian Studies* and the Princeton University Press—for permission to use segments of previously published materials; the archivists at Tokyo University and the librarians at the Universities of Minnesota, Michigan, Columbia, Harvard, Meiji, Waseda, and elsewhere—who facilitated the use of materials; Professors James Bartholomew, Jerry Fisher, and the late Wagatsuma Hiroshi as well as the members of the SSRC workshop led by Tetsuo Najita—who shared their thoughts on mine; Sheldon Garon, Kris Kade Troost, and other students—whose progress spurred my own; Professors Okita Tetsuya, Irimajiri Yoshinaga, Terasaki Masao and Mr. and Mrs. Ryūzōji Sho, Kobayashi Hiroshi, and Oda Masao—

whose hospitality and assistance during visits to Japan are deeply appreciated; Ted Farmer, Marius Jansen, Harry Harootunian, and the anonymous reader at the University of California Press—who made very useful comments on various drafts; Audrey Eyler, Jess Bell, Betsey Scheiner, Dore Brown, and Jan Kristiansson—who gave of their editorial expertise at various stages; Wallace Witham and Heta Toshio—who served as research assistants; and Sue Haskins and Eileen Walsh—who typed the earliest versions. In a very real sense it has been my teachers and colleagues at Stanford, Keiō, Waseda, Tōdai, Minnesota, El Colegio de México, and Meiji who over the years have helped shaped my thoughts on academe. But none of these individuals or groups, it is safe to say, can possibly have foreseen the results manifested here.

Introduction

This study of the politics of university self-governance and academic freedom in prewar Japan grew out of two distinct, yet interrelated concerns. One is the problem of understanding political conflict over higher education in modern Japan. I first became interested in this as a witness to the tumult of the late 1960s when Japanese campuses, like campuses elsewhere in the world, exploded in a multilateral struggle among faculty, students, and government authorities engaged in an often chaotic and seemingly incessant search for answers to the questions, Who governs the university? To what end? A striking aspect of this conflict was the continued relevance of older battles fought in the 1920s and 1930s. The deep-seated antagonisms of those prewar clashes between the imperial state and its institutions of higher education surfaced at regular intervals in the first three decades after World War II. Many postwar partisans—some of whom had also participated in the 1930s—as well as more detached commentators placed a good part of the blame for those conflicts on the institutional flaws and organizational concepts of the university as it was created under the authoritarian regime of the imperial past. The specters of "feudalism" and "fascism" were invoked repeatedly in the heated exchanges, and fears were expressed that the postwar U.S.-authored reforms would be swept away in a return to a time when, supposedly, the absence of constitutional guarantees for academic freedom rendered the academic dissenter defenseless against political oppression. Central to these fears was the question of whether, under the guise of dealing with political anarchy and organizational paralysis, a more highly centralized and comprehensive framework of proposed government controls would once again render the university captive to the will of the state.[1]

That has not been the result, as least as yet, but in the process of those struggles the prewar past came to form a significant part of the postwar ideological context on Japanese campuses. This Japanese past is also potentially relevant to an understanding of university-state relations elsewhere in the twentieth century—a century in which we have seen the imposition of Marxist dogma in Russian and Eastern European universities, the near destruction of higher learning in Nazi Germany, and systematic witch-hunts on U.S. campuses during the McCarthy era.

It would thus seem incumbent on the historian to attempt a clearer picture of the prewar Japanese experience. Unfortunately, much of the existing literature tends to treat the suppression of academic freedom in prewar Japan as a corollary of fascist politics, readily explained by reference to European patterns.[2] However useful the concept of fascism may be for analyzing the political regime of the late 1930s in Japan, my own preliminary assessment is that the patterns of state-university conflict were quite distinct from those in Nazi Germany. Indeed, at times there are closer parallels to the McCarthy era in the United States.[3] But it is not my intent to undertake any systematic comparisons here. Instead, by focusing tightly on the "takeoff and crash" of academic freedom in imperial Japan,[4] I hope primarily to clarify a single national experience, leaving comparative studies for the future.

A second set of related concerns has grown out of a long-term interest in the analysis of national elites and their ideologies, especially

---

1. See, for example, Ienaga, *Daigaku no jiyū no rekishi;* Ikazaki, *Daigaku no jisei;* Minobe Ryōkichi, *Kumon suru demokurashī;* Tanaka Kōtarō et al., *Daigaku no jiji;* Tsurumi, ed., *Tenkō.* The only broad study in English of this prewar experience is the unpublished 1952 doctoral dissertation by Suh Doo Soo, "The Struggle for Academic Freedom in Japan Universities Before 1945." Although Suh presented a wealth of information and a valuable bibliography, his work was completed too early to take advantage of the research and memoirs published over the last four decades, and my account here will differ considerably in interpretation as well as on a number of important factual matters.

2. Exceptions can be found in Kasza, *The State and Mass Media,* pp. 266–297; and in the all too brief comparative remarks in Richard Mitchell's two books: *Censorship in Imperial Japan,* pp. 341 ff; and *Thought Control in Prewar Japan,* pp. 189 ff.

3. For a recent treatment of McCarthyism and U.S. universities, see Schrecker, *No Ivory Tower;* also see Sanders, *Cold War on Campus.*

4. The metaphor is Nagai Michio's: see his *Higher Education in Japan.*

those ideals by which they attempt to justify their collective dominance of central institutions while at the same time asserting a measure of autonomy one from another.[5] In the case of Japan, the foundations of the major political, social, and economic institutions of the modern era were laid in the reforms of the Meiji period (1868–1912). Even though the subsequent decades saw considerable expansion, reconsideration, and alterations, the original designs remained until—and even, in many cases, after—the razing and rebuilding that took place under the U.S. Occupation reforms of 1945–1951. This Meiji structuring of an industrial society was accompanied by the rise of new specialized groups that laid their separate claims to status and authority as one of a set of national elites—a Western-style military officer corps, a bureaucratic higher civil service, a community of capitalists and industrial managers, and, as the parliamentary parties gained shares of power, a new type of political functionary.

All these modern elites have received systematic attention from able researchers. Far less systematic attention, however, has been paid to another integral segment of this set of national elites—the modern Japanese intellectual establishment. There is an abundance of excellent writing on individual thinkers as well as on the ideologies of various groupings. There is also much information available on the formal structure of the imperial universities that served as their institutional bases. But the roles played by academic intellectuals within these academic institutions and their interaction with other elites still have not received the attention their significance in the political system of imperial Japan warrants.[6]

In an attempt to explicate the interrelations between elite struggles and issues of academic freedom, this book will make use of research in two of the standard genres of historiography: institutional history and prosopography. The existing studies of the institutional dimension are the less stimulating of the two, partly because the potential for fruitful comparisons with the history of modern universities elsewhere has yet

---

5. See Marshall, *Capitalism and Nationalism in Prewar Japan.*

6. Passin, in one of the exceptions to the generalization about neglect of Japanese intellectual elites, made a tripartite division among (1) "the progressive, politically oriented intelligentsia," (2) "the established intellectuals," and (3) "the non-ideological intellectuals" (Passin, "Modernization and the Japanese Intellectual," p. 473). Abosch used the term *service intelligentsia* in his dissertation on one of the most prominent of these individuals ("Katō Hiroyuki and the Introduction of German Political Thought," Part 2, Chapter 1). There is also much valuable material in Bartholomew, *The Formation of Science in Japan;* and Fisher, "The Meirokusha."

to be fully explored. But this is also true in part because historians of universities too frequently forget that institutions are complexes of roles and expectations held by individuals and groups, and it is the changes in those roles and expectations—whether effected from within, without, or both—that are the truly significant processes of institutional change. Here those processes in the Japanese system of higher education will be explored through an examination of two successive generations of academics who, by virtue of their positions of leadership within Tokyo Imperial University, had significant influence on Japanese higher education as well as on other aspects of modern Japanese history. The main actors among this academic elite usually were also self-conscious intellectuals, some of whom have left lasting marks on modern Japanese thought. My focus, however, will be limited primarily to those ideas utilized in the defense of their own conception of the academic's role in society—their ideas about the purpose of the university and about freedom from outside intervention. Moreover, I am less interested in these ideas in the abstract than in those concrete contexts in which academic autonomy was perceived to be under direct threat.

Some further limitations in the scope of this book should also be clarified at the outset. Most of the individuals who will appear most prominently were faculty in *keizaigaku* (economics) and *hōgaku* (legal studies) at Tokyo Imperial University. Tōdai (the abbreviation by which this institution is most popularly known today) has occupied the dominant position in the modern Japanese system of higher learning since its beginnings in the nineteenth century. The Appendix contains some quantifiable evidence of just how hegemonic that position has been in the education of Japanese elites. Despite, or because of, the university's preeminent position, it was the Tōdai faculty that was consistently in the forefront of the most intense confrontations with the imperial Japanese government. Kyoto Imperial University (Kyōdai) will figure less prominently in this account, and the other less prestigious imperial universities of Tōhoku and Kyushu will play even lesser parts. The problem of the relationship between the state and such private colleges as Waseda and Keiō is left to future studies.

More conspicuous will be the relative absence of natural and applied scientists, on the one hand, and humanists, historians, and those social scientists within the faculty of letters, on the other.[7] Although collec-

7. My failure to treat these more comprehensively is perhaps excusable in part because of Bartholomew's excellent studies on the development of the natural sciences; see especially his *The Formation of Science in Japan*.

tively constituting a majority of the imperial university faculty, these academics outside the departments of law and economics most often played only incidental roles in confrontations between academe and state. Thus, center stage was left largely to the academic intellectuals whose specialties in what might anachronistically be termed the *policy sciences* or *public administration* led them to engage more routinely in the political discourse of their day—to play the role of, in Andrew Barshay's usage, "public men."[8] As can be seen in the Glossary and Biographical Notes, this cast included some of the most prominent individuals in their society. Because the list of actors is a long one, the temptation to eliminate more names for the sake of simplicity is strong, but too often twentieth-century Japanese history is depersonalized by such omissions.

Two other major lacunae will also become evident: the neglect of the role of students, which was crucial to the confrontations of the 1920s and early 1930s, and the exclusion of any extensive treatment of the inner workings of the government agencies or the motives of the political figures who led the campaigns against the universities. There already exists in English a body of work on these subjects.[9]

Because most readers outside Japanese studies will be unfamiliar with even the broad outlines of the history of universities in prewar Japan, chapter 1 is devoted to an overview of the two pivotal confrontations of 1905 and of 1939. The attempt to illuminate why these two clashes should have such different outcomes provides the structure for the narrative as a whole. Chapters 3 and 6 return to these pivotal events in greater detail after exploring the very different contexts in which each took place.

As the footnotes indicate, this account often relies for its source material on personal diaries and authorized biographies as well as on other partisan publications intended to justify and vindicate the actions of particular individuals and groups. I have attempted to utilize these sources with appropriate caution, cross-checking as much as possible, but it is precisely the partisanship in these treatments that reveals the importance of this story.

---

8. Barshay, *State and the Intellectual in Imperial Japan*, pp. 14ff.
9. Most notable are Smith, *Japan's First Student Radicals;* Mitchell, *Thought Control in Prewar Japan;* and Mitchell, *Censorship in Imperial Japan.*

1

Prologue:
The Rise and Fall of
Academic Freedom

On September 5, 1905, the Russo-Japanese War ended with the signing of a treaty concluded through the good offices of Theodore Roosevelt. Although the nineteen-month war had been costly for the Japanese in both human casualties and heavy taxes, peace was not welcomed with national jubilation. Instead, the news of the treaty touched off a week of widespread protests against the peace terms. The series of riots that began at Hibiya Park in front of the Imperial Palace in Tokyo constituted the most violent incidents of civil disorder Japanese cities had seen since the fall of the Tokugawa regime almost four decades earlier. Calm was restored only after martial law had been invoked and sword-wielding police had arrested some two thousand, wounding perhaps as many more.

Historians have seen these protests as a major turning point in modern Japanese history in which the urban masses emerged as a significant political force for the first time. Indeed, so dramatic were these mass demonstrations that historians have tended to lose sight of another type of dissent taking place simultaneously: the threat by the faculties of the imperial universities at Tokyo and Kyoto to close down the nation's only two major institutions of higher education in retaliation for the suspension of Tokyo University law professor Tomizu Hiroto. Yet this second challenge was potentially as serious a threat to the existing system of political rule as the mass demonstrations were because it came from within the network of interlocking elites that constituted Japan's political establishment and thus could not be easily handled by riot police.

The Affair of the Seven Ph.D.s

The Tomizu case—the Affair of the Seven Ph.D.s, as it was popularly known—was closely linked to the controversy over the war, having begun with faculty criticism of the prewar foreign policy of Prime Minister Katsura Tarō. By the time the confrontation between the academics and the government had reached its peak, however, the main issue was no longer the war but the more fundamental question of the legitimate place of the modern university in the structure of the Japanese state. In the words of a faculty petition of protest, "At the heart of the matter lies a great issue for our nation and the world: the independence of the university and the freedom of scholarship."[1]

Tomizu Hiroto, although singled out for the severest official punishment, was merely the most vocal of a group of professors who had long been thorns in the side of the Katsura cabinet. The original group had six core members, five of whom were Tokyo University law professors.[2] They had begun their collaboration in the summer of 1900 by joining a political movement dedicated to blocking the expansion of Russian influence on the East Asian continent. In July of that year the Russians had taken advantage of the Boxer Rebellion in China to dispatch troops into Manchuria, thereby posing new threats to Japanese interests in Korea as well as in the Chinese northeastern provinces. In response, a number of prominent Japanese, including Prince Konoe Atsumaro, the president of the House of Peers and principal of the

1. *Danshaku Yamakawa*, pp. 138–139.
2. The five Tōdai law professors were Kanai Noburu, Matsuzaki Kuranosuke, Terao Tōru, Tomii Masaaki, and Tomizu. Nakamura Shingo, a Tōdai graduate then teaching at the Peers School, was the sixth participant. Tomizu's own two-volume account, *Kaikoroku* and *Zoku kaikoroku,* published at the time, remains the most useful collection of materials on the activities of the group prior to the confrontation of 1905. These volumes are annotated with comments by others in the group and include selections from speeches, magazine articles, and newspaper accounts. Tomizu's version of the affair, while self-serving, is in substantial agreement on factual matters with other major sources; see, e.g., the authorized biography of Yamakawa Kenjirō, *Danshaku Yamakawa;* and Kawai, *Kanai Noburu.*

Peers School, formed the People's League (Kokumin Dōmeikai).[3] The league was a coalition of diverse political groups united in support of a hard-line policy vis-à-vis Russia.

Encouraged by Prince Konoe, the six professors resolved to use their prestige in the intellectual community as well as their contacts within the government to lobby for a dramatic counter to the Russian initiative. They began by drawing up a memorandum for presentation to Prime Minister Yamagata Aritomo, who granted the group a private interview in late August 1900. The six also coauthored a pamphlet, "A Transcription of the Views of Several Authorities on Foreign Affairs [*Sho taike taigai iken hikki*]," which, although circulated privately, drew some public attention from the Japanese press.

As relations with Russia grew more strained in the months that followed, the Tomizu group met frequently to consider further steps to influence foreign policy. On at least two more occasions the professors used their contacts to gain interviews with a prime minister or a foreign minister. They also continued their close association with Prince Konoe, who in mid-1903 urged them to redouble their efforts. The situation in Manchuria had again grown tense as the Russians delayed the withdrawal of their troops beyond the April deadline promised in the Sino-Russian agreement of the previous year.

By mid-1903 the group's composition had changed slightly and had increased to seven with the addition of two more Tōdai law professors.[4] At the end of May these seven decided again to appeal directly to the current prime minister. Katsura Tarō, a retired army general who had come into office two years earlier, responded immediately to their request for an interview. He assured the professors he had no intention of trading away Japanese interests in Manchuria even if the Russians were to promise a free hand in Korea in return. But the prime minister gave the group little other satisfaction. Instead, he made pointed references both to the limits of the compentency of academic theorists to judge practical diplomacy and to the impropriety of faculty members of an imperial university publicly criticizing government policy.[5] Thus, he

---

3. He is not to be confused with his son, Fumimaro, who served as prime minister during the late 1930s war in China and the attacks on academic freedom of that period.

4. Matsuzaki had withdrawn from active participation, apparently in anticipation of being named principal of the Tokyo Higher School of Commerce. Onozuka Kiheiji and Takahashi Sakue were the two additions.

5. Tomizu, *Zoku kaikoroku*, p. 278.

sounded two of the leitmotifs that would be heard again and again from government spokesmen in the confrontation that was to follow.

This was not the first time members of the group had been cautioned about airing their critical views in the public arena. Indeed, they themselves had been sufficiently conscious of the sensitivity of this issue to circulate their initial 1900 pamphlet privately to a select audience rather than address the general public. But the *Ōsaka Asahi shinbun* newspaper had subsequently published an account of their criticisms. This had led to police inquiries about the group's failure to submit advance copies of the pamphlet for official approval by the Home Ministry, a procedure required by the press laws. The foreign minister had spoken personally to one of the group who held an advisory post in the Foreign Ministry, warning that the publication of such views by someone with his official position might complicate the operations of Japanese diplomacy.[6] By the summer of 1903 the Katsura cabinet had apparently grown quite sensitive to public criticism, simultaneously engaged as it was in delicate negotiations with Russian representatives abroad and complex maneuvers within Japan's innermost political circles at home.

The discussion between Prime Minister Katsura and the professors had ended with a gentlemen's agreement to keep the content of their talk confidential from the press, but it was at this juncture, still seven months away from war with Russia, that relations between the government and the Tomizu group began seriously to deteriorate. The affair had begun as a debate within elite circles combined with a lobbying effort by these academics within the inner corridors of the political establishment. It had now intensified into a public quarrel between these imperial university faculty members and the leaders of the government that these professors, as members of the civil service, legally served.

Following the meeting with Katsura, the professors apparently still had every intention of being discreet in their lobbying efforts, keeping their most inflammatory views out of the public arena. They thus proceeded to draw up another private memorandum for distribution only to government leaders—elder statesmen Yamagata and Matsukata Masayoshi, the ministers of the army and of the navy, the prime minister and his foreign minister. But somewhere in the chain of commu-

6. The pamphlet cover said, "Not for sale [*hibaihin*]" (reprinted in Tomizu, *Kaiko-roku,* pp. 13–139). For the reaction of the police and Foreign Minister Katō Kōmei's comments to Professor Terao Tōru, see pp. 141–145.

nication the memorandum was leaked to one of the more vehemently anti-Katsura newspapers, which carried a garbled version of it in the June 16, 1903, edition. In retaliation, either Prime Minister Katsura or someone close to him provided a copy of the memorandum to the pro-Katsura paper *Tōkyō Nichinichi shinbun*. It was used as the basis of a June 21 editorial ridiculing the Tomizu group for the inadequacy of its analysis of foreign affairs and scolding the professors for meddling in matters where scholars should show greater restraint. Stung by the derisive tone of the *Tōkyō Nichinichi shinbun* story and angered by what they believed to be Katsura's breach of the confidentiality both sides had agreed on, Professor Tomizu and the others decided to reply in kind. They called in reporters from friendly papers for a press conference in which they detailed their side of the quarrel.

This feud with Prime Minister Katsura—which the press was quick to label *Shichi hakase jiken,* the "Affair of the Seven Ph.D.s"—now began directly to involve the administration of Tokyo Imperial University. The university president, Yamakawa Kenjirō, perhaps at the urging of an official from the Education Ministry, dispatched a note to the six of the group on his faculty, summoning them to a meeting the next morning at his home. Yamakawa was not in the least dovish on the Russian question; nor was he easily intimidated on matters involving the administration of the university. After listening to the six men defend themselves on the grounds that the prime minister's prior violation of confidence justified their own statements to the press, Yamakawa ended the meeting with only a mild reminder that, as imperial university professors, they should maintain a "sincere" attitude and should not allow the university's name to become too closely identified with partisan causes. He then defended the group's actions to Education Minister Kikuchi Dairoku, a former colleague in the university's College of Sciences as well as his immediate predecessor as university president. Yamakawa's few words of caution to the group may have had some effect, for shortly afterward Professor Onozuka Kiheiji and one other Tōdai faculty member withdrew from the group. Nevertheless, their places were quickly taken by two other Tōdai professors.[7]

Before the tensions between government and campus generated by this first open clash could fully subside, war with Russia broke out in

---

7. *Danshaku Yamakawa,* pp. 120–123; Tomizu, *Kaikoroku,* p. 302. Tomii Masaaki left with Onozuka; they were replaced by Okada Asatarō of the Law College and Tatebe Tongo, a pioneer sociologist in the College of Letters.

February 1904. Ironically, the coming of the war that Tomizu and his colleagues had sought so long served only to intensify hostilities between themselves and the Katsura cabinet. The professors stepped up their public speaking and writing activities, dividing their attention between encouraging nationwide support for the struggles on the battlefront and publishing detailed proposals for the terms they believed a victorious Japan should extract from Russia as part of any peace settlement. While the former might have been welcomed as a contribution to the government's own efforts at mobilizing the nation behind the war, the latter was seen not only as unsolicited advice for policy makers but also as a potentially serious complication for official diplomats.

Professor Tomizu in particular became increasingly vocal in championing a Japanese hegemony over Manchuria as well as over Korea. He was soon given the sobriquet *Dr. Baikal* in the Japanese press for his proposal that Russia be forced to withdraw permanently from all its territories east of that Siberian lake. The resulting embarrassment for the government went beyond any false hopes Professor Tomizu might have stirred up among the populace at home. His version of what Japan should insist on before a cease-fire was also receiving wide circulation in the newspapers of Russia, England, the United States, and China, where some confused these proposals with official Japanese policy. For instance, the *Chicago Daily Sun* had this to say in August 1904:

The University of Tokyo is a government institution and is administered by government officials. It is reasonable to suppose, therefore, that the article of its law professor, if not "inspired," at least has the sanction of men high in the councils of Japan. It may have been given out as a "feeler" or for the purpose of impressing Russia and securing easier compliance with terms somewhat less severe. On the other hand, it may, as the professor declares, represent the minimum which the Japanese government will consent to.[8]

Whatever the irony of this situation, it was lost on the Katsura cabinet, preoccupied as it was with the problem of Japan's dwindling war resources and the need to establish good faith with the neutral powers prior to any bargaining with the Russians. In October 1904 a new spate of stories in the international press cited a Tomizu speech predicting a revolution in China in the near future and urging the Japanese seizure of the Manchurian provinces. This prompted university president Yamakawa to caution Tomizu about the potential harm such newspaper accounts could do to Sino-Japanese relations. Tomizu

8. Quoted from the August 19, 1904, issue in Tomizu, *Zoku kaikoroku*, p. 302.

indicated his awareness of some need for discretion, and the two parted amicably. Within two weeks, however, the new education minister, Kubota Yuzuru, sent a note to President Yamakawa expressing concern about Tomizu, and Yamakawa once again called the professor to his office. This time the president was more pointed in urging that Tomizu refrain from utterances that could in any way undermine Japan's diplomatic efforts with China. Tomizu disclaimed any intention of disrupting such efforts but also objected to the implication that the Katsura cabinet could prohibit him from publicizing his personal views. Yamakawa denied any intention of interfering with Tomizu's freedom of speech yet insisted that arousing Chinese suspicions was not in the national interest. Tomizu then agreed that while he would continue to speak his mind, he would also take greater care not to offend Chinese opinion.[9]

In fact, Tomizu's pride in his growing international notoriety is quite evident from his memoirs, and he apparently had every intention of continuing to articulate in public forums his vision of Japan's national mission on the Asian continent even if it upset Chinese leaders. Most of these views also continued to be in conflict with official foreign policy. In early March 1905 a second memorandum from Education Minister Kubota to President Yamakawa was triggered by statements made by Tomizu and his colleague Professor Terao Tōru during a meeting of the Association for the Study of International Law (Kokusai Hōgaku Gakkai). On this occasion President Yamakawa limited his response to a brief note to Tomizu. But the pressures on the university administration to restrain its faculty were building steadily.

By June 1905 the Japanese victory in the naval battle in the Tsushima Straits had set the stage for a peace conference. The diplomatic situation consequently grew more delicate as the Katsura cabinet maneuvered to bring the United States into the process as a peace broker. When Tomizu brushed aside yet another caution, this one delivered verbally through one of Yamakawa's staff, the university president summoned Tomizu and other members of the group to another session in the president's office. On this occasion, the morning of June 12, the exchange between Tomizu and Yamakawa was less amicable than previously. Yamakawa spent the better part of an hour arguing the gravity of the foreign situation and the priority that national interests had to have over other considerations. Tomizu was equally insistent that the

9. Ibid., pp. 96–97.

main issue was now freedom of speech, a principle he claimed was itself essential to the national good. Rather than abandon his political voice, Tomizu offered to resign if Yamakawa thought it was best for the university, an offer Yamakawa refused to consider.[10]

The following evening Education Minister Kubota personally called on Tomizu at his home. Even though Kubota's demeanor was polite and the call was a brief one, it was clear he had come to underline the seriousness of the situation and to inform Tomizu directly of the contents of the official ministry memorandum Kubota had sent to the university administration that day. The memorandum clearly indicated the government's new resolve to take punitive steps against the dissenting professors unless they heeded previous admonitions "to be prudent in their speech and behavior as government officials . . . especially regarding current affairs at a time when matters of great consequence are involved in the war and the international situation."[11] Three days later the government attempted to drive the point home by announcing the Foreign Ministry no longer had use for the services of Professors Terao, Takahashi, or Nakamura Shingo, the three members of the Tomizu group who had held advisory posts within that ministry in addition to their teaching positions.

Despite these new signs that the government might take sterner action against them, group members refused to abandon the attack on the Katsura cabinet. Instead, Tomizu and his colleagues continued to protest the government's timid willingness to negotiate peace and its naive trust in Theodore Roosevelt as an intermediary. According to Tomizu, he was encouraged in his defiance of the government's attempt to muzzle him by signs of support coming from university colleagues outside the group. For example, Professor Hozumi Nobushige, former chairman of the law faculty and an imperial appointee to the House of Peers, came to the Tomizu residence to urge him not to even consider resigning his teaching position.[12]

Within a few weeks, however, Tomizu had finally strained the tolerance of the Katsura cabinet beyond the breaking point. This time the offense was the appearance of an article in which he openly predicted, "If the terms of a Russo-Japanese peace settlement differ greatly from these arguments we and others of the nation's men of high purpose

10. Ibid., pp. 251–253.
11. *Danshaku Yamakawa*, p. 128.
12. Tomizu, *Zoku kaikoroku*, p. 259.

[*shishi*] have set forth, then it probably will be impossible to avoid disorders within Japan."[13] On August 25, a little more than a week before the news of the Portsmouth Treaty terms was greeted by the civil disorders Tomizu had forecast, he was notified by the Education Ministry that he was suspended indefinitely from his professorship at the university.

The Triumph of the University in 1905

This flagrant assertion of power by the Katsura cabinet sent shock waves through Japan's academic community. Even the long series of warning signals from the Education Ministry had apparently not prepared the administration or faculty for such direct intervention into personnel matters long considered internal to the university. Faculty leaders at both Tōdai and Kyōdai hurriedly planned meetings to determine what their response should be. The Tōdai law faculty, meeting on August 31, voted to align itself solidly in defense of Tomizu and drafted a strongly worded statement. The same day President Yamakawa tendered his resignation in protest. Four days later the Kyōdai law faculty sent its own petition of protest to the education minister. During the first two weeks of September the riots over the Portsmouth Treaty diverted attention away from the turmoil on the campuses, but at the end of the month, as the Tomizu group persisted in taking part in the treaty controversy, Professor Nakamura Shingo was fired from the Peers School.

Because the Education Ministry had taken no action on President Yamakawa's letter of resignation, Yamakawa stayed at his post in an effort to moderate the crisis. At the end of September he agreed with faculty leaders to attempt a maneuver aimed at a compromise. The Law College met again and voted overwhelmingly in favor of having Tomizu continue to meet his classes despite his suspension by the Education Ministry. President Yamakawa then agreed to exercise the discretionary authority of his office to rehire Tomizu as a lecturer on irregular appointment, an action not normally requiring the approval of the Education Ministry. Tomizu himself also agreed to this temporary

---

13. "Kōwa no jikki hatashite haritaru ya," *Gaikō jihō* 192 (July 10, 1905): 174–179; reprinted in ibid., pp. 262–268.

solution. The Education Ministry made no public comment despite stories in the press interpreting this "curious" arrangement as a clear defeat for the government.[14]

The affair had yet to run its course, however. The defenders of university self-governance were now in full voice. In early October the nation's most prestigious scholarly journal, *Kokka gakkai zasshi,* put out a special issue on the principle of academic freedom. Almost all the contributors concluded by calling for Tomizu's full reinstatement. Similar demands by Kyoto faculty spokesmen were carried in the press.[15]

For two months the government made no further statement even though Tomizu remained at his post on campus. Then the Katsura cabinet once again went on the offensive in an attempt to break the impasse. On December 4 newspapers reported that President Yamakawa's three-month-old resignation request was being granted by the Education Ministry and that he was to be relieved of his duties. The dean of the Tōdai College of Agriculture, Matsui Naokichi, would replace Yamakawa. On the Tokyo campus the coals of defiance were quickly fanned into full flame. The law faculty met the same day to discuss closing down all classes. The majority, worried that this proposal smacked too much of "a strike like that of workers in a labor union," decided to postpone it at least until the views of the newly appointed president could be ascertained.

Nevertheless, some law professors proceeded to suspend their classes. Their colleagues in the Tomizu group as well as a former member, Professor Onozuka, expressed their intent to resign immediately in protest. So, too, did Hozumi Nobushige and his brother, Yatsuka, then serving as dean of the Law College. Dean Hozumi Yatsuka was one of several university representatives who met personally with Prime Minister Katsura during the ensuing week to press the faculty's demands: immediate reinstatement of both President Yamakawa and Professor Tomizu, the dismissal of Education Minister Kubota in public atonement for the government's transgressions, and guarantees against any such future government attacks on the independence of the university. The prime minister, in apparent recognition of the political perils of allowing the confrontation to continue, offered to sacrifice his education minister if both Yamakawa and Tomizu would also step down.[16]

14. *Danshaku Yamakawa,* pp. 129–136.
15. The arguments used to defend Tomizu and his colleagues are analyzed in chapter 3.
16. *Danshaku Yamakawa,* pp. 136–144.

The mood on the imperial university campuses was unreceptive to such a settlement, however, and Matsui responded by announcing his decision to decline the office of president. Fifteen professors from Letters and other colleges submitted their resignations. Faculty support was then mobilized through all-university meetings that generated a petition by some 190 professors and deans pledging to quit their posts unless Katsura capitulated on all three demands.

On December 11 the Katsura cabinet sounded the retreat. Kubota relinquished his portfolio as education minister, and the government began talks with university spokesmen and prominent educators such as Kikuchi Dairoku over the remaining issues. Yamakawa was apparently convinced that the best interests of the university and the nation would be served by his removing himself from the controversy. He thus helped convince the faculty to settle for the appointment of Hamao Arata, a former president who had long enjoyed the confidence of the faculty. No such quick compromise was forthcoming on the question of Tomizu's full reinstatement, but Yamakawa and the other moderate leaders were successful in postponing faculty resignations, while Tomizu remained in his temporary status as lecturer, and negotiations proceeded under the new president.

Ultimately, Katsura proved capable of avoiding complete surrender until early January 1906, when he himself resigned as prime minister, turning over the negotiations to his successor, Saionji Kinmochi. The defeat of the government was completed on January 29 when the new cabinet officially reinstated Tomizu to his professorship. As Professor Kanai Noburu wrote in his diary, "Today I went to the university and saw in the Official Gazette that Tomizu had been reappointed as of the 29th. Before beginning my lecture I announced this to the class, and together we celebrated the triumph of the university."[17]

The Purges of the 1930s

Thirty-four years later, in February 1939, Japan was once again a year and a half into a costly but still generally popular war on the Asian continent. Overt protest against the government's conduct of this war had been far more muted, limited for the most part to small pockets

17. Quoted in Kawai, *Kanai Noburu,* p. 181.

of intellectual moderates and avowed leftists who had long refused to support military adventurism in China. Yet once again authoritarian-minded government leaders were intent on silencing their critics, particularly those at Tokyo Imperial University. In contrast to the Tomizu case of 1905, which had ended in a resounding victory for the principles of academic freedom and university autonomy, the climax of a similar struggle in the 1930s was the Hiraga Purge, a final debacle after a long series of retreats from those same principles.

Strictly speaking, *Hiraga shukugaku* was a label given in the contemporary press only to the events of February 1939 when Tokyo University president Hiraga Yuzuru fired Kawai Eijirō, Hijikata Seibi, Honiden Yoshio, and three other senior professors from the Economics Department. In a broader sense, however, the purge at Tōdai had begun more than a year earlier with the ousting first of the colonial policy specialist Yanaihara Tadao and then of the economists Ōuchi Hyōe, Arisawa Hiromi, and Wakimura Yoshitarō. Unlike the Tomizu group of 1905, these men did not share a common agenda on foreign policy. Yanaihara Tadao was a Christian pacifist who publicly urged a peaceful approach to the resolution of Sino-Japanese problems. Ōuchi Hyōe and his group were Marxists who saw the war in terms of an aggressive imperialist stage of Japanese capitalism. Hijikata Seibi (the adopted son of Tomizu's colleague, law professor Hijikata Yasushi) and Honiden Yoshio were anti-Marxists who had vocally supported the war effort from the outset. Kawai Eijirō (the son-in-law of Tomizu group member Kanai Noburu) was a noted spokesman for Japanese liberalism who had previously most often sided with Hijikata in opposition to Marxism. More recently Kawai had articulately defended the right of academics to dissent from government policy.

It was economics professor Hijikata's support of the war in China in 1937 that touched off renewed disputes on the Tōdai campus. Disturbed by the lack of campus enthusiasm for the "troops in the front lines," he set out to organize a public show of university patriotism by having Tōdai students march through the streets of Tokyo to the Meiji Shrine. His plans for the demonstration drew very mixed reactions among the faculty, and the faculty representatives on the University Council proved reluctant to give official endorsement. The student leaders in Hijikata's own departmental club opposed the demonstration outright, as did Professors Yanaihara and Ōuchi.

In retaliation Hijikata attempted to engineer a departmental vote of censure against Yanaihara Tadao for his criticism of the war. Ōuchi took the problem to an ex-president of the university, Onozuka Kiheiji, himself a veteran of the 1905 Affair of the Seven Ph.D.s and still an influential faculty leader. Onozuka initially agreed to aid in Yanaihara's defense and helped gain the support of the current president, Nagayo Matarō. But when the issue became a public matter involving a Home Ministry criminal investigation into Yanaihara's writings and speeches, Onozuka and Nagayo both backed away, and Yanaihara was advised to resign for the good of the university.

The removal of Ōuchi, Wakimura, and Arisawa from the university came only weeks later. They were arrested and subsequently indicted by the Justice Ministry for alleged communist sympathies. Shortly thereafter Kawai Eijirō's spirited defense of both Yanaihara and Ōuchi incurred the wrath of government officials. In December 1938 the newly elected Tōdai president, Hiraga Yuzuru, advised Kawai to resign. Kawai refused and was then suspended from his duties. When the Economics Department threatened to resign en masse, Hiraga undertook to purge most of its senior faculty, including right-wing professor Hijikata Seibi.[18]

Interpretations of the Defeats of the 1930s

The debacle that took place in the Japanese academic world of the 1930s is sometimes explained by the seductively simple assertion that the Japanese imperial university had no tradition of academic freedom—"it did not acknowledge the principles of *Lehrfreiheit* and *Lernfreiheit*."[19] But the supposed presence of such traditions did not prevent the destruction of academic freedom in German elite universities in the 1930s. Nor did the supposed absence of a long tradition prevent the Japanese academic elite in 1905 from protecting its interests in an extended confrontation with the government during the Russo-Japanese War. Of course, it can be argued that despite the superficial similarities in the circumstances surrounding the 1905 Affair of the Seven Ph.D.s and the Hiraga Purge of 1939, the differences were

18. For sources on the Hiraga Purge, see notes to chapter 6.
19. Amano, "Continuity and Change in the Structure of Japanese Higher Education," p. 14.

fundamental. A somewhat more sophisticated explanation of these differences would stress that, whereas in 1905 Tomizu and his group were nationalists on the right side of a popular war, the 1939 economics professors were hapless liberals on the wrong side of a popular war. Thus, the former enjoyed the respect of the political elite, whereas the latter were victims of a state machinery of thought control designed originally to suppress Marxist radicalism.

But this generalization still leaves much unexplained. Why, if the issue was radicalism and dissent from a war of aggression, were conservative professors who supported the war in China from its beginnings and liberal academics who were not opposing it by 1939 purged together with the Marxists? Why was a government in 1939 willing to decimate an academic department, whereas the political elite in 1905 had backed down at the threat of faculty resignations? More important to an understanding of behavior within academe, why did the intervention of the government in 1905 stimulate a broad united front in defense of academic freedom and ultimately produce the public humiliation of an education minister, whereas in 1937–1939 the attacks were met with no such unified response? The following chapters will explore the factors underlying these contrasting events and the intervening processes within Japanese higher education that brought about such a change.

2

The Making of the Modern Academic Elite, 1868–1905

The historical antecedents of Tokyo Imperial University can be traced back well before the revolutionary changes that followed the Meiji Restoration of 1868. In terms of institutional organization and ideological orientations, however, the school—like the modern nation-state it was intended to serve—was a product of the political forces that overthrew the Tokugawa regime in 1867.

The policies of the new Meiji government toward intellectuals and higher education traced an erratic path in the first decade of the new era. This is not surprising given that power was initially in the hands of an amorphous coalition of domain lords, ambitious samurai, court nobles, and assorted heroes of the anti-Tokugawa campaigns. The ideological commitments of these men were almost as varied as their political origins. It is perhaps somewhat more surprising that they put such a high and an early priority on questions of education, grappling as they were simultaneously with restoring domestic peace, fending off foreign intervention, and searching for financial solvency. Yet educational issues were recognized as having tremendous import for all other priorities, the more so perhaps precisely because of the absence of an ideological consensus among the Meiji leaders. As a result, they paid considerable attention to the educational system from the outset, and it was to be a prime political battleground throughout the Meiji period.

The Meiji Restoration and
Higher Learning

From the beginning these leaders assumed that higher education fell within the purview of the new central government. Only a month after the formal proclamation of the new regime in 1868, three intellectuals who had the ear of the influential courtier Iwakura Tomomi were appointed to the Bureau of Internal Affairs and given a mandate to draft detailed proposals for government policy on higher education. This was the first move in what over the next three years was to be a consistently bitter and occasionally dramatic struggle among three major groupings of academic intellectuals competing for official sanction and government patronage: the Confucians who had served as an intellectual elite under the Tokugawa regime, the scholars of nativist studies (*kokugakusha*) who claimed the Restoration as their own on the basis of their long championship of the imperial throne, and the smaller number of specialists in Western learning (*yōgakusha*). These three broad intellectual movements had adherents in domain schools and private academies throughout the land, but the more politically significant clusterings were concentrated in two centers: the Tokugawa shogun's capital of Edo and the court city of Kyoto. In Edo stood both the seat of establishmentarian Confucianism (the two-hundred-year-old Shōheisho and the recently expanded Institute for Western Studies (the Yōgakusho). Two rival academies were located in Kyoto: the Confucian-oriented Gakushūin (or Kangakusho, as it was renamed) and the nativist Institute of Imperial Studies (Kōgakusho).

For the first few months after the Restoration the Meiji government was situated in Kyoto, and there the two Kyoto schools maneuvered for the coveted title of "Daigaku Ryō," the formal appellation of the long-defunct official university of the ancient Heian court created a thousand years earlier. The Institute of Imperial Studies was headed by Hirata Kanetane, the heir of the renowned Hirata Atsutane, and it was this faction that used its ties with Iwakura Tomomi to gain a lead on its rivals. These scholars submitted a proposal calling for nativist studies to be established as the "central body" of education, with Chinese Confucianism, the applied sciences of medicine, calendar making, and other branches of Western learning to be relegated to supplemental roles as "wings" (*ugo-yaku*).[1]

With the 1869 relocation of the Meiji government to the old Tokugawa headquarters in Edo (soon to be renamed "Tōkyō"), the scene shifted to the new capital. The disputes over higher education also took on more substance once a decision was required on the fate of the shogunate facilities and faculties already there. Faced with competing claims, the new government attempted to settle the question at least temporarily by creating a multifaculty university (Daigaku). The purpose was to represent all three main currents of the Japanese intellectual world in a single government agency and give it jurisdiction over education as a whole. Under the nominal headship of the prestigious Lord Yamanouchi of Tosa, the administration of this educational facility was entrusted at first to officials drawn from the southwestern domains of Tosa and Saga.

But this did not mean domination by scholars from either these or the other two powerful southwestern domains, Chōshū and Satsuma, that had spearheaded the overthrow of the Tokugawa regime. Although these four domains supplied the bulk of bureaucratic and military leaders at this stage in the Restoration, it was actually Hirata and his fellow nativist ideologues from Kyoto who won the first round in the competition for hegemony in higher learning. They dominated the faculty of the university's Daigakkō—referred to in the ordinances as *hongakkō*, or the "main school"—filling seven of the fifteen senior professorships. This numerical supremacy was justified by their special responsibility for "elucidating the national essence [*kokutai*] and exalting the imperial way [*kōdō*]."[2] Flanking the main unit of the new university on the organizational chart were two subordinate schools, both direct descendants of shogunate institutions devoted to Western learning—a medical college on the east campus (Daigaku Tōkō) and a general facility on the south campus (Daigaku Nankō).[3] This was not a decisive victory for the nativist scholars, however. They were forced to share their newfound preeminence in the Daigakkō with Confucian

1. Monbushō, *Meiji ikō,* vol. 1, pp. 87–92; Ōkubo, "Meiji shonen no gakkō mondai to Kōgakujo"; and Tōdai, *Gojūnenshi,* pp. 25ff.

2. Monbushō, *Meiji ikō,* vol. 1, pp. 95–96; Tōdai, *Gojūnenshi,* vol. 1, pp. 15–17.

3. These names accurately reflect the geography: the Daigaku campus was located on the grounds of the old Shōhei Academy—just northeast of present-day Ochanomizu Station where the Yushima Seidō still stands; the Daigaku Tōkō was due east of today's Akihabara Station; and the Nankō was due south at Hitotsubashi in Chiyodaku on the grounds of the old Yōgakusho.

academics from many backgrounds. As a result, within a few short months the nativist studies faculty and their students resumed the battle begun in Kyoto against these rivals.

The nativists chose to press the fight on two controversial issues: the selection and interpretation of key texts and the correct form of academic ceremonies. Both issues were symbolic manifestations of the deep antagonism the nativist scholars had long felt for the Confucian tradition. The problem of texts was more complex, involving, among other things, the proper rendering of passages in ancient Japanese works written in the classical Chinese language. In regard to school ceremonies, it had been the practice through much of the Tokugawa period for faculty and students at the Shōheisho (Tokugawa Confucian academy) as well as at many domain schools to perform public ceremonies and formal observances in honor of Confucius at specified times in the school calendar. Schools of nativist studies, by contrast, had developed their own distinguishing sets of prescribed rituals devoted to native Shintō deities. Their spokesmen expressed constant indignation that the Tokugawa regime permitted Shintō deities to be ignored at the Shōheisho in favor of Chinese figures. Nativists argued that this was an example of the manner in which Chinese "habits had perverted the national essence."[4]

Neither side was willing to compromise its principles. The Hirata nativist faction pushed the attack and eventually forced the new national deliberative body (the Shūgiin) to render a verdict on the dispute. After considerable debate this body reached a decision in the autumn of 1869, and Lord Matsudaira of Fukui, the university rector, informed the faculty, "The gods of learning of the imperial nation shall be celebrated, and the shrine of Confucius shall be abandoned. The *sodoku* [style of reciting] Chinese texts shall cease, and they shall be rendered in [the Japanese fashion]." There followed a list of specific texts to be used. Then, for good measure, the order explicitly added, "Those passages in Mencius' discussion of duty [*meibun*] that are not in keeping with the national essence shall not be permitted in the

---

4. See the memorial by Motoori Toyokai (grandson of the famous nativist Motoori Norinaga) quoted in Ōkubo, "Meiji shonen no gakushinmatsuri ni tsuite," p. 60. Ōkubo's is the best treatment I have seen on the dispute, making full use of what few sources exist. Details on rituals at the Shōheisho can be found in Monbushō, ed., *Nihon kyōikushi shiryō*, vol. 7, pp. 240ff; in English see Dore, *Education in Tokugawa Japan*, pp. 82–83, 91–96; a very convenient overview of the Shōheisho can also be found in Backus, "The Relationship of Confucianism to the Tokugawa Bakufu." For an extensive treatment of nativist studies (*kokugaku*), see Harootunian, *Things Seen and Unseen*.

curriculum, although it is not prohibited to study them on one's own."[5]

Thus having vanquished their old foes, the nativist scholars had reason to celebrate. But any celebration proved to be short-lived. They soon became painfully aware of the growing official patronage being given to the faculty of Western studies. These eclectic scholars of European science and culture had in the past sometimes served as useful allies in the struggle against the Confucians; but with the Confucians vanquished, Western studies at the university were now perceived as the main threat. By the summer of 1870 the university was once more in turmoil, and members of the faculty and students of nativist studies again petitioned the rector to support their claims to hegemony.[6]

The ideological hostility felt by these nativist scholars toward the Western specialists may well have been exacerbated by the fact that the majority of the latter were men who had once served the Tokugawa shogunate. Despite proscriptions on interaction between Japanese and foreigners from the seventeenth century onward, the old regime had maintained an official interest in European learning. In particular the shogunate had subsidized such practical studies as medical science and astronomy, the latter especially useful for calendar making. When Russian and British pressure on the seclusion policy intensified at the turn of the nineteenth century, an additional bureau for the translation of European writings was created. When the opening of diplomatic contact and trade was forced on the Tokugawa regime by the United States in the 1850s, the shogunate consolidated these heretofore peripheral agencies into the new Institute for Western Studies. Library holdings of Western texts and translations were expanded, and efforts were made to recruit Japanese with special skills in languages and natural sciences as well as more general knowledge of Western institutions and thought. Under this faculty a training program was launched for talented students from many backgrounds.[7]

5. Tōdai, *Gojūnenshi*, vol. 1, pp. 51–52. For a witty, yet clear explanation of the *sodoku* method of studying classical Chinese, see Dore, *Education in Tokugawa Japan*, pp. 127–136, and the illustration following p. 154. The problem with the Mencius texts doubtless had to do with that philosopher's explanation of how the Mandate of Heaven might pass from one dynasty to another—a Confucian notion at odds with the insistence on the unbroken dynastic line in Japan.

6. Tōdai, *Gojūnenshi*, pp. 75–90.

7. For materials in Japanese on the institute—known variously after 1850 as the Bansho Shirabesho, the Yōsho Shirabesho, the Yōgakusho, and the Kaiseijo—see Monbushō, ed., *Nihon Kyōikushi shiryō*, vol. 7, pp. 660ff; and Hara Heizō, "Bansho Shirabesho

By 1866 the staff and trainees at the Institute for Western Studies numbered more than sixty with a great diversity of backgrounds. Kikuchi Dairoku, for example, was the young son of a second-generation instructor at the institute. Sugi Kōji was an orphan adopted by a Nagasaki watchmaker then serving as a purveyor to the shogunate; Sugi joined the institute after studying at a private medical academy in Osaka. Nishi Amane was the eldest son of the personal physician to the lord of a small outer domain and was recruited at the institute after resigning a domain teaching post, thereby cutting his ties to his lord to study Dutch and English on his own.[8]

The institute had no monopoly on knowledge of the Western world in the 1860s, however. Satsuma was an example of a domain subsequently victorious in the anti-Tokugawa movement that had earlier launched its own program of Western studies. Nevertheless, the institute was clearly in the forefront nationally. Its library and other physical facilities were the most impressive for the times, and, more importantly, the institute offered unequaled access to study abroad in the 1860s.

Beginning in 1862 a program was launched to send promising trainees under government sponsorship to England, France, Holland, and Russia. More than half of all those Japanese who have been identified as studying abroad with shogunate or domain support in this period prior to the 1868 restoration went under the auspices of the institute. It was from this nucleus of faculty and students at the institute in the late 1860s that the first generation of the Meiji intellectual elite later emerged. Of the fourteen senior faculty on the staff between 1864 and 1866, no fewer than ten left impressive marks on post-Restoration political and intellectual worlds. Five were given significant positions in the bureaucracy in the early years of the Meiji regime, including three who were later rewarded with seats in the House of Peers in the 1890s. Among the best known were Tsuda Masamichi, for his part in the compilation of legal codes in the Ministry of Justice; Kanda Kōhei (Takahira), for his work relating to education and the drafting of the Meiji Constitution; and Nishi Amane, for his long service in the Army

---

no sōsetsu," pp. 1–42. In English there is interesting detail in Abosch, "Katō Hiroyuki"; and in Jansen, "New Materials for the Study of the Intellectual History of Nineteenth-Century Japan."

8. On Nishi, see Havens, *Nishi Amane and Modern Japanese Thought*. There is also much biographical material on some of those who studied at the institute in Fisher, "The Meirokusha." (I wish to thank Professor Fisher for sharing parts of earlier versions with me.)

Ministry. Five others were retained on the senior staff of the university's south campus, including Katō Hiroyuki, who later became a very prominent figure in educational policy making and served as president of Tōdai.[9]

The nativist scholars at the university were not alone in protesting the patronage granted to Western specialists who had formerly served the Tokugawa regime. There were many antiforeign voices in the larger political world objecting to the priority being placed on Western knowledge. But these voices were in the minority, and the Meiji government, like the Tokugawa shogunate before it, generally recognized the importance of the broadly defined cultural as well as technological knowledge from abroad. It is nevertheless somewhat surprising that these specialists who had served the shogunate were not replaced by scholars whose political loyalties were more clearly with the southwestern domains that had led in the overthrow of the Tokugawa regime. Certainly higher education was politically quite sensitive, as attested by the attention government leaders paid to the strife among the various intellectual factions in this initial phase and by continuing concern for the political aspects of Western learning over the next decades. Moreover, the uppermost echelons of the Education Ministry were staffed with men possessing Restorationist credentials—nine of the eleven ministers and three of the five vice ministers between 1868 and 1885 were from one or another of the four southwestern domains.[10]

Nevertheless, we should not assume that all Western specialists employed by the Tokugawa shogunate had strong political allegiances to one side or the other. Although some, such as Tsuda Masamichi and Nishi Amane, did follow the Tokugawa House into its temporary provincial exile in Shizuoka before being recalled to the capital by the new government, cautious neutrality or even antipathy to both sides may have been the more prevalent attitude during the Restoration struggles.[11] What is evident is that the Meiji leadership thought the talents

9. Of the other four, one died in 1871, and the subsequent careers of three are unclear. Information on these shogunate scholars has been based on the list of Kaiseijo faculty in Monbushō, ed., *Nihon kyōikushi shiryō,* vol. 7, pp. 670–673; the materials on the Kaisei Gakkō in Tōdai, *Gojūnenshi,* vol. 1, pp. 117–118, 350; entries in *Daijinmei jiten* and similar biographical sources cited in the List of Works Consulted.

10. For a convenient list, see Ijiri, ed., *Rekidai kenkanroku.*

11. In addition to Tsuda and Nishi, these included Toyama Shōichi, Nishimura Keiu, and Sugi Kōji. On Nishi's attitudes see Havens, *Nishi Amane and Modern Japanese Thought,* pp. 66–67. For a comment on the lack of political consciousness, see Tōyama, "Ishin no henkaku to kindaiteki chishikijin no tanjō."

and skills assembled at the institute too valuable a resource to be ignored even if some of these men originally had been, at best, lukewarm toward the Restoration movement. Hence the Meiji government, rather than attempt further compromise with intramural strife, responded to the protests of the nativist scholars by disbanding the university.

The closing of the first Meiji government–sponsored university in 1871 represented much more than a reorganization of the formal structure of higher education. It was simultaneously a disestablishment of the Confucian tradition and a rejection of the proprietary claims to the Restoration advanced by the nativists. The senior faculties in both these fields were dispersed, the majority to minor posts as archivists or ritualists in the imperial court or within the Shintō shrine system.[12] Hirata Kanetane and four others retired to private scholarship. Only two of the fifteen reemerged in the 1880s to serve as professors in the reconstituted Tokyo University and/or to be honored in the new system of doctoral titles created in 1888. The most important role performed by any of the group was work in the Shūshikyoku, a bureau of historical compilation that eventually developed into the Historiographical Institute (Shiryō Hensanjo) attached to Tokyo University.[13]

The nativist scholars had aspired to dominate a university devoted to their version of intellectual purity and standing at the apex of a national system of education. These hopes were shattered in 1871. Yet it was to be another decade before the newly emerging Western-oriented intellectual was to have an institutional home to rival the first university.

The Creation of Tokyo
Imperial University

Between 1871 and the early 1880s the still small corps of specialists in the new knowledge were scattered among a wide range of government bureaus and teaching facilities. Those ministries primarily

12. For a recent account of Meiji government patronage of Shintō, see Hardacre, *Shintō and the State*.

13. The two who reemerged were Kimura Masakoto (1827–1913) and Kawada Ōkō (Takesui, 1830–1896), both appointed professors of letters at Tōdai in 1886 and subsequently made recipients of the *hakushi* title. The details of the later careers of seven of the other fifteen senior men are unclear, as are those of thirteen of the twenty-seven junior faculty. But of the total of forty-two, twenty-two were put to work in historical compilation or agencies attached to the court and the Shintō shrines.

concerned with reforming Japanese institutions with the aid of European and U.S. models tended to establish separate advanced training programs. In 1871 a school of engineering was built by the Ministry of Public Works, and a law school was established by the Ministry of Justice; in 1873 a foreign language institute was attached to the Ministry of Foreign Affairs; in 1874 the Finance Ministry began offering courses in Western economic principles; and both the army and the navy created officer candidate schools in this same period. A large number of other medical, military, technical, and foreign language schools, both public and private, sprang up in the capital and the provinces. The single most important school under the jurisdiction of the Education Ministry was now the Kaisei Gakkō. This was the nucleus for Western studies that had survived the transition from the Tokugawa Institute for Western Studies to the university's south campus and then the subsequent collapse of the university in 1871. Now, however, Western studies were being pursued within a decentralized structure.

The other crucial change was that those specialists in Western studies now had to share the roles of policy advisers and classroom educators with foreigners recruited in large numbers from Europe and the United States. Considerable systematic research on the Meiji government's use of foreign advisers and functionaries is available elsewhere, and here we need take note only of two of the more significant aspects of this foreign interlude.

First, although government leaders in the 1870s saw their most immediate needs for imported knowledge in terms of military defense and public works, a sizable portion of public expenditures was allocated to long-term investment in Western humanities, social sciences, and theoretical natural sciences, apart from applied technologies. In other words, these leaders were committed to social engineering and cultural reform as well as to the importation of material technology. Along with armaments, steamships, and telegraph lines, Japanese leaders sought to acquire a working understanding of those basic principles underlying Western civilization that might be of use in reshaping Japan's economic life, legal system, political structure, and even aesthetic standards. Half the foreign advisers and teachers employed under the Ministry of Education were actually specialists in, to use today's terms, either the humanities or the social sciences.[14]

---

14. This figure is calculated from Umetani, *Oyatoi gaikokujin*, Chart 4, p. 88; see also p. 222. The Education Ministry itself, while ranking second in these years in the break-

Second, in the educational, no less than in the military or economic, sphere, the ultimate goal was always indigenization—the filling of these new roles with native Japanese. Almost immediately after coming to power the Meiji government reinstated the overseas scholarship program inherited from the Tokugawa regime. In 1869–1870 a total of 174 students were sent abroad at government expense. The heavy costs of this program, however, forced a temporary suspension, and at one point all students studying abroad were ordered home. The program resumed in 1875, but the number of students was drastically reduced, and the program was placed under the tight control of the Education Ministry, which in turn delegated considerable responsibility to the Kaisei Gakkō. Between 1875 and 1885 only 58 students, mostly of the Kaisei Gakkō, were sent abroad by the ministry.[15] It was primarily from this small pool that the late Meiji generation of the academic elite was recruited.

The decentralization and foreigner domination of higher education lasted less than a decade. By the beginning of the 1880s the reverse processes of centralization and indigenization had become quite evident. At the top of a new education pyramid slowly taking shape under the overall direction of the Ministry of Education, the Kaisei Gakkō began to reemerge as preeminent. In 1877 the school was given the name Tōkyō Daigaku (Tokyo University). A year earlier official English publications had already begun referring to the school as "the Imperial University of Tokio," although it did not officially receive the Japanese equivalent of this designation, "Teikoku Daigaku," until 1886.[16]

This newly elevated school expanded rapidly over the next dozen years, primarily by absorbing its rivals. In 1877 the College of Western Medicine, which had been functioning separately after the breakup of

---

down by ministry, consumed only 12 percent of the foreigners in terms of "person years." But if one adds to these the legal, economic, and social policy advisers in the Ministries of Justice, Finance, and Home Affairs, the percentage rises to 24 percent (calculated from Jones, "The Meiji Government and Foreign Employees," Table 2, p. 98; Table 13, p. 188).

15. Monbushō, *Gakusei hachijūnenshi*, pp. 64–67; and Tōdai, *Gojūnenshi*, vol. 1, pp. 163–181; see also Jones, "The Meiji Government and Foreign Employees," pp. 352–357; Table 7, p. 177; Table 18, p. 384.

16. Nakayama Shigeru has pointed out that foreigners were already referring to the "Imperial College of Engineering" in the 1870s and suggested the usage derived from nineteenth-century British practice (Nakayama, *Teikoku daigaku no tanjō*, pp. 25–31). Mori Arinori's biographers attribute it to him (Mori, *Mori Arinori zenshū*, vol. 2, p. 482).

the first post-Restoration university, was reamalgamated. In 1886 the Engineering School begun under the jurisdiction of the Ministry of Public Works was incorporated. In the same year the government's Bureau of Historical Compilation was brought under the control of the Education Ministry and attached to the new school. This jurisdiction extended to the nativist studies experts on traditional texts and other such potentially sensitive subjects as the history of the imperial throne. In 1890 a faculty of agriculture was created within the university to replace the Agriculture Ministry's school at Komaba. By this time the other divisions—law, letters, science, medicine, and engineering—had all been physically relocated onto a single campus in the Hongō district of Bunkyō Ward (which has remained the main campus to the present day).

The most significant step in this centralization of higher learning—as judged either by its long-term implications for the political role to be played by the Tōdai academics or from the perspective of an Education Ministry always jealous of facilities outside its own jurisdiction—was the closing of the Justice Ministry law school in 1884. *Hōgaku*, although translatable as "legal studies," was never meant merely to be the narrow study of jurisprudence for prospective lawyers. Rather, the study of law entailed the broadest study of comparative government, economic systems, and social thought—what might somewhat anachronistically be termed the *policy sciences* or *public administration*. The closing of the Justice Ministry's facility and Tokyo University's 1886 assumption of supervisory, inspection, and accreditation functions relating to private law schools in the capital were official confirmations of the dominating position Tōdai faculty members were intended to have in all these fields.[17]

Concomitant with this process of centralization was the phasing out of dependence on foreign teachers and administrators in higher education. The senior ranks of this expanding university were steadily filled with Japanese professors. Whereas foreign professors had constituted approximately two-thirds of the 1877 faculty, by 1890 the appointment of newly trained Japanese had reduced the proportion of foreign academics to one-fifth in law and letters and one-third in medicine, sciences, engineering, and agriculture combined (see Table 2-1.) These

17. Fuller detail on this process can be found in the various official histories of Tokyo University; see Tōdai, *Gojūnenshi*; and Tōdai, *Gakujutsu taikan*. For the situation regarding legal studies, there is a convenient summary in English in Spaulding, *Imperial Japan's Higher Civil Service Examinations,* pp. 70–71.

Table 2-1 *Professors at Tōdai, 1877–1890*

	1877	1881	1884	1886	1890
Law and letters					
Foreigners	23 (66%)	13 (48%)	29 (58%)	9 (15%)	19 (21%)
Japanese	12 (34%)	14 (52%)	21 (42%)	51 (85%)	70 (79%)
Sciences, medicine, engineering, agriculture					
Foreigners	4 (67%)	6 (42%)	6 (35%)	8 (38%)	13 (35%)
Japanese	2 (33%)	8 (58%)	11 (65%)	13 (62%)	24 (65%)

SOURCE: Tōdai, *Gojūnenshi,* pp. 114, 588–594, 675–684, 714–721, 835–850, 1141–1145, 1194–2000, 1264–1269, 1317–1320, 1360–1363, 1396–1399. Engineering dates are from 1885; agriculture, from 1890.

NOTE: These figures include all foreigners regardless of rank or duties but only Japanese with the title of professor (*kyōju*) or associate professor (*jokyō*) and no Japanese on irregular appointments. The ratio would thus change even more rapidly if Japanese instructors of all ranks including part-time lecturers from various government agencies were included and/or foreigners whose service elsewhere in the government made them part-time employees were excluded.

Japanese Tōdai academics constituted the core of the intellectual establishment for the remainder of the Meiji period.

The Recruitment and Training of the New Academic Elite

The men who staffed this new university in the 1880s and 1890s shared much in common in their career patterns. With some notable exceptions in the early years, they had all studied at Tōdai or its predecessor institutions—entering at an early age, acquiring a basic knowledge of foreign languages and Western learning, then being among the very few sponsored by the government for study abroad.

This pattern is well illustrated in the career of Hozumi Nobushige (1856–1926). Nobushige, the elder of the two Hozumi brothers who played such a large role in the controversies over the Meiji law codes, was only fourteen when he first attended the university's south campus in 1870. The school already had some 300 students, but he was one of 310 newly matriculated *kōshinsei,* or "tributary students," from the daimyo domains. Each domain had been invited to send at its own expense one or two students, depending on its size, with the thirteen largest being permitted three each. Hozumi had been chosen for a scholarship by his domain of Uwajima, a smallish fief on the island of Shikoku, which despite having no active part in the Meiji Restoration was nevertheless invited with all the other domains to send talented youths to the capital. Hozumi's family was not politically prominent, although the fact that the father was a teacher in the famed Motoori tradition of nativist studies may have influenced the selection. The family's emphasis on education was more clearly an important factor in the academic success of its offspring, for Yatsuka followed the same path to Tōdai a few years later.[18]

Among Hozumi Nobushige's schoolmates was Kinoshita Hiroji (1851–1910), later president of Kyoto Imperial University during the Affair of the Seven Ph.D.s. The nineteen-year-old Kinoshita, who had transferred after one year at the French-oriented Justice Ministry Law School, was from Kumamoto. This was a much larger domain than Hozumi's, but Kumamoto had been so politically polarized in the 1860s that it also had remained on the sidelines during the Restoration, thus contributing few political leaders to the new regime. Like the Hozumis, Kinoshita came from a family with scholarly aspirations, albeit one that was more orthodoxly Confucian in persuasion.

As offspring of scholarly families these three men were not typical of the early students at the university's south campus. Most of their classmates could claim only the educational background common to the great majority of young samurai males. To what extent the student body was actually chosen on the basis of intellectual potential is impossible to determine. That few of their classmates seem to have had particularly distinguished national political connections does suggest that they must either have come from locally prominent families or have demonstrated some particular scholastic aptitude.

Whichever the case, Hozumi's schoolmates were a motley array, at least as seen through the eyes of one of their future U.S. teachers. William Elliot Griffis, a Rutgers graduate who was passing through Tokyo in January 1871 on his way to teach a year in the Fukui domain, lodged briefly at the university's south campus and recorded his initial shock:

A little after three o'clock, hearing a strange noisy clatter, I ran out by the gate to see what is going on. The school is being dismissed. What a sight for a

18. For the Hozumi family background, see Minear's intellectual biography of Yatsuka, *Japanese Tradition and Western Law.*

schoolmaster! Hundreds of boys, young men, and men of older growth, all in high wooden clogs, are shuffling and scraping homeward. . . . All [are] dressed in the native costume . . . with shaven midscalps and topknots like gun hammers. . . . Each has two of the murderous-looking swords, one long and the other short, stuck in his belt.

Most of Griffis's first impressions of the school were negative. On the one hand, he may have been affected by the political tensions in the city that made bodyguards mandatory for foreigners. On the other hand, he had little respect for the staff at the south campus and was disdainful of the level of the curriculum:

It was called a "university," but its proper name was a school of languages. The Japanese had very primitive ideas concerning the fitness of men to teach. The seclusion of Japan for nearly three hundred years had its effect in producing generations of male adults who, compared to men trained in the life of modern civilization, were children. Anyone who spoke English could evidently teach it. The idea of a trained professional foreign teacher was never entertained by them. . . . The "professors" at first obtained were often ex-bartenders, soldiers, sailors, clerks, etc. When teaching, with pipe in mouth, and punctuating their instructions with oaths, or appearing in the classroom top-heavy, the Japanese concluded that such eccentricities were merely national peculiarities. As for Japanese "wives," they were in many houses, and this the native authorities never suspected was wrong, or different from the foreign customs.[19]

Griffis nonetheless did give some evidence that the school was attracting good students from the provinces. He complained during his year in Fukui that "all my best students are continually leaving Fukuwi [sic] for Yedo [sic], thus spoiling my plans."[20] The government was also attempting to attract better foreign teachers to the school. By February 1872, when Griffis arrived to take a post there, the situation had apparently changed considerably for the better. The political atmosphere in what was now the official capital had settled down, and in Griffis's view at least the moral character and teaching qualifications of the foreign faculty had improved greatly. Nevertheless, the school's main goal was to impart basic information and the all-important language skills without which there was no entry to the corpus of Western scholarship because so little was yet available in Japanese translations. For advanced study the student would have to be sent abroad.

The opportunity to study abroad with official support remained closely controlled by government regulations in the early 1870s. After

19. Griffis, *The Mikado's Empire,* p. 371.
20. Quoted in Beauchamp, *An American Teacher in Early Meiji Japan,* p. 77.

high costs and the need to systematize the government-sponsored program of overseas study had led to the recall of all students in 1873, no students were sent until the fall of 1875. New regulations promulgated that August gave Kaisei Gakkō students an advantage in the new competition: their school, the successor to the university's south campus, was placed in charge of the required qualifying examination. Eight of the eleven in the 1875 group were from this school. All of the ten selected in 1876, the last government group until 1879, were from Kaisei Gakkō, including the twenty-year-old Hozumi Nobushige and the twenty-five-year-old Kinoshita.

Kinoshita was sent to study law at the Sorbonne in Paris, while Hozumi traveled to London to enter Middle Temple to become a barrister. Although there are no published accounts of their sojourns, there is an interesting record by another member of the 1876 group. Sakurai Jōji—a Tōdai science professor, a representative to the University Council during the Affair of the Seven Ph.D.s., and eventually the Tōdai president—recalled vividly the excitement that sustained him during the twenty-five-day ocean voyage from Yokohama to San Francisco, the transcontinental rail trip to the Atlantic coast to sail for London, and the five-year stay in England:

It was, however, not the scientific training alone that I received in England, [*sic*] was a period in which some of the greatest and most illustrious men and, also, of women were to be met with in almost every field of human activity. . . . Having had the rare fortune of being in England at such a glorious time, I could not and would not confine myself to scientific studies alone, but wishing to look upon England with more widely opened eyes, I studied something of English History, of English Literature, of English Art, and even, of English drama.[21]

Hozumi Nobushige, after almost four years in London, moved to the University of Berlin for two additional years of foreign study. In 1881, then twenty-five years old, he returned to Japan and was immediately assigned to a post in the bureaucracy. This was mandatory at that time for those who had received government support abroad. His first post was in a section of the Education Ministry charged with the supervision of all private law schools in Japan, but he was also asked to lecture at his alma mater, Tōdai, as was common in this period of few

21. Sakurai, *Omoide no kazukazu*, pp. 345–346. For information on individuals sent abroad in the 1860s, see Ogata Hiroyasu, "Seiyō kyōiku inyū no hōhō," especially Tables 1 and 2, p. 15; Hara Heizō, "Tokugawa bakufu no Eikoku ryūgakusei"; Hara Heizō, "Wagakuni saisho no Rokoku ryūgakusei ni tsuite"; and Watanabe Shūjirō, "Bakumatsu jidai oyobi Meiji shonen no yōkō ryūgakusei."

Western-trained Japanese. The following year, despite his young age, Hozumi was appointed both full professor and head of the Tōdai law faculty. Much of the teaching at this time was still being done by either foreigners or part-time lecturers who, as Hozumi had done the previous year, held other posts in the government bureaucracy.

Among the latter were two of his schoolmates—Kinoshita Hiroji, who joined the faculty in 1883, and Hatoyama Kazuo, who became a full-time member in 1886. Hatoyama (1856–1911), who eventually relieved Hozumi Nobushige of some of his burdens as head of the law faculty, had been one of those Kaisei Gakkō students chosen to study U.S. law in 1875. He had attended Columbia University and then had earned a doctorate at Yale. After his return to Japan he had served as president of the Tokyo Association of Lawyers and as head of the Tokyo Municipal Assembly.[22]

The Tōdai law faculty continued to expand steadily throughout the 1890s, but the same pattern persisted. Almost all the new recruits were Tōdai's own students who had been selected for postgraduate work in the West before returning to join the faculty themselves. This was true of six of the eight Tōdai law professors active at one time or another in the Tomizu group. Tomizu himself was the son of a samurai of the Kanazawa domain, one of the few professors from a domain that had taken part in the overthrow of the Tokugawa shogun. After taking his degree at Tōdai in 1886, Tomizu attended Hozumi Nobushige's alma mater, Middle Temple.

Tomii Masaaki (1858–1935), by contrast, was the son of a Tokugawa shogunal official. He had attended the Tokyo Foreign Language School, rather than the Kaisei Gakkō, but in 1877 had been chosen to study at the University of Lyons. After six years abroad, Tomii returned to take a post in the Justice Ministry and serve as part-time lecturer at Tōdai. In 1885, at twenty-seven, he was assigned to the school full time and was promoted to professor. Terao Tōru (1858–1925) was the other member of the Tomizu group who was not an alumnus of Tōdai. He had come to the law faculty via the Justice Ministry law school and service in the Yokohama courts.

Kanai Noburu (1865–1933), another politically active member of the law faculty, was born to a rural official with quasi-samurai standing in present-day Shizuoka Prefecture, a district then governed by a high-

22. On Hatoyama's career, see Hatoyama, ed., *Hatoyama no isshō*.

ranking retainer of the Tokugawa house. Kanai's father is said to have
been a man with a knowledge of the Chinese classics and some political
ambition, and when the Restoration destroyed the Tokugawa shogunate, he set off for the capital to seek a position with the new regime.
He found a minor post in the new Education Ministry. Thanks to a
connection in the Shrines Office, he was able to house his family in a
tenement taken over by the government to shelter the influx of Shintō
priests who helped crowd the city. The mother died a few years later,
but the elder Kanai kept his son at home until he was ten, tutoring him
in classical Chinese as well as Japanese. Evidently recognizing that the
path to success lay through the mastery of Western languages, he enrolled Noboru in a private academy and subsequently at the English
Language School in Hitotsubashi, which soon became the official pre-
paratory school for Tokyo University. The cost proved a considerable
burden despite the government subsidy to students at this school, and
the young Kanai was forced to drop out in 1879 to return to his
hometown. Family friends raised funds to send him back to school in
Tokyo, but his father's illness and heavy debts continually threatened to
end Kanai's education. It was finally assured, however, by a financially
advantageous marriage to the daughter of the Shrines official who had
previously befriended the family.

Kanai's higher education began at the Tōdai College of Letters,
which when he entered in 1881 housed the courses of his major interest, political economics. Over the next four years he maintained a very
respectable grade average of nearly 90 percent and was accepted to
graduate school in 1885. The following year he received a coveted
government fellowship to study political economics and economic history in Germany. There, as was common among German students, he
spent his three years shifting from one university to another—first
Heidelberg, then Halle, and finally Berlin, where Hozumi Nobushige
had studied seven years before. Kanai rounded out his sojourn abroad
with a year in a second country, England—a pattern not uncommon for
the holders of such fellowships. By the time he returned in 1890 at the
age of twenty-five, the formal study of economics had been transferred
to the College of Law. There a full professorship awaited him. He later
became chairman of the first Economics Department at a Japanese
imperial university.[23]

Onozuka Kiheiji (1871–1944), the son of a small-town merchant

23. Kawai, *Kanai Noburu*.

who had married the daughter of a village headman, was the youngest of the Tomizu group members. He also represented the first of a new academic generation, for his secondary education had taken place at the First Higher School. The higher schools, five in the original plan, had been designed in 1886 as a new type of public school whose mission was to routinize the selection and preparation of university students. Because of the extensive prerequisites, the stiff entrance examination, the relatively high (compared to other public schools) tuition fees, and the demanding curriculum as well as the assurance of entry into the imperial university on graduation, these higher schools ultimately became the new proving ground for Japan's future bureaucratic and academic elites.[24]

The pattern of recruitment established in these early years remained the routine throughout the next half century in the Tōdai College of Law: from elite higher school to Tōdai College of Law, from graduating class to graduate assistantship, advanced training in European or U.S. universities, then back to Tōdai as College of Law professors—all under the patronage of the professors these students would eventually succeed. The pattern was similar in the other divisions of the university. Among the early appointees to the College of Sciences was its first dean, Kikuchi Dairoku. Only twenty-two years old when promoted in 1877, he had studied as a young boy at the Tokugawa Institute for Western Studies and had completed two sojourns as a government-sponsored student in Europe.[25]

The College of Letters actually comprised two quite disparate groups in the 1886–1890 period.[26] But this proved a temporary phenomenon. The seven Japanese who served as professors of Western philosophy, history, psychology, literature, and sociology were, like their colleagues in law or sciences, men in their midtwenties to early thirties who had been among the earliest students sent abroad by the government. The other thirteen, all appointed after 1881, were older specialists in Chinese or Japanese studies who had received their educations prior to the Restoration in a variety of settings, including the

24. Nanbara et al., *Onozuka Kiheiji*. For details on the organization and educational climate of the Meiji higher schools (*kōtō gakkō*), see Roden's often brilliant description in *Schooldays in Imperial Japan*.

25. For family ties in the Medical School, see Bartholomew, *The Formation of Science in Japan*, pp. 168–176.

26. *Bungaku* has a broader meaning than the usual English translation, "literature," connotes.

Shōheisho. Only two had traveled in the West. The one conspicuous attribute common in their backgrounds was that five had been employed by the Bureau of Historical Compilation prior to its being transferred to Tokyo University in 1886. After 1894, however, the career profile of the majority in the College of Letters became more similar to that of their colleagues in law: 76 percent of all those appointed between 1894 and 1918 had studied at Tōdai, and many had been abroad. For example, Anesaki Masaharu (1873–1949), who was one of the more vocal supporters of academic freedom in the Affair of the Seven Ph.D.s, held the first Tōdai chair in Buddhist studies. He had attended the Third Higher School in Kyoto, had taken his degree in the Tōdai College of Letters, and had spent three years studying comparative religion in England and Germany before receiving a professorship.

Family Ties Within the Meiji Academic Elite

Within this Meiji academic elite there were complex networks of family relations. Evaluating the significance of such family ties is, of course, a complicated task, but in lieu of a more comprehensive quantitative study of the biographical data, some tentative generalizations may be of interest here.

First, as has already been suggested, although most of the men who joined the Tōdai faculty in the 1880s and 1890s came from families with at least nominal samurai status in the old social system, few, if any, of their families seem to have had substantial wealth or political prominence. There is evidence, as can be seen in the Mitsukuri family tree in Figure 2-1, that many came from families in which scholarship, either as a hereditary occupation or a socializing influence, was very important.

Second, very few of the Tōdai academics enjoyed the political advantage of being from any of the four southwestern domains that produced so many of the leading government figures in the Meiji period. Whereas almost 67 percent of the men who held cabinet minister posts between 1885 and 1906 were from Satsuma, Chōshū, Tosa, or Saga, of the seventy-four Japanese professors on the 1890 Tōdai faculty, only five (6 percent) were from those four domains (see Table 2-2). Far

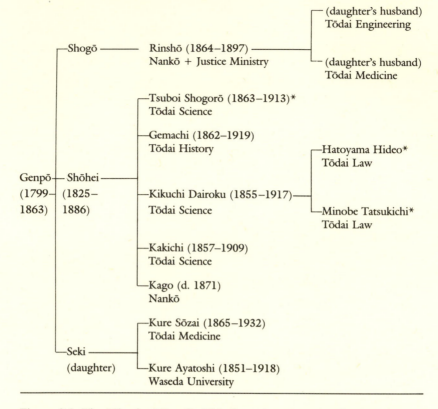

Figure 2-1 The Mitsukuri Family. This figure is reconstructed primarily from Ōtsuki, *Mitsukuri Rinshō kun den,* and Kure, *Mitsukuri Genpō.* For an informative discussion of the Tokugawa tradition of adoption with special reference to samurai and scholars, see McMullen, "Non-Agnatic Adoption."

*Daughter's husband

more were sons of Tokugawa shogunal retainers (if one includes specialists in Western studies employed by the shogun before the Restoration), a total of seventeen (23 percent).

Tōdai's predecessor institutions in the early 1870s at first recruited students exclusively from the samurai class; gradually commoners were also admitted. In either case there is no persuasive evidence of favoritism toward any particular geographical or political region.

Third, a remarkable number of Meiji academics were interrelated either by birth, adoption, or marriage. The outstanding case is the genealogy of Kikuchi Dairoku, the first chairman of the College of

Table 2-2   *Regional Origins of Meiji Elites*

	Tōdai Professors[a] (1890)	Political Elite[b] (1890)	Cabinet Ministers[c] (1895–1906)
Kagoshima (Satsuma)	1	19	12
Yamaguchi (Chōshū)	2	22	13
Kōchi (Tosa)	0	12	10
Saga (Hizen)	2	6	6
Subtotals (4 domains)	5 (6%)	59 (29%)	41 (64%)
Kyoto	0	17	1
Other prefectures	58	124	22
No information	11	2	0
Totals	74	202	64

SOURCES: [a]From Teikoku Daigaku, *Teikoku Daigaku ichiran* (1891) and standard biographical references. [b]Calculated from Takane, "Factors Influencing the Mobility of the Japanese Political Elite," Table 6-1, p. 209 (see pp. 42–58 for his definition of "political elite"). [c]From Ahn, "The Japanese Cabinet Ministers," Table 7, p. 56. See also the data reported in Silberman, *Ministers of Modernization;* and Silberman, "Elite Transformation."

Sciences who later went on to serve as president of Tōdai and of Kyoto Imperial University as well as education minister. Although Dairoku had taken the surname Kikuchi when adopted by his uncle, he was actually the second son of Mitsukuri Shōhei and the grandson of Genpō, both of whom had taught at the Tokugawa Institute for Western Studies. Mitsukuri Shōhei had six other sons or sons-in-law who taught at Tōdai or its predecessor, the Daigaku Nankō (see Figure 2-1).

Albeit an extreme case, the Mitsukuris were by no means unique. As had been true in the Tokugawa era, sons frequently followed their fathers into scholarly pursuits. Nor was it uncommon for Meiji academics to have brothers or brothers-in-law who were also academics. They themselves often chose promising young scholars, either from among their own students or others, as husbands for one or more of their daughters.

The Law College offered many examples of what were sometimes multiple family ties. Terao Tōru's brother was director of the Tōdai astronomical observatory. The two Hozumi brothers have already been noted. Nobushige's son Shigetō joined the faculty in 1908, as did Hatoyama Hideo, son of the former professor Hatoyama Kazuo as well as son-in-law of Kikuchi Dairoku. Hideo's sister was later married to Suehiro Izutarō, who was appointed to the same faculty in 1914. Hideo's wife's sister was married to law professor Onozuka Kiheiji. Another of Kikuchi's sons-in-law had been on the law faculty since 1899. Kawai Eijirō and Hijikata Seibi, two students who joined the Tōdai law faculty in the 1920s, were both adopted heirs of professors.

Professors and Social Status in the Meiji Period

Once on the faculty the Tōdai professor enjoyed high status and an income well above average. Under the 1890 revised schedule of civil service ranks, those faculty members serving as head of one of the five faculty divisions were accorded *chokunin* status—"appointed by [imperial] decree," the second highest echelon. All other full and associate professors were ranked among the *sōnin* grades—"appointed by memorial," the third echelon. As a group this placed them in the top 8 percent of the ranks of the imperial bureaucracy. The base salary of Tōdai full professors ranged from ¥1,000 to ¥3,000 per year—all above the *sōnin* average of ¥940. By comparison, the private college of Waseda was able to pay its senior men only ¥720 each in 1889, and the total 1891 budget for salaries at the Keiō "university division" was only ¥11,366.[27] Income from supplementary salary scales, from outside lecturing, and from publishing augmented these Tōdai base salaries.

Information on the marriage ties of Tōdai faculty members suggests, moreover, that their high status as scholars with official rank could be translated into some measure of additional material security for their families through marital alliances with the elites of big business, the civil bureaucracy, military officers, and political party leaders. The brothers Hozumi, to cite the outstanding examples, married into two of the most prominent families in the Meiji business community: No-

27. Tōdai, *Gojūnenshi*, pp. 944–946. For detailed information on the civil service ranks as a whole, see Spaulding, *Imperial Japan's Higher Civil Service Examinations,* especially Table 8, p. 95; pp. 327–329. For information on Waseda and Keiō, see Waseda Daigaku, *Hanseiki no Waseda*, pp. 58–64; and Keiō Gijuku, ed., *Keiō Gijuku hyakunenshi*, vol. 6, pp. 3673–3676.

bushige to the eldest daughter of Shibusawa Eiichi and Yatsuka to the eldest daughter of Asano Sōichirō.[28]

Tōdai academics were also frequent recipients of various special honors bestowed or sanctioned by the government and the imperial throne. These included receipt of the coveted *hakushi* title and sometimes appointment to the House of Peers. The *hakushi* title in the first years of the Meiji period had been a professorial rank. It became an academic degree under a new system initiated in 1888. But it was not yet a degree received by all on the completion of advanced graduate studies. Rather, as in the German system, it was supposedly conferred only following demonstration of outstanding scholarly contribution. Recipients during the Meiji period, however, included individuals then serving as Supreme Court judges, vice ministers, and other top-echelon civil bureaucrats. Between 1888 and 1917—after which the system was modified—there were a total of only 275 *hakushi* in the two categories of law and letters combined. Of these, a third were on the Tōdai faculty. After 1897 academics at the new Kyoto Imperial University were also among the lists, if less frequently, accounting for some 16 percent of the 275. The exclusiveness intended for the title is suggested by the fact that among the private colleges as late as 1917, only Waseda and Keiō could boast more than two *hakushi* recipients who had served on their regular faculties: Waseda having 15 (6 percent) and Keiō having 5 (2 percent).[29]

28. One measure of the Tōdai academics' social status in their own times was their regular inclusion in the contemporary "who's who" listings, publications that paid particular attention to marital connections (e.g., the 1903 edition of *Jinji kōshin roku*).

29. The great majority of those awarded the doctorate in legal studies from 1888 to 1905, fifty-four of sixty-nine, were neither from the four southwestern domains nor from the Tokugawa domain:

Place of Employment	From Southwest Domain	From Shogunal Domain	Educated at Tōdai	Studied Abroad
Tōdai (N = 26)	2	2	23	25
Kyōdai (N = 13)	2	0	12	13
Other public schools (N = 2)	0	0	1	1
Bureaucratic posts (N = 14)	3	2	8	7
Private schools (N = 8)	1	0	7	6
Other (N = 3)	0	1	1	2
Unclear (N = 3)	0	2	2	1
Totals (N = 69)	8 (12%)	7 (10%)	54 (78%)	55 (80%)

"Tōdai" includes the predecessor institutions: Kaisei Gakusho, Daigaku Nankō, and Kaisei Gakkō.

These data are compiled from the lists in Izeki, ed., *Dai Nihon hakushi roku*, vols. 1 and 2, supplemented by entries in *Daijinmei jiten* and other biographical sources. For rules regarding the conferral of the *hakushi*, see Tōdai, *Gakujutsu taikan*, pp. 89ff; and Monbushō, *Daigaku kankei hōrei no enkaku*, vol. 1, pp. 26ff.

Yet another type of status was conferred on leading figures among this academic elite when in 1890 and 1891 fifteen current or former Tōdai faculty members were named imperial appointees to the first House of Peers.[30] The seating of these academics was by no means merely a symbolic reward for orthodox scholarship or passive loyalty to the Meiji government. In the eyes of the architects of the Meiji Constitution, the powers and prerogatives of the Upper House were of crucial importance in the functioning of the new political system, most especially as a counterbalance to the feared radicalism of the political parties that dominated the House of Representatives. These appointments must thus be seen as a recognition that the prestige and expertise of these intellectuals could be a significant influence on the Diet regarding the political, social, economic, and educational issues facing Meiji Japan. The role of these establishment intellectuals in the House of Peers, in other words, was another in a set of elite roles they were expected to perform.

The Political Roles of the Tōdai Faculty, 1880s–1900s

The most studied and richly documented function performed by this intellectual elite was that of educating other elites. Throughout most of the preceding Tokugawa period, positions in the political and social hierarchy within Japanese society had been distributed primarily in accordance with inherited status. Until the Tokugawa system began to disintegrate, the function expected of the Tokugawa educator was to prepare samurai youths for roles that, more often than not, had already been reserved for them. During the Meiji period the new institutions of higher education rapidly became central to recruitment into the national elites. This is not to say that inherited family connections and wealth no longer counted—they could count for a great deal. But the emphasis was now squarely on achievement, and elite qualifications had to be demonstrated first in the competitive obstacle course of the formal educational system.[31] During the first half-

30. Shūgiin, *Gikai seido shichijūnenshi.*

31. See Dore, *Education in Tokugawa Japan,* Chapter 6, where he also discusses changes over time; see also his other writings on education and social mobility cited in my critique, "Universal Social Dilemmas and Japanese Educational History." Silberman's

century after the Restoration, this educational system was dominated by those educators who served on the faculty of Tokyo University; in their hands rested the tasks of advanced schooling and screening of the bulk of future members of all other elites except the military.

Tōdai preeminence in this regard has often been asserted, but for these decades it can hardly be exaggerated. A sample of four thousand individuals who received their education in the 1880s indicates that more than half of all Tōdai graduates achieved high status, with one out of every four attaining membership in the upper elites. By contrast, only one of five students from Tōdai's chief rivals in this period, the private schools of Waseda and Keiō, rose into the elite, and only one of twenty-five made it into the upper elites.[32]

Tōdai's dominance was particularly marked in the recruitment of civil bureaucrats, as can be seen in Table 2-3.[33] Tōdai graduates also dominated the ranks of educators at other state-supported institutions of higher education, as is demonstrated in Table 2-4. Thus, Meiji government leaders, deeply concerned with national unity and consensus as well as with the shortage of funding, chose to centralize the training and recruitment of elites. In the process they gave the Tōdai faculty a crucially important integrative function.

Yet the relationship between this educational function and the influence of the Tōdai academic has sometimes been obscured by the generalization that actual decision-making power rested in the Ministry of Education. The implication is that Tōdai, like other state schools, was held captive to the will of Education Ministry bureaucrats. This generalization does not fit the realities of the late Meiji period, however. Indeed, whereas in more recent periods (including our own) critics have lamented the degree of ministry control over Tōdai, in the late Meiji

statistics on post-1899 gubernatorial appointees who entered the bureaucracy in the 1880s showed 96 percent as having a university education ("Bureaucratic Development and the Structure of Decision-Making in Japan," p. 353).

32. Asō, "Meijiki ni okeru kōtō kyōiku kikan no erīto keisei kinō ni kansuru kenkyū." See also the Appendix.

33. In his work on the civil service Spaulding was primarily concerned with the workings of the examination system, but the point should be made here that even prior to the maturation of that system in the 1890s, Tōdai was the primary mechanism for formal screening of would-be bureaucrats. After the screening became systematized in the examination system, moreover, Tōdai faculty members continued their earlier function by serving as civil service examiners, as Spaulding described in Chapter 21, especially p. 234. For a good summary of the importance of the bureaucracy as an elite and the eventual centrality of examination men within it, see Spaulding, "The Bureaucracy as a Political Force."

Table 2-3 *Education of Civil Bureaucrats*

Individuals Educated Before 1900	% Studied at Tōdai
Successful candidates in the administrative examinations for the higher civil service, 1894–1901 (N = 319)	60[a]
All vice ministers of finance, home, justice, education, railroads, communications, commerce and agriculture, and foreign affairs, 1901–1926 (N = 76)	92[b]
All vice ministers and key bureau chiefs in Ministries of Finance, Home, Justice, Commerce and Agriculture, and Foreign Affairs, 1901–1926 (N = 208)	71[b]

SOURCES: [a]Computed from Spaulding, *Imperial Japan's Higher Civil Service Examinations,* Table 15, p. 131. [b]Calculated from lists in Ijiri, *Rekidai kenkanroku.*

NOTE: "Tōdai" includes the predecessor schools—the Kaiseijo, Daigaku Nankō, and Kaisei Gakkō.

Table 2-4 *Education of Educators*

Educators at State Schools	% Studied at Tōdai
Presidents, deans, and chairmen at elite schools, 1897–1926 (N = 105)	78
Presidents/principals at 84 other state colleges or higher schools, 1897–1926 (N = 255)	61

SOURCE: Calculated from lists in Ijiri, *Rekidai kenkanroku.*

NOTE: "Tōdai" includes the predecessor schools—the Kaiseijo, Daigaku Nankō, and Kaisei Gakkō. The elite schools comprise the imperial universities of Kyoto, Hokkaido, Tōhoku, and Kyushu plus the Tokyo Higher School of Commerce (Hitotsubashi).

period the protests were more often aimed at Tōdai influence over the ministry. Such protests appear to have had solid bases during the two decades between the elevation of Tōdai to the stature of an imperial university in 1886 and the Russo-Japanese War in 1905.

Those were critical years when new relationships were being worked out between the structure of higher education and the newly institutionalized form of bureaucratic monarchy. During this time the key bureaus within the Ministry of Education that dealt most directly with higher education were most often filled by scholar-educators whose careers were inextricably linked with Tōdai. Between 1886 and 1893 the chief of the Bureau of Professional Education (Senmon Gakumu), which handled matters pertaining to higher education, was Hamao Arata (1849–1925), an important figure in the early development of

Tōdai who was to be the faculty's candidate for university president in 1905. When Hamao returned to duties at the university in 1893, his place in the ministry was taken by Kinoshita Hiroji, the Tōdai professor who had previously served as principal of the First Higher School. When Kinoshita assumed the presidency of the new Kyoto Imperial University in 1897, Kikuchi Dairoku, dean of the Tōdai College of Sciences, took over as head of this key bureau. Kikuchi in turn was succeeded as bureau chief by Matsui Naokichi, a Tōdai professor of science. In 1901 a major reshuffling of personnel in the Education Ministry placed Tōdai professors in three of the top offices simultaneously: chief of the Bureau of Professional Education, chief of the Bureau of Technical Education (Jitsu Gakumu), and the post of minister.

In quantifiable terms six of the eight men who served as the administrative head of the bureau most closely concerned with formulating policy and supervising the operations of higher education in these two decades were either professors or, as in Hamao's case, long-term administrators from Tokyo University. As a group these Tōdai men held that post for seventeen and a half of the twenty years under investigation here. In addition, Tōdai intellectuals were appointed minister of education in three different cabinets and vice minister twice during these years.[34]

This situation did not go unnoticed, and there were frequent demands in the press and the parliament for broader consultation on educational policy. When the government responded by creating the new Council for Education in 1896, however, its core membership was composed of academics from Tōdai.[35] Tōdai academics also dominated the ministry's Commission on Ethics Textbooks that toiled from 1900 to 1910 to produce a moral orthodoxy for the educational system as a whole.[36] Being members of government commissions as well as admin-

---

34. Tallied from Ijiri, ed., *Rekidai kenkanroku*.

35. Seven of the twenty-four seats on the Kōtō Kyōiku Kaigi, the largest single bloc, were reserved for the Tōdai president and faculty chairmen; four others went to Kyōdai academics, some of whom were former Tōdai faculty members; four went to the ministry; and the remaining nine were distributed among the presidents and directors of other state schools, museums, and the Imperial Academy. Of the thirty-eight individuals who sat on the council during its first four years (1897–1901), twenty-two had been educated at Tōdai, and nineteen had served on its faculty. See Monbushō, *Gakusei hachijūnenshi*, pp. 164–165; and Abe, *Teikoku Gikai*, vol. 1, pp. 112–113; vol. 2, pp. 266–273.

36. The most useful survey of the work of the Shushi Kyōka Chōsa Iinkai is in Karasawa, *Kyōkasho no rekishi*, pp. 146–233. In English, see Fridell, "Government Ethics Textbooks in Late Meiji Japan."

istrators within the Education Ministry, these Tōdai academics moved frequently between the role of scholar-educator and that of adviser-official. It was in part because of this involvement within the Ministry of Education that they were able to resist government intervention when it became blatant in 1905.

As important as the educational system was at this juncture in modern Japanese history, there were other critical areas of Meiji social policy where Tōdai academics also had a direct hand in shaping the course of national affairs. For example, Tōdai professors frequently were influential members of the many important government commissions created to analyze and make proposals on critical problems. Professor Yoshino Sakuzō, a Tōdai undergraduate in 1900, recalled how this dual role even caused the cancellation of classes:

The government continually borrowed the strengths of their scholars and kept them busily engaged in such innovative work as the revision of the treaties, the compilation of laws, or the reform of the monetary system. Thus, the professors were usually involved in work of one sort or another for the government, either officially or behind the scenes. We were often left gazing enviously at a professor's back as he went flying out to the rickshaw that had come to fetch him halfway through the lecture because, as he would say, "There's a cabinet meeting today."[37]

Naitō Konan, who later became a professor at Kyoto Imperial University and a celebrated commentator on Chinese politics, was more critical of this phenomenon of serving simultaneously as professor and bureaucrat: "[They] assume the honorific name of university professors, but . . . for wealth, fame, and protection, they accept the esteem of the vulgar political world."[38]

Especially conspicuous were the Tōdai law professors who played adviser-official and partisan roles in formulating social legislation. Meiji leaders had committed themselves early in the 1870s to a sweeping reform of the Japanese legal system. When the actual drafting of new legal codes began in earnest in the 1880s and 1890s, it was accompanied by stormy political controversies, for contemporaries were quite sensitive to the critical issues involving both domestic and foreign affairs. The drafting of the codes became intricately intertwined with the

37. Quoted in Tanaka Sōgorō, *Yoshino Sakuzō*, p. 76. Yoshino also said that before his graduation in 1903 he noted a somewhat more relaxed atmosphere, and his professors did not seem so deeply involved in such work.

38. Quoted from a 1901 article in the *Ōsaka Asahi shinbun* in Fogel, *Politics and Sinology*, p. 117.

ongoing negotiations with the Western powers to revise the unequal treaty system, the single most heated foreign issue of the late 1880s and early 1890s. The question of whether, as critics claimed, foreign diplomats were to be allowed to dictate the timing and content of such important legal reforms was quickly used to good advantage by the fledgling political parties in their struggle with the government.

More broadly, the legal reforms raised the complex set of issues that have since come to be labeled problems of "cultural identity." Opponents of the draft codes insisted that the unique values constituting Japan's heritage would be destroyed by the indiscriminate borrowing of the European customs and Christian beliefs they saw underlying Western law. More narrowly, the sticky problems of settling on the proper formal procedure for ratifying the new codes were seized on by champions of the prerogatives of the Diet, while the government bureaucracy suffered from continual inter- and intra-agency rivalry over jurisdiction. Finally, disagreements at the level of legal philosophy concerning the theoretical underpinnings of law served to split the small world of Meiji legal scholars, judges, and private lawyers into warring camps.

Work on these legal reforms had been undertaken in the 1870s by a Justice Ministry task force that included Mitsukuri Rinshō and several other Western specialists formerly employed by the Tokugawa shogunate. The Justice Ministry's direction of these reforms, however, was seriously threatened in the mid-1880s, first by the transfer of its law school to Tōdai in 1884 and then by the Foreign Ministry's attempt in 1886 to take jurisdiction over the final drafting. The Justice Ministry regained jurisdiction in 1887, only to suffer a major defeat in 1890 when the new parliament refused to ratify the proposed codes. The campaign against the 1890 drafts was spearheaded by the Barristers Club (Hōgakushikai), whose leadership was composed primarily of Tōdai law professors Hozumi Nobushige, Hijikata Yasushi, and Kikuchi Takeo plus a number of former Tōdai students whom they had helped to open a private law school in 1885. Around this core were prominent Tōdai faculty members, including Hamao Arata and Tomii Masaaki, who, like Hozumi Nobushige, were able to use their seats in the House of Peers to carry on the struggle within the Diet itself. When in 1893 the Itō cabinet gave in to pressure to abandon the Justice Ministry's drafts and established a commission to revise them, it turned to Tōdai law professors to produce a compromise. Hozumi Nobushige and Tomii Masaaki, leading opponents of the original drafts, and Ume

Kentarō, a colleague who had earlier helped to formulate them, were chiefly responsible for writing the final version of the revised codes that went into effect in 1898.[39] In the long controversy over the legal codes the Tōdai academics moved out beyond their positions as advisers within government commissions and agencies to take part as political partisans in a struggle involving a major ministry, both houses of the Diet, and a number of the most influential government leaders of the time, including the cabinet of Itō Hirobumi.

Another instance of the Tōdai professors' involvement in equally significant political action can be found in the later Meiji controversy over labor relations and government social policy. As early as 1880 the Ministry of Finance had raised the issue of government intervention into labor relations in the private sector of the economy when it sought the opinion of the Tokyo Chamber of Commerce on the government's role in enforcing labor contracts. In 1884 the question of broader labor legislation was on the agenda of a series of regional conferences on the promotion of industrial growth held under government auspices. Business representatives were generally opposed to government regulation, and no further action was taken in the 1880s. In 1891 the Ministry of Agriculture and Commerce circulated a draft of a law regulating working conditions in factories. This, too, was withdrawn in the face of business opposition. But in 1896 bureaucrats within the ministry were insisting that, although labor strife in Japan was still minimal, the history of class strife and social disorders that marked industrial development in the West was a clear warning of what would befall the Japanese nation if it did not create "laws necessary to maintain in the future the balance between between capital and labor and ensure harmonious relations between employers and employees, thereby protecting in advance against any disorders."[40] In October 1898 the Third Plenary Conference on Agriculture, Commerce, and Industry was called. The

39. Epp has ably summarized the process and the various perspectives at the time and later in "Threat to Tradition." I have also used Hoshino, *Meiji minpō hensanshi kenkyū;* and Higashigawa, *Hakushi Ume Kenjirō.* The private law school was the Igirisu Hōritsu Gakkō, later to become Chūō University. Other Tōdai professors who opposed the Justice Ministry drafts included Hatoyama Kazuo, Hozumi Yatsuka, Kinoshita Hiroji, and Okano Keijirō. The Tōdai law faculty was by no means united on the issue, however, and supporters of the original drafts included Isobe Shirō as well as Ume Kentarō.

40. For details and sources, see the references in Marshall, *Capitalism and Nationalism in Prewar Japan,* pp. 51–55, 94–96; Dore, "The Modernizer as a Special Case"; and Taira, "Factory Legislation and Management Modernization During Japan's Industrialization."

thirty-six participants included representatives from several ministries and the business community and three Tokyo University professors—Kanai Noburu of the law faculty and Yokoi Tokiyoshi and Tamari Kizō of the faculty of agriculture.

Kanai Noburu was part of a circle of young political economists from Tōdai and other schools who in 1896 had organized the Association for the Study of Social Policy (Shakai Seisaku Gakkai) on the model of the Verein für Sozialpolitik of Bismarckian Germany. Between 1898 and World War I Kanai and his allies used the association both as an elite forum for discussion with prominent businessmen and senior bureaucrats and as an effective lobby for social legislation in the Diet. Some of their influence doubtless stemmed from the fact that they also took it on themselves to engage spokesmen for the nascent Meiji socialist movement in public debate over European and American social thought, thus providing an intellectual counter to radical programs for social change. As incidents of labor strife, albeit on a small scale, increased in the 1900s, the arguments of Kanai and his colleagues gained a wider audience within the civil bureaucracy and the Diet. Eventually, in 1911, a compromise factory act was passed.[41]

Tōdai faculty members did not, however, limit their participation to political struggles over domestic policy. As individuals and groups in the late 1890s and early 1900s, Tōdai professors were also engaged as partisans in controversies over foreign policy. It was a prime instance of this involvement that led to the 1905 Tomizu affair, the first major direct confrontation between the modern academic elite and a Meiji cabinet on the issue of university autonomy.[42]

41. See Marshall, *Capitalism and Nationalism in Prewar Japan*, pp. 94–96. Pyle also shed some light on the role of the Shakai Seisaku Gakkai in influencing government policy toward rural society in "The Technology of Japanese Nationalism." Tōdai law professors active at one time or another in the association during these years included Wadagaki Kenzō, Takano Iwasaburō, Onozuka Kiheiji, Matsumoto Jōji, Tachi Sakutarō, and Tomizu Hiroto.

42. This excludes both the 1870 crisis that led to the closing of the first university and the Kume affair of 1892. The 1870 conflict, as previously described, was part of the birth pangs of the modern academic system—a purging of older claimants to government sponsorship. The 1892 incident, which involved the forced resignation of Kume Kunitake, a scholar in the Historical Compilations Institute with a joint appointment as Tōdai professor of Japanese history, occurred after his publication of an article labeling the conventional sources on the early history of the imperial house as "myths." Kume's case was definitely a challenge to academic freedom but one to which Tōdai faculty made no overt response, perhaps because Kume's primary appointment was in this specialized institute; see Ienaga, *Daigaku no jiyū, no rekishi,* pp. 38–39; and Nakano, *Kume hakase kyūjūnen kairoku,* vol. 2, pp. 556–557.

Cohesiveness Within the
Meiji Academic Elite

It is sometimes suggested that family ties, patron-protégé relations, and other vestiges of feudal practices were constant factors in promoting disruptive factionalism within the academic world of imperial Japan. Factionalism in the 1920s and 1930s will be explored in later chapters, but if such ties were factors at all in the Meiji period, they seem to have enhanced an already existing set of interconnections built out of common early education, shared experiences abroad, and similar professional career patterns. These interconnections seemed to serve the Meiji academic elite well in 1905 when it was confronted with a challenge to its status from outside the university. This cohesiveness could not have existed, however, without shared perceptions of what such an elite status entailed; the next chapter will focus on the ideology of academic freedom expressed by the spokesmen for this intellectual elite.

3

The Assertion of Academic Autonomy, 1905–1918

Interpersonal ties, shared educational backgrounds, or similar career patterns among Meiji academics by no means ensured ideological homogeneity. The Meiji academic elite was certainly not of one mind on the political and social issues facing Japan. Nevertheless, by 1905, if not before, these Tōdai academics had manifested a common identity as an intellectual elite and a consensus on the need to achieve an autonomous status for their university base. This consensus cut across disciplinary lines and political differences, and the attack by the Katsura cabinet on Tōdai law faculty was met by faculty members of different departments and various political persuasions as if the attack had been on themselves. Professor Tomizu's defense also received support from Tōdai's sister institution at Kyoto, where many, if not most, of the 1905 faculty were Tōdai alumni.[1] There was also support from faculties at private colleges, despite the resentment the latter sometimes felt toward the elite status of the imperial universities. This

1. Three of the first six Kyoto University presidents were Tōdai alumni. The percentage was even higher among the chairs of departments during the period 1887–1902 (source: Ijiri, ed., *Rekidai kenkanroku,* pp. 727, 728, 730, 732):

	Total Appointees	Tōdai Alumni	%
Chair of law	13	10	77
Chair of letters	5	5	100
Chair of economics	7	5	71
Totals	25	20	80

show of unity was as unprecedented as the confrontation itself. But it was by no means the first time academics had raised the issues of the independence of scholarship and university self-government. This chapter surveys the earliest attempts by the modern Japanese academic elite to assert a measure of institutional autonomy vis-à-vis the administrative agencies of the state, examines their claims of academic freedom made in the 1905 confrontation, and then suggests some reasons for their success in gaining a significant measure of self-governance by 1918.

University Governance Prior to 1905

The question of the proper relationship between the scholar and his government in the new Japan was first raised in a systematic fashion in a debate between members of the Meirokusha, an association of some of the most prominent of Japan's modernizing intellectuals organized in 1873. The early argument centered on the consequences of the government's monopoly on the services of scholars who, if they remained in the private sector, might better serve the nation in the role of independent critic.[2] Fukuzawa Yukichi, founder of what was to become the prestigious Keiō University and one of the best-known proponents of this latter view, was particularly critical of the government for treating Tokyo University as simply another agency within the bureaucratic structure. In 1883, for example, Fukuzawa wrote a series of newspaper editorials entitled "Scholarship and Politics Should Be Separated," arguing, "Scholarship and politics both have as their object the advancement of the nation's good, but scholarship is not politics and men of scholarship are different from men of politics. . . . It is as if the man of politics uses his strength as a medical practitioner treating an illness, while the scholar is the one who imparts the methods of regular hygiene." Typical of modernizers of his day, Fukuzawa buttressed his argument with references to Western practices: "If one considers the situation in the civilized countries of Europe and America, it is extremely rare in those foreign countries to find the government creating schools, assembling the students, controlling

---

2. An English translation of the major portion of the debate can be found in Braisted, trans., *Meiroku Zasshi;* the debate is analyzed in Fisher, "The Meirokusha."

them through administrative agencies, and having scholars as officials of those agencies do the teaching."[3] Fukuzawa's proposed solution was to place the government schools under the legal protection of charters from the throne and subsidize them directly from the wealth of the imperial household, thereby effectively removing them from partisan political control.

Scholars within the imperial universities were also well aware of European notions of corporate autonomy in general and the German concept of *Lehrfreiheit* (scholastic freedom) in particular. As early as 1872 Katō Hiroyuki had translated an influential work by the Swiss author Johann Kaspar Bluntschli that included a section on "the right of independence of scholarship within the university."[4] As the new imperial university increased in organizational complexity and as its faculty grew through appointments of Japanese who had received their advanced training and professional socialization in European and U.S. centers of higher learning, the problem of defining the relationship between scholarship and politics increasingly became a source of tension.

Despite the absence of formal guarantees regarding academic autonomy, all indications suggest that throughout the 1870s and the early 1880s the government actually delegated a large measure of de facto self-government to the Tōdai administrators and senior faculty members. Powers in such critical matters as personnel, curriculum, and the internal funding of research were entrusted to the university president. According to the early ordinances governing the university, decisions on appointment and termination of faculty were made by the minister of education on the "recommendation [*gujō*]" of the president; yet despite this legal requirement for formal approval by the minister, there are no recorded cases of serious conflict over recruitment or tenure in these early years. Although the university president was a ministry appointee, his substantive powers were actually circumscribed by the formal and informal organization within the university. Under the

3. Fukuzawa, *Fukuzawa Yukichi zenshū*, vol. 5, pp. 369–370. The series was reprinted as a pamphlet entitled *Gakumon no dokuritsu*, and an earlier article had called for the abolition of the Education Ministry. The question of academic freedom was also raised in spring 1882 in the political platform of the Rikken Kaishintō Party, which included the following pledge: "To free the national university from state control, promote academic independence, and raise the level of education in the nation" (Davis, *Intellectual Change and Political Development in Early Modern Japan*, p. 176).

4. Bluntschli, *Allgemeine Staatslehre*; see quotations in Ienaga, *Daigaku no jiyū no rekishi*, pp. 16–18.

1877 regulations only the Medical School had its own head—the Schools of Science, Law, and Letters being directly under the president. But in 1881 each of the separate faculties was given its own divisional head, and senior faculty members of each were constituted into a divisional consultative committee (*gakubu shijunkai*). A university consultative committee was also created to advise the president, and at its first meeting almost all the senior Japanese faculty members were seated.[5]

This pattern of relations between the university and the government was threatened briefly when Mori Arinori took over as minister of education at the end of 1885. Mori was well known in Japanese intellectual and political circles for his vigorous advocacy of modernization, and his views were by no means incompatible with those of Tōdai faculty leaders—indeed, he was said to have been on very good terms with a number of the most influential professors. Nevertheless, Mori was also known as extraordinarily strong-willed and deeply committed to a plan for reforming Japan's entire educational system. In this he had the full backing of the powerful Itō Hirobumi, who was then serving as prime minister. There was therefore good reason to fear that Mori would attempt to place the stamp of his own personality on the university. Mori's appointment on December 22, 1885, did precipitate Katō Hiroyuki's resignation as president, and Mori chose as Katō's successor Watanabe Kōki, an outsider to the university. Watanabe had been a pre-Restoration student of medicine at the Tokugawa Institute for Western Learning and had also served briefly as the head of the Peers School. But Watanabe was not noted as either a scholar or an educator, and his most recent post had been that of chief administrative officer of the city of Tokyo.[6] When Mori's new university ordinance was finally enacted in 1886, it actually had much less radical consequences for the university than did his reforms at other levels of the educational system.

Yet there were changes that gave cause for alarm to defenders of

5. The relevant regulations are reprinted in Tōdai, *Gojūnenshi*, vol. 1, pp. 258–288, 459–462, 507–510. Ivan Hall, in his very valuable biography of Mori Arinori (p. 404), suggested that foreign teachers held the positions of divisional head until Mori's reforms of 1886. According to the records published by the university, however, these were filled in 1881 by Japanese professors, and no foreign teachers were listed as having attended the 1881 Shijunkai meeting (Tōdai, *Gojūnenshi*, vol. 1, pp. 512, 524; vol. 2, pp. 1229–1230).

6. Mori's friends on the faculty included Toyama Shōichi, dean of the College of Letters; Kikuchi Dairoku, dean of Sciences; and Professor Yabe Ryokichi. See Ōkubo, *Nihon no daigaku*, pp. 304–305; and I. Hall, *Mori Arinori*, pp. 390–397, 414.

university autonomy. The 1886 regulations made no formal provision for the consultative committees at the level of the colleges, or *bunka daigaku*, as the faculty divisions were now renamed. Moreover, the university Shijunkai was replaced by the smaller Hyōgikai (or University Council), which was to consist of only two representatives from each college. These representatives were to be appointed by the minister of education to five-year terms. In reality, over the following six years the College of Letters was represented only by Dean Toyama Shōichi (Masakazu), and when the College of Agriculture was added in 1890, its dean was also the single representative from that college. Furthermore, although the law faculty was well represented under Mori's reorganization, the university president served ex officio as the dean of the Law College. The 1886 imperial university ordinance also differed from previous regulations in the changed wording regarding faculty appointment to the senior ranks. Whereas earlier ordinances had included provision for the "recommendation" of the president in appointments, no such phrase appeared in Mori's ordinance.[7]

Mori's reforms were part of a larger reorganization of the Japanese government structure in the late 1880s, a preparation for the first modern constitution that was to establish a national parliament, the Diet. Political tensions were thus running high. At the same time, a number of prominent Tōdai professors were deeply involved in the struggle over the new civil law code, which included very controversial provisions regarding the family. These developments formed a new political context for questions about academic autonomy within the framework of the new government bureaucracy.

In 1888 a dozen younger Tōdai faculty members recently returned from advanced training abroad met in private with Finance Minister and longtime influential statesman Matsukata Masayoshi, seeking his support for the adoption of European-style institutional arrangements to ensure faculty participation in university policy making. Matsukata is reported to have been markedly unsympathetic as the arguments were presented: according to one account their requests were like "wind in a horse's ear."[8] In early 1889, Mori Arinori was suddenly removed from the scene by a political assassin. Shortly thereafter a group of prestigious professors at Tōdai put forth a detailed proposal on reform of

7. Tōdai, *Gojūnenshi*, vol. 1, p. 936; vol. 2, p. 1242. Terasaki Masao has made a careful analysis of the recorded minutes of the Hyōgikai in his "Nihon no daigaku ni okeru jijiteki kankō no keisei."
8. Quoted in Bartholomew, *The Formation of Science in Japan*, p. 134.

the ordinances governing the imperial university. It, like Fukuzawa Yukichi's earlier suggestion, would have removed the imperial university entirely from the supervision of the Education Ministry as well as from the new Diet by granting it a special charter and financial endowment from the imperial household. Five crucial elements of self-governance were proposed:

1. The president would be appointed by the imperial throne, but a vice president would be elected by faculty ballot and would preside over a senate (*sanjikai*).
2. The Senate would consist of twenty-five representatives elected by their respective colleges.
3. The five college deans would be elected to three-year terms by a majority vote of their faculties.
4. Each college would have formal faculty meetings (*hyōgikai*) of all full professors, who would be empowered to make faculty appointments subject only to the approval of a fourteen-member board of trustees.
5. Five of the trustees would be elected from the university faculty itself.

A final version of this set of proposals was presented to the education minister in May 1889 with the signatures of thirty-nine Tōdai professors, including Deans Toyama (letters), Hozumi (law), and Kikuchi (sciences).[9]

There is no record of an immediate government response to these proposals, but in the following four years the cause of university autonomy was substantially advanced. In 1890 Katō Hiroyuki returned to the presidency of the university, replacing Mori's political appointee. Then in September 1892 the government made a major concession when it amended the rules for the University Council to give the professors in each college the right to elect by ballot one of the two council representatives.[10] Further concessions came in 1893 as part of the reformulation of the imperial university ordinance under yet another influential education minister, Inoue Kowashi. Unlike Mori, Inoue was a senior statesman rather than a self-conscious intellectual reformer, and

9. Ienaga, *Daigaku no jiyū no rekishi*, pp. 29–34, 37n, 267n; and Tanaka Kōtarō et al., *Daigaku no jiji*, pp. 4–9. The drafters of the initial proposal also included one senior professor each from the faculties of medicine, engineering, and sciences.

10. Tōdai, *Gojūnenshi*, vol. 1, p. 938.

in his approach to Tokyo University he was primarily concerned with administrative and financial matters. He thus gave careful attention to the problems of organizational lines of authority and procedures for decision making. At one point, it is said, Inoue actually gave thoughtful consideration to a draft regulation that would have given faculty members what they wanted: the formal right to vote on new appointments as well as to elect their own deans.

In its final form, it is true, the 1893 ordinance stopped short of granting formal rights to conduct such elections. Yet it did grant important sanctions for faculty participation. Official faculty meetings (*kyōjukai*) were reestablished at the college level with specific responsibilities for curriculum decisions, degree requirements, and examination procedures. The mandate of the University Council was expanded, and the council emerged more clearly as a vehicle for faculty input on a whole range of administrative matters, meeting every two weeks with a varied agenda. Although half the seats were still occupied by college deans who continued to be appointed directly by the ministry, the anomaly of having the president serve concurrently as dean of law was ended, and a stipulation was inserted that the deans had to come from "among the professors of that college."[11]

Documentary records of faculty participation in the selection of deans before 1919 were not available to me, but there is strong circumstantial evidence that most, if not all, of the deans who served between 1893 and 1919 had solid support among the full professors: more than half (three-quarters if the Medical School is excluded) were men whose colleagues had previously or subsequently elected them by ballot to serve other terms as representatives to the University Council.[12] The wording in the 1893 ordinance also made significant concessions to the sensitivities of the proponents of greater autonomy in at least two other instances: the phrase "The president . . . serves under the orders [*mei*] of the education minister," which had appeared in previous ordinances, was altered to read "under the jurisdiction" (or "supervision," *kantoku*); and the earlier clause specifying that faculty appointments and dismissals were made by the minister "on the recommendation" of the president—wording that had been removed in 1886—was restored.[13]

11. Terasaki, "Kōtō kyōiku," pp. 317–325, 333–340.
12. Calculated from the lists in Tōdai, *Gojūnenshi;* and Tōdai, *Gakujutsu taikan.*
13. Terasaki, "Nihon no daigaku ni okeru jijiteki kankō no keisei."

Neither of these clauses, anymore than the more substantive concessions to faculty participation in academic governance, altered the fact that legal decision-making authority remained ultimately with the minister of education if he chose to intervene. It is thus true that the specific proposals made by the faculty in 1889 were not accepted. Yet in terms of de facto power there is little question that the Tōdai senior faculty members had secured a very large measure of collective control over the internal workings of their university. This was even more obviously the case as such champions of academic self-government as Professors Toyama Shōichi, Kikuchi Dairoku, and Yamakawa Kenjirō came to occupy the office of president.[14] (Toyama and Kikuchi later went on to serve as ministers of education.) The influence of Tokyo Imperial University on the ministry was further increased by the standing practice in this period of selecting Tōdai professors to serve as head of the Bureau of Professional Education, the section within the ministry most directly concerned with formulating policy for and supervising higher education.

Even with the considerable degree of university autonomy achieved by 1905, there were still important legal restrictions on faculty behavior. The 1881 ordinance had incorporated the faculty of Tōdai into the civil service, thus giving professors the same legal status and subjecting them to the same official limitations as other functionaries in the upper ranks of the government bureaucracy. Under the provisions of a series of government regulations dating from 1873, government appointees were strictly prohibited from public criticism of domestic or foreign policies. Between 1884 and 1905 the Education Ministry had interpreted these prohibitions to preclude those at the state schools under its supervision from taking part in public debates or from making public speeches, except for those that were scholarly in nature. The April 1884 version of the instructions from the ministry also admonished professors in their classrooms to keep educational objectives and the public good firmly in mind. Once the national parliament was created under the constitution of 1889 and the political opposition challenged the

14. Ivan Hall described the Tōdai president in these years as "chosen for his administrative talents" ("Organizational Paralysis," p. 318). This was no doubt true in Mori's appointment of Watanabe Kōki, but one could just as plausibly argue that after 1893 rapport with the faculty was the critical attribute in the appointments of Professors Toyama Shōichi (1897–1898), Kikuchi Dairoku (1898–1901), and Yamakawa Kenjirō (1901–1905 and 1913–1920). As we shall see, the reappointment in 1905 of Hamao Arata was part of the settlement in the Affair of the Seven Ph.D.s.

government at the polls, the ministry issued regular directives prior to general elections to remind both teachers and students of the legal ban on their participation in political campaigns. Ironically, the justification given for this admonition was the need to prevent "damage to the independence of education."[15] Nonetheless, in the years prior to 1905 no Tōdai faculty member had ever been charged with any misconduct under these provisions despite frequent participation in heated political controversies over such issues as the revision of the civil codes and the creation of factory laws.

Thus, the evolving relationships between state and university were complex and fraught with ambiguity. Until 1905 there was little basis for any prediction on what would be the outcome in the event of a major confrontation over the key issues of academic freedom and university autonomy. The 1905 Affair of the Seven Ph.D.s provided the first open testing of the limits of academic autonomy possible for the imperial university under the Meiji state.

The Issues Defined in 1905

In suspending Professor Tomizu in 1905, the Katsura cabinet issued no official statement beyond the formal announcement that the government was acting in accordance with Article II, Section 1, Paragraph 4 of the Education Ministry Regulations for Personnel. That paragraph provided for suspension or even dismissal "when necessitated by the circumstances of the government agency."[16] Despite the absence of further explanation, the rationale for Tomizu's suspension was evident from many sources. These included Minister Kubota's memorandum to President Yamakawa in June 1905, several speeches in the Diet supporting the disciplinary action, and the editorials of pro-Katsura newspapers.

None of these charged Tomizu with actually taking part in any acts violating any criminal laws, although in a speech to the House of Peers, General Viscount Tani Kanjō—a venerable hero of the Meiji Restoration and a former president of the Peers School—did point to the

15. See Okada, "Bungei no kaishaku to kyōju no genron," p. 13.
16. The original phrase in the Monbushō Bunkan Bungenrei read, "*Kanchō no tsugō ni yori hitsuyō.*"

Hibiya Park riots and condemned all irresponsible teachers who condoned to their students such "defiance of government and resistance to authority."[17] Tomizu does not seem to have ever actually advocated violence in the resistance to Katsura's foreign policy, notwithstanding a 1905 article in which he did predict civil disorders. He later admitted that he had gone to the headquarters of the organization planning the mass rally on the morning of the riots, but he claimed his intention was to attend a peaceful demonstration against the Portsmouth Treaty. As it turned out, according to his memoirs, a stomach ailment caused him to return home without ever reaching the rally.[18] Nor was there significant participation by students in the antitreaty riots.[19] In any case Tomizu's suspension came more than a week before the riots took place, and the riots themselves were not the main focus of the ensuing controversy.

Rather, Tomizu and his fellow activists were accused of meddling in affairs of state beyond their scholarly purview and of abusing their status as university professors to mislead domestic and foreign opinion on Japanese goals in the Russo-Japanese War. The newspaper *Kokumin shinbun*, in an October 3, 1905, editorial that Tomizu believed summed up the government's case against him, reiterated the point Prime Minister Katsura had made privately to the group months earlier: "Scholars bear a responsibility greater than that of ordinary people. At the same time that scholars have an obligation to learn as much as possible . . . they also have an obligation not to [claim] what they do not know. The ordinary person can be forgiven when he expresses as an amateur a hypothesis about something he does not know, but [not] a scholar professing to be a specialist."[20] The more serious aspect was the potential damage to the operations of foreign diplomacy at a time when, as Education Minister Kubota had phrased it, "matters of great consequence are at stake."[21]

Tomizu disclaimed any intention of misleading foreign opinion, but it is evident from his memoirs how much he relished the attention his

17. The 22nd session of the House of Peers, January 7, 1906; reprinted in Abe, *Teikoku Gikai*, vol. 2, pp. 266–273.

18. Tomizu, *Zoku kaikoroku*, p. 298.

19. Gordon listed 10 students among 327 arrested or tried in Tokyo riots during 1905 and 1906 (*Labor and Imperial Democracy*, p. 37). Eight of 308 actually indicted were identified as "students"; see the table in Okamoto, *The Japanese Oligarchs and the Russo-Japanese War*, p. 214.

20. Tomizu's comment and the editorial appear in his *Zoku kaikoroku*, pp. 341–346.

21. *Danshaku Yamakawa*, p. 128.

views received in the world press as well as the additional pressures this produced on the Katsura cabinet. Nor was there any question that Tomizu and his fellow activists had been determined from the outset to make conscious use of their prestige as holders of the *hakushi* degree and as professors at an elite institution. On several occasions he reported that group members discussed the special advantages their position gave them as spokesmen for their cause and considered it carefully in their choice of tactics.[22] Tomizu also explicitly embraced a role for scholars that entailed "leading" public opinion, although he denied "temporary fame" should ever be a motive.[23] Terao Tōru, in his defense of his own participation in the group, also spoke of academics as occupying a "position as leaders of the nation's people."[24]

The questions here were whether such a role was possible for a scholar whose appointment to the faculty of an imperial university conferred on him the status of a civil official and whether such officials were explicitly prohibited from taking part in partisan politics or even publicly criticizing government policy. Tomizu's adversaries thus accused him of violating the code of proper and lawful behavior for a civil servant.

In response, Professor Terao attempted a distinction between politics (*seiji*) in the sense of party struggles for power, on the one hand, and a nonpartisan critique of government policy, on the other. In the latter case, he asserted, scholars did not lose their freedom of political expression merely because they held official rank.[25] The scholar's right to voice his political opinions was defended by another Tōdai law professor, Minobe Tatsukichi, as a corollary of the absolute right of all citizens to criticize their government.[26] This stance was rare, however. More frequently, arguments for the right to speak were premised on the right to academic freedom—a freedom that, by implication at least, did not necessarily extend to the ordinary individual.

Philosophy professor Inoue Tetsujirō, better known to historians for his contributions to the ideology of nationalism than to any defense of civil liberties, was in this case unequivocal in his support of academic

22. For example, see Tomizu, *Zoku kaikoroku,* p. 97.
23. In an interview that the *Chūōkōron* published on April 1, 1905, under the title "Shakai ni taisuru gakusha no seiryoku"; reprinted in Tomizu, *Zoku kaikoroku,* pp. 608–612.
24. Terao, "Gakusetsu to seiron."
25. Ibid., p. 10.
26. Minobe Tatsukichi, "Kenryoku no ran'yō to kore ni taisuru hankō."

freedom. In Inoue's analysis the values of scholarship took precedence over political limitations because the scholar was concerned with a higher order of eternal and universal truths that transcended national boundaries. Writing in a popular magazine, he did add, nevertheless, "I believe professors who serve the university are every bit as devoted to the national good as the officers of the army or navy."[27]

Law professor Kanai Noburu, himself the subject of attacks in the press for his membership in the group, also spoke of academic freedom as an absolute good: "The independence of learning is sacred [*gakumon no dokuritsu wa jitsu ni shinsei nari*]." Yet Kanai was not willing to carry this to any logical conclusion that might challenge the legitimacy of existing peace preservation or press laws. Rather, he conceded there should be limits "where a scholar's speech sullies the dignity of the imperial throne, undermines the political system [*seitai*], or clearly violates the imperial constitution."[28]

The more common explication of the rationale for academic freedom in the 1905 confrontation depended less on the premise of absolute rights and more on the assertion of such freedom's instrumental value to the nation—that is, the argument that scholarship was an essential means to Japan's progress toward material and cultural goals. Anesaki Masaharu, a young specialist in Buddhism in the Tōdai College of Letters, declared that all academics should put aside their differences to defend academic freedom because "it is obvious the university is the central sphere of the country's scholarship, and its results can be applied to the advancement of the country's cultural and material civilization. There is a very close connection between a nation's progress and the university [serving] as the critic [*hyōsha*] of the intellectual world and the guide [*kyōdō*] for the minds of the populace."[29]

Law professor Takahashi Sakue pointed out the relationship between the protection of academic freedom and the strength of nations in the Western world. In England, he noted, an Oxford professor could even criticize his government's naval defense plans in the London *Times*.[30] Kahei Katsuhiko warned that wherever academic freedom was stifled, the vigor of the nation declined.[31] Kanai Noburu claimed that, with the notable exception of the recently defeated czarist Russia, the

27. Inoue, "Teikoku Daigakuron."
28. Kanai, "Gakusha no genron ni appaku o kawauru no fuka naru o toku."
29. Anesaki, "Daigaku kyōju no jiyū to sono seisai," p. 43.
30. Takahashi, "Kokusai hōgakusha no genron."
31. Kahei, "Gakusha no kokka ni okeru chii o ronzu."

suppression of academic freedom in Europe and the United States had not been practiced since the eighteenth century. He particularly pointed to the German example, where opposition to Bismarck's policies was permitted even at Berlin University in the nation's capital. To practice suppression, Kanai predicted, would cause the nation to lose the respect of foreign scholars who had great contributions to make to Japan.[32]

The main thrust of all these arguments was that the freedom to disseminate the results of the pursuit for knowledge was a sine qua non to the pursuit itself; ergo, the Japanese scholar had to be guaranteed freedom of speech. Nor could political topics be placed out of bounds. To hold academics accountable to the strict interpretations of the civil service regulations would be logically contradictory because professors of law, economics, history, and similar disciplines inevitably treated controversial political issues in the course of their studies and could not otherwise properly perform their research or teaching duties.[33]

Some of these authors apparently were willing to accept the logical implications of the argument based on national interests: if academic freedom was a means to further the national welfare, then considerations of national interests might dictate limitations on this freedom in some circumstances. They nonetheless denied that there existed any such circumstances in the Tomizu case. Because the national good could never be equated automatically with any specific policy of a particular cabinet, the Katsura administration was not justified in suppressing the results of Tomizu's studies on international affairs merely because his conclusions were not in accord with current foreign policies.[34]

Finally, the defenders of university autonomy attempted to take the offensive, accusing Education Minister Kubota of exceeding his legal authority when he unilaterally suspended an imperial university faculty member. Here their arguments focused on whether the Education Ministry had jurisdiction in this case. Some claimed it did not because Tomizu's appointment was to the Law College of the university, not directly to the Education Ministry. Because the university president and the Law College had agreed that "circumstances" in the school "neces-

32. Kanai, "Gakusha no genron ni appaku o kawauru no fuka naru o toku."
33. See, for example, *Kokka Gakkai zasshi* 19, no. 10, pp. 9–10, 51, 91–92, 96.
34. For examples of this line of reasoning, see the contributions to the October 1905 issue of *Kokka Gakkai zasshi* by Onozuka Kiheiji and Takano Iwasaburō as well as that of Terao Tōru already cited.

sitated" the continued service of Tomizu in his post, the faculty petition argued, the suspension was invalid.[35]

Spokesmen for the opposing camp professed themselves unimpressed by this or other arguments put forth by these faculty spokesmen. For men such as Viscount Tani and the thirty members of the House of Peers for whom he spoke, the discussion of Western practices was not relevant: "The ambition of these university professors is to have the university independent like the universities in the West—in other words, something like the papal organization in Rome. . . . Perhaps these university professors are thinking of themselves as university professors in the West, but what about in Japan?" Their answer was quite definite: "The university is merely a facility under the jurisdiction of the Education Ministry. It is by no means an independent organization. The professors have been appointed in accordance with Article 10 of the imperial constitution and are all equally government officials."[36]

The essential point here is not whether on this occasion the ideological assertions of academic freedom swayed Prime Minister Katsura or his supporters but rather that these Meiji academics were able to invoke a well-articulated set of values to sanction their social function as an intellectual elite in the service of the nation. This elite had to be distinguished from ordinary civil bureaucrats, these men asserted, because it fulfilled a set of roles that logically required a degree of autonomy for the university and even the right for individual academics to dissent publicly from current government policies despite their legal status as officials of that government. The Meiji academics effectively used this ideology to rally their colleagues on the campuses of both imperial universities as well as in some private colleges in a common front against their adversaries. In the face of such a clear demonstration of solidarity and under the threat that the irreplaceable services of the universities would be withheld in a faculty strike, Katsura and his successor, Prime Minister Saionji, backed down.

The 1905 victory at Tokyo Imperial University has often been discounted in histories written after the disastrous events of the 1930s. For example, the eminent historian Ienaga Saburō, himself a participant in a momentous series of lawsuits over textbook censorship beginning in

35. See the faculty petitions quoted in Kawai, *Kanai Noburu,* pp. 175–176; and in *Danshaku Yamakawa,* pp. 137–140. Also see the detailed discussion by Okada, "Bungei no kaishaku to kyōju no genron," pp. 13–24.
36. Abe, *Teikoku Gikai,* vol. 2, pp. 266, 272.

the 1960s, treated the Affair of the Seven Ph.D.s as a hollow victory. Because no constitutional guarantees for academic freedom were granted, Ienaga viewed the clash as merely an anomalous event in the authoritarian history of the Meiji state.[37] But the Tōdai faculty at the time did not hold such a perception; its sights were set less on de jure guarantees than on maintenance of existing procedures of de facto self-governance. Although the flaws in the legal supports for self-governance would become evident in the 1930s, the trends of the next decade and a half, culminating in the legal changes wrought by the university reforms of 1918–1919, seemed clearly to favor the participants' optimistic interpretation of what had transpired in 1905. There were to be several new challenges between 1905 and the end of World War I, but each time the partisans of faculty participation in university governance proved themselves equal to the occasion.

Progress Toward Self-Governance, 1905–1918

The first of these new challenges came in 1907. That year the special accounts law enhanced the imperial universities' control over their own financial affairs.[38] But in the autumn the Education Ministry fomented new tensions through its choice for president of Kyoto Imperial University. Kinoshita Hiroji, who had served in that post since the school's founding in 1897, had died suddenly, and Dean Kuhara Mitsuru of the College of Sciences had been named acting president during the summer vacation. In October, apparently without consulting Kyoto faculty leaders, the education minister appointed Okada Ryōhei as Kinoshita's successor.

Okada Ryōhei (not to be confused with Professor Okada Asatarō) was a career bureaucrat who had moved up the career ladder rapidly to become bureau chief of technical education and then, in 1901, vice minister of education. In 1904 he received imperial appointment to the House of Peers. Okada's prior academic experience was limited to some postgraduate study at Tōdai and a brief period of teaching at the First

---

37. Ienaga, *Daigaku no jiyū no rekishi*, pp. 42–43.
38. For the significance of the special accounts law of 1907, see I. Hall, "Organizational Paralysis," pp. 318–319.

Higher School in the 1890s. His appointment to the Kyoto presidency was openly resented by many there who considered him an intruder. Some professors were even said to have denied him access to their classrooms on the grounds he was an "outside official." Okada is also said to have alienated Tōdai professor Hozumi Nobushige when Okada called the young Tōdai graduate Yoshino Sakuzō home from teaching in China to offer him a job at Kyoto without proper consultation with Yoshino's mentors on the law faculty. Hozumi managed to block the move and secured Yoshino a position at Tōdai instead, saying he would not tolerate "a president who was an administrative official deciding the appointment of a professor."[39]

After a tense nine months in Kyoto, Okada was recalled in July 1908 to serve again as vice minister of education. Eight weeks later the situation was resolved to the satisfaction of the faculty with the selection of Kikuchi Dairoku, the former Tōdai president, to head the Kyoto school.[40] Because the decision to give the Kyoto post to a distinguished academic was made shortly after a change in cabinets brought Katsura Tarō back into power, it might indicate that Katsura personally preferred to avoid any disharmony that might mar his return to the prime ministership. As it turned out, however, conflict over the government's power to designate imperial university presidents was merely postponed a few years. In the so-called Sawayanagi Affair (or first Kyōdai Affair) of 1913–1914, the issue flared into a confrontation comparable in importance to the Affair of the Seven Ph.D.s, albeit with far less drama.[41]

The stormy national political scene that formed the backdrop for the opening scenes of the Sawayanagi Affair almost rivaled the political intensity of the Russo-Japanese War era. The reign of the new Taishō emperor had scarcely begun before a complex constitutional crisis took place. It was caused initially by military demands on the Diet for in-

---

39. Attributed to Yoshino in Tanaka Sōgorō, *Yoshino Sakuzō,* pp. 118–120.

40. The Okada incident is described in *Danshaku Yamakawa,* p. 257; Sumiya, "Kyōdai hōgakubu Konjaku monogatari"; and Suh, "The Struggle for Academic Freedom," p. 321.

41. Primary materials for the Sawayanagi Affair are contained in the *Kyōto Hōgaku zasshi* 9, no. 1 and no. 2; lengthy excerpts from that are translated in Suh, "The Struggle for Academic Freedom," pp. 321–327. Although these are on the whole literally accurate, some portions quoted here are retranslated in an attempt to reflect something more of the flavor of the rhetoric in the original. For other sources, see *Danshaku Yamakawa,* pp. 257–273; Ienaga, *Daigaku no jiyū no rekishi,* pp. 43–50; and Sasaki Sōichi et al., *Kyōdai jiken,* pp. 37–39.

creased appropriations and by the withdrawal of the army minister from the Seiyūkai Party cabinet of Saionji Kinmochi. Saionji, unable to find a senior officer on active duty willing to serve, resigned in December 1912. When the navy tried the same tactic to block the formation of a third Katsura cabinet, Katsura countered with an attempt to manipulate the new Taishō emperor into publicly backing Katsura's side. By thrusting the throne into the midst of a partisan political controversy, Katsura enraged both his military opponents and the Seiyūkai Party. Public support mounted for the principle of having cabinets selected by the Diet and thereby "protect constitutional government" and "destroy clique government." Prominent Diet members, liberal newspapers, progressive intellectuals, and some influential businessmen denounced Katsura. Massive public rallies were held, and the press drew parallels with the antitreaty riots of 1905. In the end Japan's political elites maneuvered to oust Katsura from office after less than three months.[42]

The events of this "Taishō Political Change" are of interest here for three reasons. First, a number of Tōdai professors were deeply involved in debates over interpretations of constitutional law and provided some of the intellectual framework for the advocates of parliamentary government. Second, this Movement to Protect Constitutional Government helped spawn activity aimed at more radical demands for "Taishō democracy," which in subsequent years involved academics in even more partisan activities.[43] Third, and most immediately, the confusion of the 1912–1914 period in national politics was reflected in the government's bungling approach to campus issues in those years.

Between the spring of 1911, when the administrative burden was increased by the creation of two new imperial universities in Kyushu and Tōhoku, and June 1915, when the Sawayanagi Affair was concluded, six different men held the post of education minister. During the same time span the presidents of all four imperial universities were replaced at least once. The turnover in imperial university presidents began at Tōdai when President Hamao Arata was elevated to the Privy Council in August 1912. Science dean Sakurai Jōji was appointed acting president and remained in that post for fifteen months as the Education Ministry deliberated over a permanent replacement. In May

42. For one of the clearer analyses in English of this "Taishō political change," see Najita, *Hara Kei in the Politics of Compromise*, pp. 100ff.

43. For a provocative reassessment of the concept of Taishō democracy, see Gordon, *Labor and Imperial Democracy*, especially pp. 5–9.

1912 Kyoto president Kikuchi Dairoku was named to the Privy Council, and the Education Ministry filled that position temporarily with science dean Kuhara Mitsuru. In May 1913 Education Minister Okuda Yoshindo suddenly announced simultaneous appointments of new presidents for all four schools. Yamakawa Kenjirō, who had been serving as the first president of Kyushu Imperial University, agreed to return to his old post at Tōdai, a move welcomed by faculty leaders who remembered his efforts during the Affair of the Seven Ph.D.s. But the announcement that Sawayanagi Masatarō was being transferred from Tōhoku to Kyoto had quite the opposite impact.

Sawayanagi was a longtime Education Ministry official and school administrator who had previously served in various secondary-level institutions before becoming the first head of the Tōhoku Imperial University. Whatever irritation the Kyoto faculty felt at the ministry for once again sending an "outsider" to head the university soon flared into outrage at Sawayanagi's actions. Shortly after his arrival faculty members became aware that he intended to force the early retirement of seven professors from various disciplines, men who Sawayanagi later claimed were "fatigued by mental or physical strain in their research and cannot keep pace with the development of learning and skills nor show progress in their scholarship."[44]

Led by professors from the Law College, faculty members reacted on August 2 with a statement of their objections to this abuse of presidential authority. They emphatically identified the issue as one of academic freedom and reminded the president that faculty tenure was a prerequisite to the advancement of knowledge. Without that security, "scholars will come to think it foolish to exert efforts on scholarship, those who would become scholars will decrease steadily, and not only will it be impossible to recruit men of genius in the future but those capable men who are presently holding posts as professors will be dissatisfied with their status here and look elsewhere for a position." The faculty spokesmen conceded, "It is in the proper nature of things that there should be revitalization [*shinchin taisha*] in keeping with the advance of world progress," but they insisted nevertheless that academic tenure was "necessary to protect professors from intervention by government officials or coercion by vulgar [public] opinion." Only a scholar's peers could judge his competency, and that judgment should properly be made by a college faculty meeting. For the president to

44. Suh, "The Struggle for Academic Freedom," p. 324.

undertake such judgments in cases of appointment unilaterally without faculty consultation was to violate "an article of common law [*fubunhō*]." This same principle applied equally to cases of dismissal. The authors continued by warning Sawayanagi that the university could not perform its mission unless mutual cooperation and consultation existed between the faculty and the office of the president. If the president, "acting as the delegate of the government," destroyed the spirit of cooperation by abusing his powers in personnel matters, then not only would the morale of the faculty suffer but also professors would lose the respect of their students and the wider public because they would be reduced to the status of "ordinary bureaucratic functionaries [*jinjō gyōseikan*]."[45]

The summer vacation period allowed Sawayanagi to delay his reply until late October, when he issued his own carefully argued rebuttal. Surprisingly, he denied there was any issue of academic freedom involved because he could assure the faculty that personnel decisions would be made with the "utmost care and fairness": "So long as I occupy this office there will be no dismissals of professors from their posts through government intervention or outside pressures." He did agree faculty tenure was generally a good practice, but the failure to dismiss incompetent professors was potentially more damaging to the prestige of the university than their retention in the name of academic freedom. As to the procedural question central to the faculty's argument, Sawayanagi simply rejected the claim that existing practices required faculty participation in the dismissal of professors, stating "it is unreasonable" to insist on the consent of college faculty meetings and asserting "there has never been such a system in any country."[46]

In response to Sawayanagi's unbending posture, faculty spokesmen appealed directly to Education Minister Okuda Yoshindo. Their statement of early December 1913 reiterated the claim that consultation regarding dismissals was the logical extension of the role faculty already played in recommending candidates for new appointments. They cited at some length precedents in Germany, France, and Austria. Thus, they concluded, it was Sawayanagi, not the faculty, who was guilty of attempting unilaterally to change the existing practices at Japan's imperial universities.

Minister Okuda was too sensitive to the potential for an embarrass-

45. Sasaki Sōichi et al., *Kyōdai jiken,* pp. 38–40.
46. Quoted in Suh, "The Struggle for Academic Freedom," p. 324.

ing clash with Japan's academic elite to act hastily. He took the matter under advisement while he sounded out feelings at the Tokyo campus. Leading figures at Tōdai sided with their colleagues in Kyoto and proposed amending the university regulations to clarify the role of the faculty in personnel matters. Faced with this united front, Minister Okuda began maneuvering toward a compromise. In late January 1914 he informed a delegation from Kyoto that he had "no objections [*sashitsukaenaku*]" to the president consulting with faculty meetings in questions regarding the dismissal as well as the appointment of faculty.

Not surprisingly, the faculty was pleased. But this attempt at compromise set off a minor tempest in the House of Representatives, where thirty-one members signed a formal interpellation. They demanded to know whether the education minister was taking it on himself to alter the civil service regulations that specified the administrative prerogatives of the school president regarding imperial university staff. If not, then why were Kyoto faculty members being allowed to behave, in the words of one speaker, like "ordinary employees of the government tobacco agency"? Their threats of strikes could not but "disturb the minds of the people" and "spread an ominously evil influence among the youths of the nation."[47] Other speakers reminded the House of Representatives of the turmoil that had prevailed during the Affair of the Seven Ph.D.s.

Minister Okuda responded by disclaiming any intention of proposing changes in the civil service status of imperial university professors. He conceded that in this case harmony had been lost through a combination of his own carelessness and Sawayanagi's tactless response to the faculty's initial petition. But he quickly added that he agreed with those members of the House of Representatives who thought the professors were acting with less than full concern for propriety.[48]

The Sawayanagi Affair was allowed to drag on until the change of cabinets in April 1914 brought Ōkuma Shigenobu to the prime minister's office. Sawayanagi was then dismissed from the Kyoto post. But this by no means resolved the dispute. The issue now shifted from the prerogatives of the university administration to the method of selecting the president. As a result, no decision on Sawayanagi's replacement was forthcoming for another fourteen months.

---

47. Speech by Morita Kotarō to the 31st session of the House of Representatives, January 30, 1914; reprinted in Abe, *Teikoku Gikai*, vol. 3, pp. 199–202.
48. Ibid.

During this period the new education minister was Ichiki Kitokurō, ironically the elder brother of the Okada Ryōhei who had been driven from the Kyoto presidency six years earlier. Unlike his brother, however, Ichiki had some credibility in academic circles. He held a doctorate in law and had served on the Tōdai faculty before devoting himself full time to a very successful bureaucratic career. Ichiki immediately entered into lengthy negotiations with representatives of the faculty from both Tokyo and Kyoto over the latter's proposal for formal faculty elections for the presidency. In the interim a compromise was struck when the Kyoto faculty agreed to the unprecedented arrangement of having Tōdai president Yamakawa serve concurrently as president of Kyōdai. In reality Yamakawa was primarily a mediator between the ministry and the faculties at the two imperial universities. In this role he was unsuccessful in getting any agreement from Minister Ichiki to undertake a formal amendment to the imperial university regulations, but in February 1915 Yamakawa did persuade the minister to consider an informal arrangement peculiar to the Kyoto campus. Under this compromise the Kyoto faculty might vote to put forth a candidate for ministry approval. In April the Kyoto University Council discussed candidates for president. Ironically, in view of the long struggle by faculty leaders to gain control over the nomination process, the council was unable to agree on a nominee.

The deans at Tōdai now began to put pressure on the ministry by complaining that the agenda of business at their school required the attention of a full-time president. Yamakawa formally asked to be relieved of his dual responsibilities in May, and Minister Ichiki finally gave in to a new proposal. Rather than the University Council picking the candidate, Kyoto faculty members would nominate by direct ballot.

The education minister was soon pressed by the House of Peers to defend his bargain with the academics. The former Kyōdai president, Sawayanagi Masatarō, was a member of that body and at one point in the debate took the floor. Suppressing any signs of bitterness about ministerial capitulation to faculty demands, Sawayanagi inquired only whether such an arrangement could produce an "appropriate person." Ichiki blandly replied that he hoped it would prove workable. On June 15, 1915, the government brought the Sawayanagi Affair to a close by officially designating science dean Araki Torasaburō, the candidate chosen by a vote of the faculty, president of Kyoto University.[49]

49. *Danshaku Yamakawa*, pp. 262–273; Tanaka Kōtarō et al., *Daigaku no jiji*, pp. 32–34.

Clearly, once again the combined weight of the faculties at Kyoto and Tokyo had been felt on an issue fundamental to the cause of university autonomy. This time the victory had not required the dramatic tactics of a decade earlier. And it was made even sweeter that same summer when the Education Ministry announced its plans for a high-level commission to consider reforms within the entire system of national education. The advocates of greater university independence were more than ready to use the occasion to press their previous victories.

The ministry's Extraordinary Commission on Education (Rinji Kyōiku Kaigi) deliberated for many months before producing the set of reforms that opened a new era in Japanese higher education. Major changes were made in existing schools, and a dramatic expansion of the number of universities took place. As might be expected, the Tōdai faculty was very much involved in lobbying for proposed reforms relating to the imperial universities.

President Yamakawa, an influential member of the commission, was advised by a special Tōdai faculty committee. Created by an action of the University Council, the committee consisted of five representatives from each of the six colleges of the university. The report of this committee was then discussed in each college faculty meeting as well as in the University Council.[50] Amid recommendations on a wide variety of questions, the report called for several key changes in the existing regulations for policy and personnel decisions:

1. A system for the direct election of the university president by ballot of all full professors for a specified term of five years.
2. The election of the new department chairmen—the equivalent of the college deans under the old system—by the faculty of their departments for specified terms of three years.
3. The expansion of the University Council to include two elected professors in addition to the chairmen sitting ex officio.
4. An explicit recognition of the right of the department faculty

---

50. For example, see the minutes of the Tōdai Hyōgikai for March 10, 1914, September 28, 1915, and December 3, 1918. Unfortunately, no records have been available for the departmental faculty meetings, and the minutes of the Hyōgikai that are available tend to be very sketchy for these years, with little detail on any discussions that might have taken place.

meeting to make recommendations on both appointment and termination of professors and associate professors.[51]

When the commission deliberated on these issues, however, it reached no consensus. Thus, the commission's final report to the government made no mention of procedures for selection of either university presidents or professors other than to endorse education minister approval as part of the ministry's responsibility to oversee all universities, public or private. The new regulations, issued in a series between December 1918 and March 1919, were substantially the same on the subject of appointments for the imperial universities as had been previous ordinances. The major legal change in university governance was the expansion of elected faculty representation on the University Council by the addition of a second faculty member from each department. Hence, the council became a body of which two-thirds were elected directly, and the ex officio chairmen were reduced in proportion from one-half to one-third.

Despite the absence of new legal sanctions, faculty participation in selecting the Tokyo University president was in actuality assured after 1918 by the firmly established practice of determining by faculty secret ballot a single nominee for education minister approval. After 1918 all Tōdai presidents were faculty members appointed only after nomination by ballot of the university faculty. Including Yamagawa, who stayed on until September 1920, none of the five presidents between the two world wars served more than eight years. Moreover, as a result of an informal practice of rotation, no two came from the same college within the university. The terms for department chairmen continued to vary among the seven faculty divisions, but three to four years had become the norm by the 1930s. Here, too, faculty balloting was the accepted procedure.[52] Recruitment and promotion of faculty also remained firmly in the hands of the separate departments, with a tacit understanding that the University Council and president would normally rubber-stamp departmental decisions.

As these procedures for academic self-government became routine in the early 1920s, the faculty of Tokyo Imperial University had good reason to believe it had secured a large measure of de facto, if not de jure, autonomy in the appointment of faculty and selection of school

51. Tōdai, *Gojūnenshi*, vol. 2, pp. 84–85, 553; Nanbara et al., *Onozuka Kiheiji*, pp. 135–137; and Yamanouchi, "Daigaku to senmon gakkō."

52. See the lists of presidents and chairmen in Tōdai, *Gojūnenshi*.

officials. In the sense of formal institutional mechanisms, it can be argued this was indeed the case. Although it had taken more than a decade to complete the triumph of the 1905 confrontation, the proponents of university self-government who had fought the Katsura government so energetically seemed to have finally achieved most of their objectives.

The next chapters will describe how difficult it was to maintain these gains. There remains to this chapter the task of identifying some of the key factors behind these early successes.

The Bases for Elite Status

In assessing the circumstances that forced the Katsura cabinet in 1905 to capitulate in its confrontation with the Tōdai faculty, later analysts have usually emphasized the political unpopularity of Katsura Tarō and the nationalistic appeal of Tomizu and his fellow hawks. Certainly no analysis of the Affair of the Seven Ph.D.s can ignore that those faculty activists were on what turned out to be the popular side of the war issue. Nevertheless, these considerations alone do not explain the restraint shown prior to the autumn of 1905 by the Katsura cabinet, which was not known for its tolerance of critics of any stripe. Nor do they explain the remarkable unity of Katsura's academic adversaries, who included men such as Onozuka Kiheiji who did not always share Tomizu's bellicosity. Furthermore, the peace settlement was a fait accompli by the time the Tomizu confrontation was fully joined. However important the war issue, it became secondary to the academic elite's insistence on its independence. Nor does the popularity of Tomizu's stand on the Russo-Japanese War in 1905 explain the academic victories of 1908 and 1913–1914. What must be weighted more heavily in the final balance are two other factors: the cohesiveness of these academic intellectuals when attacked and the ensconced nature of their positions within the political establishment of late Meiji Japan.

This academic elite included professors from a wide variety of disciplines: medicine, engineering, literature, economics. Although their main institutional locus was Tōdai, they also had the support on the issue of academic freedom from faculties at the newer Kyoto University and at private colleges. As intellectuals, men such as Hozumi Yatsuka, Minobe Tatsukichi, Inoue Tetsujirō, and Takano Iwasaburō were often in opposing philosophical and political camps. Nevertheless, in the Meiji period they shared a conscious identity as an academic elite and a consensus on the need to struggle for greater university autonomy. Underlying this cohesiveness were the personal ties formed while students together at the early Tōdai, when the student body and faculty were still small and when the number of Japanese trained at foreign universities was as yet quite limited. This affinity was further strengthened by interaction as social peers and colleagues in an academic community that in 1905 was still not very large. In many cases, family ties and intermarriage also contributed to this cohesiveness.

Cohesiveness, while essential, was of course not sufficient to protect this academic community in confrontations with the Meiji state. Here the importance of the political, economic, and social roles performed by the Western-trained experts on the faculty of Tokyo Imperial University cannot be overemphasized. To have allowed the imperial universities at Tokyo and Kyoto to have remained closed, in effect dispensing with the services of these intellectuals, was simply not a viable option for government leaders in the late Meiji period. There was a constant and critical need for the expertise of imperial university faculty; and it was this need that gave the Tōdai academics an influential voice in Japanese social policy in this period. The analyses of Bernard Silberman and Ronald Dore are very helpful in understanding this crucial point.

Silberman has cogently argued that the bureaucratic elite of late-nineteenth-century Japan had reached a consensus on national goals in the abstract but that there were "a lack of consensus on and absence of knowledge necessary to achieve the goals." The need for expertise thus stemmed from a situation in which "the goals agreed upon required the use of Western models and therefore the use of Western systems of knowledge."[53] But as late as the turn of the twentieth century, the ability to comprehend and apply Western experience remained in the possession of relatively small numbers of Japanese who had the requisite training abroad and the familiarity with Europe and the United States to speak with authority. Silberman's studies of the backgrounds of elite bureaucrats between 1868 and 1900 lead to the conclusion that, granted the large percentage who had been exposed to Western ideas, on the whole their education was "spotty and not very profound."[54]

53. Silberman, "Bureaucratic Development and the Structure of Decision-Making in Japan," pp. 357–358.
54. Ibid., pp. 353, 357.

The more important criterion for achieving the highest offices in the various ministries between 1868 and 1900 was being from one of the four leading southwestern domains and/or having been active in the Restoration movements of the 1860s. In direct contrast, the academic elite seldom shared these regional or political credentials; rather, these academicians owed their positions more clearly to their early acquisition of specialized information and skills then in short supply.

This is not to imply that the academics who composed such a large part of the Meiji reservoir of scarce expertise were used simply as technicians implementing policies already determined or as mere consultants having no influence on goals. The Meiji academic elite took a very active part in debates over both means and goals in such critical areas as mass education, legal reform, constitutional law, and industrial relations. And the Tōdai faculty was very much involved in justifying both goals and means—providing an ideology that would explain why foreign models were required in the first place and how a sense of cultural and national identity could be preserved despite the abandoning of so much of Tokugawa tradition. In this integrative function the establishment intellectual of the Meiji period served in ways analogous to his Tokugawa predecessor, the Confucian literatus who was both scholar-educator and ritualist-moralist.[55]

It can also be argued that the influence of Tokugawa tradition on political discourse in the Meiji period legitimated for the academic expert an authority even beyond that bestowed by his mastery of Western knowledge. As Ronald Dore has pointed out in his study of the debates over factory legislation in the 1890s and 1900s, "The debates took place in an intellectual climate in which the distinction between fact and value was not conventionally made." This meant the academic was called on to treat policy issues in the broadest context:

The Confucian scholar was entitled to pronounce not only in matters of fact, but also, even more especially, on matters of value. The high prestige of the Confucian tradition . . . was another special feature of Japan's early development not commonly duplicated elsewhere. . . . The authority of scholarship might not often assume the proportions that it did in Japan where it could borrow from the traditional authority which had always attached to the role of the scholar.[56]

55. See J. Hall, "The Confucian Teacher in Tokugawa Japan."
56. Dore, "The Modernizer as a Special Case," pp. 447–448. For the contrary view—that Confucian scholars were traditionally viewed as mere "specialists"—see Backus, "The Motivation of Confucian Orthodoxy in Tokugawa Japan," p. 290.

Despite the very great changes that took place in the decades immediately preceding and following the Meiji Restoration of 1868, the
ideal of the intellectual combining in himself the separate roles of
scholar-educator, adviser-official, and moral-cultural arbiter was sustained. The major changes were not in the perception of the proper role
of the academic as elite but rather in the displacement of the Confucian
literati by men with new intellectual paradigms and by a very dramatic
increase in the social and political demands for the functions they performed.

This does not mean that their elite position within the system of
political power in Meiji Japan was one that was easily maintained. On
the contrary, in the 1930s Japanese universities would prove all too
often vulnerable to political attacks. Nonetheless, the causes of that later
vulnerability cannot simply be attributed to flaws in the formal structures of universities as originally instituted in the Meiji period. Rather,
the key to understanding the inability of the university faculties to
repulse such attacks in the 1930s must be found in historical developments subsequent to the Meiji period.

4

The Transformation of the Academic Community, 1919–1931

The history of conflict over academic autonomy in the years following World War I cannot be adequately comprehended without recognition that a fundamental transformation was taking place within the Japanese system of higher education. The clashes between the university and the state in these years involved a new generation of academics functioning in a significantly altered institutional setting as well as a new ideological climate. It will be the purpose of this chapter to examine the institutional and intellectual developments that mediated the struggles between state and university in this period.

Although both its dates and significance are subjects of controversy, the new climate of opinion has most often been labeled Taishō *demokurashī* or Taishō liberalism, after the reign name of the emperor on the throne between 1912 and 1925.[1] Actually this climate prevailed until the end of the 1920s but was quite diverse in content, ranging from anarcho-syndicalism and communism on the Left through Fabian socialism and contemporary British liberalism and on toward the Center of the political spectrum. When the holders of these various stances did find common ground, it was in their shared antagonism toward the concentration of political power in the hands of political and economic elites that were unwilling to address the social problems of an increas-

---

1. See Gordon's reassessment and provocative argument for what he termed *imperial democracy* in the Taishō period (*Labor and Imperial Democracy*, especially pp. 5–10).

ingly industrial nation. The mainstream of this movement thus demanded an end to the veto power held by the nonelected House of Peers, the expansion of suffrage for the House of Representatives to include at least all male adults, and cabinet ministers more directly accountable to the majority in the Diet. These reformers also tended to agree on the need for stronger labor unions, tighter regulation of factory conditions, and more protection from the exigencies of a capitalist economy for workers and the deserving poor.

In part this new climate was fed by world tides moving away from the authoritarianism of the German kaiser or the Russian czar, both ousted in the aftermath of the victory won on the battlefield by the democracies of Britain, France, and the United States. That victory gave the democratic ideals and, to a lesser extent, the actual political practices of these nations unprecedented prestige among Japanese intellectuals and activists. Simultaneously, the Bolshevik Revolution focused their attention on the necessity as well as desirability of new approaches to the problems of farmers and workers in an industrial economy.

Not surprisingly, the faculty at the elite universities played an integral role in the processes of translating and expounding on these new ideas. Nor was it surprising that when some of the more radical of these professors and their students carried their convictions into political action, conservative elements within the established parties and the bureaucratic elite attempted to assert greater control over the universities. Thus, part of the story of clashes between the state and the imperial university in the 1920s revolves around the predisposition of a conservative elite to suppress intellectual freedom when it is utilized to challenge the status quo.

Table 4-1 *Expansion of Higher Education, 1908–1933*

	No. of Schools			Total Students	% Increase (5 years)
	Daigaku	*Senmon Gakkō*	*Kōtō Gakkō*		
1908	3	65	8	46,504	
1913	4	86	8	53,188	14
1918	5	96	8	65,180	23
1923	31	121	25	106,698	64
1928	40	153	31	165,885	55
1933	45	171	32	181,455	9

SOURCES: Calculated from Monbushō, *Wagakuni no kōtō kyōiku*, Table 1, p. 254; Table 2, pp. 262–267; Table 8, pp. 290–291; Table 12, pp. 184–185.

The latter section of this chapter is devoted to chronicling the growing tensions these political changes produced among faculty members at Tokyo Imperial University. As significant as this new intellectual and political climate was for the academic activists involved, however, what is too often lost in accounts of their activities in the 1920s is a recognition of the importance of the concomitant shifts taking place in their own institutional environment. The first part of this chapter is thus devoted to describing the changes in the structure and governance of Japanese higher education from 1919 to 1930.

Structural Change in Higher Education

A glance at the numbers in Tables 4-1 and 4-2 affords the quickest insights into what was certainly one of the most important processes at work in higher education—the great increase in scale. The total number of students in officially recognized universities (*daigaku*), colleges (*senmon gakkō*), and higher schools (*kōtō gakkō*) jumped more than 240 percent between 1913 and 1933, with rates over some five-year periods as high as 64 percent.

As can be seen from these tables, the process of segmentation through the proliferation of new schools was even more dramatic, albeit the result, in part, of the upgrading of existing *senmon gakkō*. While such segmentation was the primary means of accommodating growth in scale, the imperial universities at Tokyo and Kyoto also experienced large increases in their student bodies, as are evidenced in Table 4-3.

Table 4-2 *Expansion of Universities, 1908–1933*

	Schools (number)	Students (number)	Faculty Members (number)	Expenditures (100,000s)
1908	3	7,517	533	1,744
1913	4	9,472	815	2,554
1918	5	9,040	970	2,171
1923	31	38,731	3,224	9,669
1928	40	61,502	4,905	14,234
1933	45	70,893	6,285	19,646

SOURCES: Calculated from Monbushō, *Wagakuni no kōtō kyōiku*, Table 1, p. 254; Table 2, pp. 262–267; Table 8, pp. 290–291; Table 12, pp. 184–185. Expenditures are given in 1961 yen, which in that year were officially traded at ¥360 per U.S. $1.

Table 4-3 *Growth of Tokyo and Kyoto Universities, 1913–1933*

	Tokyo		Kyoto	
	No. of Students	*% Change*	*No. of Students*	*% Change*
1913	5,223		1,791	
1918	4,904	−6	2,033	+14
1923	5,981	+22	2,548	+25
1928	7,820	+31	5,170	+103
1933	8,269	+6	5,710	+10
Cumulative change		+158		+489

SOURCE: Naikaku Tōkei Kyoku, *Nihon teikoku tōkei nenkan*, vols. 45, 49, 50, 54.

Changes in the Governance of Higher Education

Such rapid growth in scale and segmentation of any social system poses serious challenges for coordination and control. Given the inadequate response to these challenges in the 1920s, it is not surprising that the Japanese system of higher education became more vulnerable to conflict in this period. Growth was accompanied by two other developments. One the one hand, there was an increasing trend toward bureaucratization within the Ministry of Education. On the other hand, there was a steady drift away from effective centralized authority within the universities.

One measure of the bureaucratization of authority vis-à-vis the universities is the proliferation of formal, standardized rules intended to routinize procedures of governance within the system (see Figure 4-1). This proliferation of standardized rules was, in part at least, a response to a system growing increasingly complex merely because of its scale and segmentation. But it was also an indication of a fundamental shift toward more formal mechanisms of coordination between the Education Ministry and the universities—a shift necessitated by the loss of earlier informal channels of communication of the Meiji period.

One way in which those channels were lost was through differentiation between the personnel of the Education Ministry and the faculty at Tōdai. This process was well under way by the end of the Meiji period as the staff of the ministry simultaneously grew and became

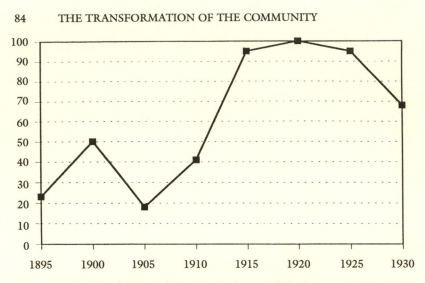

Figure 4-1 Index of New Edicts, Regulations, and Ordinances, 1895–1930
(ten-year averages). Calculated from Monbushō, Chōsa
Fukyūkoku Chōsaka, *Daigaku kankei hōrei no enkaku.*

more professionalized. Although the Education Ministry and the imperial universities had been formally distinct since at least 1885, when
the government was reorganized, administrative personnel were actually often treated as if interchangeable before 1905. Between 1880 and
1905 the Bureau of Professional Education was headed almost exclusively by men with prior experience as administrators or by faculty
members from the imperial university. Nor was it rare in that period to
find Tōdai personnel even in the top post of education minister. By the
end of the Meiji period, however, the minister's post had become increasingly politicized as prime ministers in the Taishō period used the
education portfolio to draw influential civil servants or political party
supporters into the cabinet.[2] These were men whose views on educational policy were often at odds with those of Tōdai leaders, as were
those of the two academics drawn from private schools to serve as head
of the ministry in this new period.[3] At the same time, recruitment to the

2. Among the influential civil servants were Makino Nobuaki (who served as minister, 1911–1912), Okuda Yoshindo (1913–1914), Ichiki Kitokurō (1914–1915), and
Okada Ryōhei (1916–1918). Nakahashi Tokugorō (1918–1922) was a businessman
turned party politician.
3. Takada Sanae, president of Waseda, was appointed minister in 1916; Kamata Eiji,
president of Keiō, served in 1923–1924.

chief of the bureau most closely concerned with the universities, the Bureau of Professional Education, became a routine part of the bureaucratic process of promotion within the permanent staff of the ministry. Thus, Fukuhara Ryōjirō, a career bureaucrat, headed that bureau from 1905 until 1911, when he moved up to vice minister. His successor, Matsuura Chinjirō, was promoted to vice minister in 1924, turning the post over to the current chief of the Bureau of Technical Education.[4]

If the Bureau of Professional Education became more professionalized and differentiated from the Tōdai faculty in these years, there are also indications that its relative position within the Monbushō was reduced as other units grew in size and budget (see Figure 4-2). Even though it is true that expenditures for higher education rose rapidly in the Taishō era, it is also the case that expenditures for other parts of the school system grew even faster. The Bureau of Professional Education, one of only four ministry bureaus in 1908, was one of seven by 1928. The size of its staff, which constituted approximately 13 percent of the ministry higher civil servants in 1906, grew so slowly it represented less than 6 percent in 1926.

The Education Ministry had also yielded ground to other government agencies now more closely involved than previously in matters affecting students and faculties at the universities. Beginning in 1911 the task of controlling dissidents in Japan's institutions of higher education shifted gradually but steadily away from the jurisdiction of the Education Ministry. The Special Higher Police (Tokubetsu Kōtō Keisatsu), which was charged with the investigation of ideological crimes, was expanded, and the 1920s saw the creation of the Thought (Shisō)

---

4. Another measure of the professionalization of Education Ministry staff in these years can be seen in the relative stability of tenure in the posts of vice minister, chief of the Bureau of General Education (Futsū Gakumu Kyokuchō), and chief of the Bureau of Professional Education (Senmon Gakumu Kyokuchō). The average years of tenure were as follows (source: Ijiri, ed., *Rekidai kenkanroku*):

	1886–1906	1906–1926
Vice minister	1.7	5.0
Chief of Bureau of General Education	1.7	2.9
Chief of Bureau of Professional Education	2.0	6.7

For yet another indication of the decline of Tōdai's influence on educational policy, compare the proportion of Tōdai faculty on the Kōtō Kyōiku Kaigi of 1897–1901 with the list of participants in the government conferences of 1910 and 1918: Kaigo, ed., *Rinji Kyōiku Kaigi no kenkyū*, pp. 1019–1036; Monbushō, *Meiji ikō*, vol. 5, pp. 1139ff; vol. 6, p. 1177; Monbushō, *Gakusei hachijūnenshi*, pp. 164–165; and Abe, *Teikoku Gikai*, vol. 1, pp. 112–113; vol. 2, pp. 266–273.

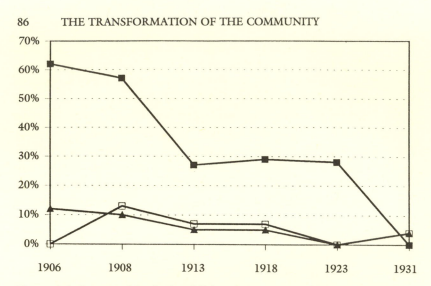

Figure 4-2 Bureau of Professional Education as a Percentage of the Ministry
as a Whole. Calculated from Monbushō, *Meiji ikō,* vol. 4, pp.
73–740; Naikaku, *Nihon Teikoku tōkei menkan;* and Monbushō,
Monbushō nenpō, various years.

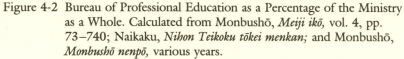

■ Expenditures on universities
☐ Percentage of Ministry salaries
▲ Percentage of Ministry staff

Section of the Justice Ministry. During this process there were frequent
interagency rivalries over jurisdiction and disagreements over tactics.
These frictions sometimes posed obstacles in coordinating government
efforts to cope with intellectual radicalism in a vastly expanded system
of higher education.[5]

These changes within the national educational bureaucracy were accompanied by an even more significant trend toward decentralization
and delegation of authority in the internal governance of the imperial
universities. The result was greater faculty control over a variety of
other critical matters, including the selection of presidents, deans, and
faculty. Prior to 1897 Tōdai presidents had been men selected by the
Meiji political elite in part because they enjoyed close ties to that elite.
Katō Hiroyuki, who served a total of twelve years in two separate
terms, was a model of what has been labeled the "service intelligentsia"
of early Meiji.[6] Watanabe Kōki had been the chief administrative official
for the city of Tokyo before being appointed in 1886 by Minister Mori

5. Mitchell, *Thought Control in Prewar Japan.*
6. Abosch, "Katō Hiroyuki and the Introduction of German Political Thought."

Arinori. Hamao Arata, who served between 1890 and 1897, had long held posts in the Education Ministry as well as within the Tōdai administration. But after 1897, with only one exception, the presidency of Tōdai went to a member of the regular faculty: first to professor of letters Toyama Shōichi, then science professors Kikuchi Dairoku and Yamakawa Kenjirō. The one exception took place in 1905 when Hamao Arata was brought back to office in the wake of the confrontation between the Katsura cabinet and the Tōdai faculty over the government's attempt to fire Tomizu Hiroto. But Hamao's reappointment was less a reversion to a previous pattern of nonfaculty presidents than a temporary compromise with the Tōdai faculty, which accepted Yamakawa's departure in return for that of Education Minister Kubota and the reinstatement of Professor Tomizu.[7] In 1913 the Tōdai faculty succeeded in having Yamakawa Kenjirō reappointed as Tōdai president, and as part of the 1918 reforms faculty balloting for the presidency became the accepted norm. Neither Tokyo nor Kyoto Imperial University was ever again headed by anyone other than the majority candidate of its respective faculty.

The delegation of this important authority to the faculty was only one of a number of shifts toward greater self-governance during the years between 1905 and 1920. Indeed, a general move away from the "authoritarian-bureaucrat" pattern of early Meiji and toward one much closer to "collegial" or "participatory" governance occurred at Tōdai and Kyōdai.[8] This can be seen quite clearly in two related developments already described: the expansion of the membership and powers of the university Senate (Hyōgikai) and the increased formal participation after 1918 of the faculty in the selection of deans or, more accurately, department chairmen.

Changes in the Educational Roles of Academics

If the growth and structural changes in the system of higher education rendered it more vulnerable to conflict because of the

7. See chapter 1.
8. These terms are used in the sense defined in Baldridge, *Power and Conflict in the University*. See also the study of postwar institutions by Iwauchi and Cummings, who use a somewhat more complex paradigm ("Decision-Making Structures in Japanese Universities").

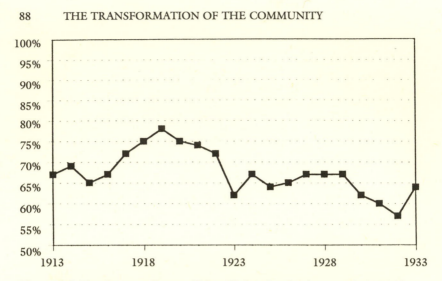

Figure 4-3 Employment Rates of New University Graduates, 1913–1933.
(Excludes those entering military service or postgraduate study.)
From Ministry of Education, *Demand and Supply for University Graduates,* Figure 19, p. 17.

difficulties in coordination and control, there is also sufficient evidence to suggest that the growth and change were accompanied by some significant losses of key academic roles. The easiest of these changes to quantify was the erosion of Tōdai hegemony over the placement of future elites. In the Meiji period Tōdai professors had served as mentors to youths whose Tōdai credentials gave them, once they graduated, unparalleled advantages in vying for positions in the higher civil service and other elite structures. This became far less true in the 1920s. The increase in the supply of university graduates could hardly have come at a worse time in terms of market demand. Although the government bureaucracy as a whole continued to expand in this decade, the pace of its expansion was much slower than in earlier periods, and the competition was correspondingly greater. One consequence was that Tōdai graduates tended more often to seek jobs in the private sector. But in the 1920s the Japanese economy suffered a series of sharp business cycles that limited opportunities here as well. As a result, there were more graduates than jobs for them. Figures 4-3 and 4-4 reflect that excess in supply and the unemployment (but not the underemployment) it produced.

The problem was particularly acute for degree holders in law and

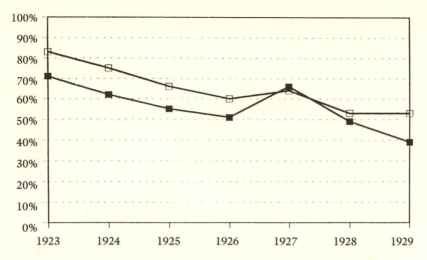

Figure 4-4 Employment Rates of College Graduates, 1923–1929. From
Abe Isoo, *Shitsugyō mondai,* p. 195, quoted in Bamba, *Japanese
Diplomacy in a Dilemma,* Appendix XII, p. 392. For comparable
figures, see Smith, *Japan's First Student Radicals,* p. 214.

☐ All departments
■ Law and economics

economics. Yet in the 1920s more than 40 percent of the student body
at both Tōdai and Kyōdai continued to major in these "public administration" fields despite the relative decline in employment opportunities (see Table 4-4).

By the end of the 1920s the unemployment problem had come to
be seen by academics as well as others as a major cause for student
discontent and the growth of Marxist influence on campus. For
Marxist academics such as Ōmori Yoshitarō, the crisis at least had the
salutary effect of freeing students from the "delusion" that Japanese
higher education was truly dedicated to higher learning. The
overcrowded private universities had become mere commercial
enterprises cynically dedicated to turning a profit. Even students in the
state-supported schools, when faced with unemployment, could now
see the realities:

The prestige of the [state-supported] schools as well as that of their professors
has been totally destroyed. Previously the schools were respected as institutions
of learning and the professors as seekers of truth. Now . . . students fully
understand that the higher schools and universities are nothing more than
organs for maintaining control by the ruling classes, the same as the military

Table 4-4 *Enrollments by Department in Tokyo and Kyoto, 1919–1933*
(as percentages of total students enrolled at school)

	1919	1923	1928	1933
Tokyo Law	34	31	29	28
Tokyo Economics	10	13	15	16
Kyoto Law	32	20	28	32
Kyoto Economics	21	27	18	18

SOURCE: Naikaku Tōkei Kyoku, *Nihon Teikoku tōkei nenkan*, various years.

and police, and the faculty (with the exception of a few Red professors [*sekishoku kyōju*] are merely watchdogs for the learning of the ruling class."[9]

Some non-Marxists, such as Kawai Eijirō, used language only slightly less strong in arguing that the unemployment crisis signaled it was time for basic reform, although what he advocated was not as radical as that envisaged by Ōmori. In Kawai's view, what was needed was, in essence, a better product. Whereas in Meiji times, "the universities, especially the imperial universities, were necessary organs for training assistants" to serve in subordinate roles under the great "pioneers" within the government and business community, this was no longer the case in the 1920s:

The universities consciously or unconsciously came to consider their function that of producing technicians for society . . . graduates who were nothing more than assistants. . . . Now the supply of such narrowly trained products has increased beyond the demand [because], in addition to the oversupply of university graduates, the supply from outside the universities has also increased. The university students cannot retain a monopoly [because] numerous competitors have appeared from outside the university.[10]

Thus by the end of the 1920s, if not earlier, faculty members at elite schools such as Tōdai, who once had expected their students to move all but automatically into roles with considerable potential for influencing the affairs of state and society, were now faced with a very real reduction in their own functional roles as mentors to future elites.

Nor could this loss be considered entirely the unintended consequence of incremental policy making. The greater competition in the higher civil service examination system was at least partly the result of

9. Ōmori Yoshitarō, "Gakkō sōdō uraomote," p. 216.
10. Kawai, "Shūshokunan to daigaku kyōiku." For a similar comment by Ōuchi, see his *Watakushi*, pp. 73–74.

Table 4-5 *Higher Civil Service Examiners (%)*

	1906–1917	1918–1928
Tōdai faculty members	66	45
Faculty members from other schools	23	25
Government officials	11	30

SOURCE: Spaulding, *Imperial Japan's Higher Civil Service Examinatons*, Table 34, p. 249.

conscious reforms. The privileged position of Tōdai as a personnel agency for the bureaucracy had been under steady attack since the 1890s. In those early years opponents of such "imperial university privileges [*teidai tokken*]" as exemptions from certain qualifying examinations had been unsuccessful in forcing any reforms. In 1910, however, the House of Representatives passed a bill extending exemptions to all graduates of certified private law schools. Although the bill was resisted by the government and did not survive the House of Peers, Robert Spaulding has pointed out the underlying significance of the lower house vote: "After 1903 [the anti-imperial university] cause was taken up by . . . private university alumni already established in a profession or business, moving into political parties and the lower house of the Diet. . . . The new critics gave the protest movement the respectability, continuity, and political influence it had lacked."[11]

In 1914 such pressure began to bear fruit as men such as Hara Kei (Takashi), then home minister, supported the attempt to reduce the role of Tōdai, apparently as part of a larger effort to open the top echelon of the civil bureaucracy to more party supporters. When the government stalled in implementing the 1914 reform, which would have ended special privileges in the examinations for imperial university graduates, this occasioned mass demonstrations by private college students outside the Diet and vehement attacks from Diet members within on policy favoring the imperial universities. The government slowly gave ground in 1918 and again in 1923. By this time official university status had been granted to most of the private schools involved in the original campaigns. Spaulding's exhaustive research on the subject did not yield hard data on relative numbers of Tōdai graduates affected, but competition from graduates from other schools was not insignificant. Moreover, the role of Tōdai professors as civil service examiners was

11. Spaulding, *Imperial Japan's Higher Civil Service Examinations*, p. 139.

reduced somewhat as the overall proportion of civil bureaucrats and others increased during the 1920s (see Table 4-5).

Changes in the Political
Roles of Academics

The role played by the lower house of the Diet in bringing about these reforms in civil service recruitment in particular and the expansion of higher education in general was part of a larger shift in the political environment—a shift that adversely affected the political roles of the Tōdai academic. As political parties emerged as a means for aggregating the special interests of various groups within society, the Diet became more and more a central forum for public debate over social legislation. At the same time, the civil bureaucracy, which still drafted as well as implemented much of such legislation, grew increasingly independent of the older Meiji style of oligarchic coordination as the higher civil service itself moved toward greater specialization and professionalization. This emergence of the political parties and the maturation of the civil bureaucracy altered the processes of policy making in a way that reduced opportunities for academic experts to exert the type of direct influence on the broad range of social policy they had in the Meiji period.

One indication of this change has already been described in the differentiation between Tōdai professors and the Education Ministry staff. A similar trend took place within the Justice Ministry, whose personnel had once frequently appeared as instructors in Tōdai law classrooms and had regularly turned to Tōdai academics for expertise in revising the legal codes of the mid-Meiji period. In the post-Meiji era such interchange of personnel was rare.[12]

Yet another important sphere where academic expertise carried less weight in the decades of the 1920s and 1930s than in the 1900s was that of industrial relations and labor legislation. In the earlier period Tōdai professors had been ex officio participants in major government-sponsored conferences on labor policy and, as members of the influential Social Policy Study Association, had taken a leading part in pres-

---

12. For the Justice Ministry in the Taishō period, see Mitchell, *Thought Control in Prewar Japan*, pp. 34ff; and Yasko, "Hiranuma Kiichiro."

suring the bureaucracy for action on factory legislation. By the early 1920s, however, the association had been disbanded, and bureaucratic agencies within the Home Ministry and the Agriculture and Commerce Ministry, as well as the quasi-official Kyōchōkai (Conciliation Society), had taken over much of the function of preparing policy positions for Diet action.[13]

The historian Tsurumi Shunsuke has summarized succinctly these trends in his comments on the frustrations of academic intellectuals in the 1930s (although the change should be dated somewhat later than Tsurumi has dated it and the frustration was certainly felt as early as the 1920s): "Between the Meiji Restoration and the mid-Meiji period was an era in which specialized scholars [senmonteki gakusha] had participated fully in national policies as they took shape in the government. But this contact turned into a mere exchange of formalities."[14] What Tsurumi did not mention was that, ironically, this change was made possible by the increased supply of university-trained expertise within the bureaucracy in the 1920s and 1930s.

If the maturation of Japan's civil bureaucracy and the parliamentary parties reduced the opportunities for academics to participate directly in elite decision making in the style of the Meiji period, in the 1920s there was a reciprocal increase in their involvement in popular political movements. In the Meiji era prior to 1905, politically active academic intellectuals such as Hozumi Nobushige and Kanai Noburu had focused their efforts primarily on influencing government planning from within the circle of ruling elites. Beginning with the Affair of the Seven Ph.D.s but not cresting until the late 1910s and 1920s, imperial university professors such as Yoshino Sakuzō and Takano Iwasaburō assumed prominent leadership roles in partisan political efforts to mobilize mass support behind reform movements aimed at opening the system to nonelite participation. Indeed, for such young idealists as Ōuchi Hyōe, Kawai Eijirō, and Nanbara Shigeru, the academic world offered a greater opportunity for influencing social reform than did posts in the government bureaucracy.[15] Because these activities extended to the

13. In addition to my treatment in *Capitalism and Nationalism in Prewar Japan* (Chapters 4 and 5), see Kinzley, *Industrial Harmony in Modern Japan;* and Garon, *State and Labor in Modern Japan.*

14. Tsurumi et al., *Tenkō,* vol. 2, p. 179.

15. Hirai also made this point in her biography of Kawai Eijirō, *Individualism and Socialism,* p. 216, n46. Also see Barshay's intellectual portrait of Nanbara in *State and the Intellectual in Imperial Japan.*

organization of student groups that played a remarkably significant role in the antiestablishment politics of the 1920s, the overall effect was to politicize the imperial universities in unprecedented ways.

Perhaps the best remembered of these Taishō liberal activists has been law professor Yoshino Sakuzō (1878–1933). Yoshino's early personal career was hardly typical of his fellow Tōdai law professors.[16] Baptized as a Christian during his school days at the Second Higher School in Sendai, he married a young coreligionist while both were still students. By the time he entered Tōdai as a political science major in 1900, he was already a father. His path from student to professor was even less smooth than that of Minobe Tatsukichi or the other exceptions to the dominant pattern of recruitment described in the previous chapter. The burden of family expenses led Yoshino after graduation in 1904 to accept a post in Tientsin as tutor-adviser to the eldest son of Chinese strongman Yuan Shih-k'ai. Tutor and pupil found themselves at loggerheads from the very outset, and Yoshino consequently spent three long years in academic and financial limbo, teaching part time at a Chinese school.

Yoshino's career as an academic was put back on track when his former professor, Hozumi Nobushige, sponsored him for an associate professorship at Tōdai. The financial problem of supporting his family during the tour of study abroad expected of all young faculty was solved when some of Japan's most influential Christians arranged for a financial subsidy from a prominent civil bureaucrat.[17] Returning from England in 1913 to a full professorship, Yoshino plunged into what were to be the three central political controversies of the coming decade: the reform of labor relations, the expansion of suffrage, and the new political activism of university students.

Yoshino's connections as a young Christian doubtless had much to do with his concern for the laboring classes. On arrival in Tokyo in 1900 he almost immediately began to associate with the various socialists and other social reformers who orbited around two of the best-known Christians of the day: Ebina Danjō (1856–1937), then pastor of the Hongō church in the same district as the Tōdai campus, and

---

16. Among the many writings on Yoshino, see Tanaka Sōgorō's biography, *Yoshino Sakuzō;* Najita, "Some Reflections on Idealism in the Political Thought of Yoshino Sakuzō"; and Silberman, "The Democracy Movement in Japan."

17. See Tanaka Sōgorō, *Yoshino Sakuzō,* pp. 118–120. The part played by Ebina Danjō and Tokutomi in securing a ¥1,500 gift from Gotō Shinpei is discussed on pp. 123–124.

Uchimura Kanzō (1861–1930), whose home was the center for a tightly knit group of student converts. Both men stressed a combination of Bible study with social idealism, and the intellectuals and students who gathered around them had enormous influence on progressive and left-wing movements in subsequent years.[18] Among the younger ones was Suzuki Bunji, the labor organizer. Suzuki had been born and raised in the same small town in Miyage Prefecture as Yoshino, was also baptized while at Yoshino's alma mater in Sendai, and was subsequently helped by Yoshino to enter Tōdai.[19] Thus, they were close personally as well as ideologically. When Suzuki created the Yūaikai (the Friendly Society) to organize workers for their mutual aid, Yoshino was one of a number of supporters who lent prestige to Suzuki's cause by serving as councillors.[20] It was out of this early Yūaikai that Japan's first full-fledged labor union movement developed in the 1920s.

For Yoshino, however, popular participation in Japanese politics was even more basic than social welfare legislation or the trade union movement. His greatest efforts were spent in the campaign for universal male suffrage. In June 1915 he and his friend at Kyoto University, law professor Sasaki Sōichi, organized the University Extension Society (Daigaku Fukyūkai). It published a magazine, *The People's Lectern (Kokumin kōdan)* aimed at increasing the influence of academic intellectuals among the more literate public by publishing faculty views on current political issues and social problems. *The People's Lectern* was not a financial success, but similar articles and reports on public speeches appeared with increasing regularity in the more widely read monthlies and newspapers of the day. Henry Smith succinctly summarized the change:

The novelty of the Taishō democrats lay . . . in the extensive use of journalism to propound their views. Whereas the members of the Social Policy Study Association and other early reform advocates had put forth their ideas in scholarly periodicals and abstruse theoretical tomes, Taishō democrats like Yoshino Sakuzō . . . preferred to utilize more popular media. . . . For the first time the

18. For a good treatment of the relationship between Meiji Christianity and social idealism in the Meiji period as well as specific information on the teachings of Ebina Danjō, see Scheiner, *Christian Converts and Social Protest,* especially pp. 243–247; and Notehelfer, "Ebina Danjō." Uchimura Kanzō is discussed in Arima, *The Failure of Freedom.* Also instructive is Barshay's treatment of the influence of Christian thought on Yoshino and others in this period in *State and the Intellectual in Imperial Japan.*

19. Suzuki Bunji, *Rōdō undō nijūnen.*

20. See Large, *The Yūaikai,* p. 31.

dissident views of university professors were becoming widely popular through the distribution of such publications.[21]

Yoshino was joined in these activities by dozens of other academic intellectuals, including Tōdai professors Hozumi Shigetō (law), Watanabe Tetsuzō (economics), Morito Tatsuo (economics), Anesaki Masaharu (letters), and Ōshima Masanori (letters). There were also active faculty members from the leading private colleges of Keiō and Waseda. In December 1918 these academic liberals formed the Society for Enlightenment (Reimeikai) to sponsor public lectures. It was soon to receive considerable publicity, much of it the result of attacks on the society by right-wing nationalist groups. What provoked the political Right is evident from the Reimeikai manifesto. It boldly proclaimed that its members were dedicated to adapting Japan "to the new conditions of the postwar world" that had resulted from the victory of "liberalism, progressivism, and democracy." What was needed, the manifesto demanded, was "to destroy the . . . concepts which are contrary to the present trends of the world [*sekai no taisei*]," outdated notions clung to by "the many conservatives, obstinate advocates of despotism and militarism . . . in our society who despise freedom of speech and thought."[22] A number of student groups quickly sprang up embracing these goals, the most influential being the Tōdai New Men Society (Shinjinkai), which was founded the same month as the Reimeikai with a nucleus drawn from Tōdai Law College students closely associated with Professor Yoshino.[23]

In reaction to this new tide of liberalism and radical ideas, a counteroffensive arose among the politically conservative faculty and students on the Tōdai campus. In the early years after World War I these right-wing students tended to gravitate toward Tōdai law professors Uesugi Shinkichi and Kahei Katsuhiko.[24] Uesugi (1878–1929), the more prominent of the two, was the son of a traditional physician from Kanagawa, where he attended the Fourth Higher School before entering Tōdai Law College in 1898. He graduated at the top of the 1903

21. Smith, *Japan's First Student Radicals,* p. 32.

22. Silberman, "The Democracy Movement in Japan," p. 160; and Kyōchōkai, ed., *Saikin no shakai undō,* p. 537.

23. For Yoshino's early connection to these groups, see Smith, *Japan's First Student Radicals,* pp. 45–46. Later Yoshino and the Shinjinkai parted political company.

24. Right-wing academic factions have received far less attention than their liberal or radical counterparts (as Smith also noted in his study of the Taishō student movement), and information on Uesugi and his followers is gleaned from a number of sources whose accuracy is, in Smith's apt characterization, "modest" (ibid.).

class, although an illness had delayed his progress for a year. Thanks to the financial support of a wealthy patron, he was able to spend 1906 to 1909 in Heidelberg studying constitutional theory. On his return he was appointed associate professor and took over the seminar of Professor Hozumi Yatsuka when the latter fell terminally ill. Uesugi soon emerged as Yatsuka's successor in the long-term debate within the college and the Japanese intellectual community over the proper interpretation of imperial sovereignty.

Uesugi's chief academic opponent was Minobe Tatsukichi, who had himself taken over the mantle of his own mentor, Ichiki Kitokurō, when Ichiki left the school in 1908 to devote himself full time to a remarkably successful bureaucratic career. Minobe summed up the more crucial differences between himself and the camp of Hozumi Yatsuka in an early article:

> The state is the subject of governmental power and the monarch is an organ of the state. . . . Japan's national policy in its historical base is not like that of the states of Europe. . . . But historical bases are not adequate to explain the present state. . . . In present legal terms, Japan's national polity does not differ in pattern from the constitutional monarchies of Europe.[25]

Minobe's own liberalism was constrained by his reluctance to participate in popular movements and by his belief in the authority of the state. Nevertheless, his "organ theory" had important ramifications for intellectuals searching for a justification for the growing share of political power being acquired by the parliamentary parties.

Uesugi's views were antithetical, stressing the primacy of the throne and the transcendental quality of the emperor while rejecting the comparative approach to constitutional interpretation. These ideas were less influential among intellectuals and political leaders in the 1910s than in the 1930s when they became the political fashion. Yet Uesugi was not reticent in carrying on the attack against the then more respected Minobe. By 1912 the debate had taken on the character of a personal feud, with Minobe labeling his opponent an advocate of "disguised despo-

---

25. Quoted in Miller, *Minobe Tatsukichi*, p. 27; see ibid., pp. 25–38, for an incisive analysis of these early debates with Uesugi. Hozumi Yatsuka's writings are treated comprehensively in Minear, *Japanese Tradition and Western Law;* see especially pp. 191–192 for a summary of the basic differences between the two camps. There is also a thoroughly documented account in Miyazawa Toshiyoshi (himself a Minobeite), *Tennō kikansetsu jiken,* vol. 1, pp. 9–68. Hijikata, *Gakkai shunjūki,* pp. 69–75; Tanaka, *Yoshino Sakuzō,* pp. 53–55; and Ōuchi, *Keizaigaku.* All these reveal clearly the influence these debates had on younger contemporaries.

tism," while Uesugi, in Minobe's words, "charged me as a treacherous rebel [and] raised the great sword of national polity [*kokutai*] from on high."[26] Uesugi's views and style did win him adherents in the military academies, where he regularly lectured, and among right-wing patriotic students at Tōdai who frequently met at his home for discussion. In 1919 such students formed the Kōkoku Dōshikai (Colleagues in Support of the Nation) with the specific intent of countering the liberal following of Yoshino Sakuzō. Like the Yoshino camp, Uesugi also had prominent allies off campus, notably Justice Minister Hiranuma Kiichirō, who served as a councillor to the student group and later recruited members from it to other nationalist organizations.[27]

Thus, a cleavage that had begun with different interpretations of constitutional monarchy between two early Tōdai theorists had taken on new political relevancy in the 1910s and then became institutionalized into formal groups that engaged often in bitter and sometimes violent clashes in the highly politicized atmosphere of the Tōdai campus of the 1920s. As politicization intensified, so did the intramural factionalism within the faculty, and it was this factionalism, especially in the new Economics Department, that had such pernicious effects on academic cohesiveness.

The leftist student groups formed immediately after World War I moved steadily toward a more radical political orientation under the influence of a tide of Marxist and other socialist ideas in the 1920s. This was also true of a number of young faculty activists. Among the most radical at Tōdai were Ōmori Yoshitarō, Hirano Yoshitarō, and Yamada Moritarō, who collectively acquired the sobriquet *The Three Tarōs*. The three were actually part of a network of politically active Tōdai graduates who became teachers at other imperial universities in the 1920s: most notably, Sakisaka Itsurō (b. 1897, graduated Tōdai economics 1921), Ishihama Tomoyuki (b. 1895, Tōdai political science 1920), Sasa Hiroo (b. 1896, Tōdai political science 1920), and Imanaka Tsugimaro (b. 1893, Tōdai political science 1918), all of whom taught at Kyushu Imperial University. In addition to maintaining contact with the student movement on campus, some of these young social scientists formed close ties with off-campus radicals. Ōmori, for instance, became a leading member of the Rōnōha (Labor-Farmer Faction), an important splinter group of communists and other radicals estranged from

26. Miller, *Minobe Tatsukichi*, pp. 29, 33.
27. Ibid., pp. 207–210; see also Yasko, "Hiranuma Kiichirō."

the Japanese Communist Party because of their refusal to accept Comintern policy. Ōmori also took part in efforts to organize tenant farmers against their landlords, and it was at his home in November 1927 that plans were laid for the publication of *Rōnō*, a "theoretical journal of militant Marxism" for which he wrote under the pseudonym Naruse Mitsuo.[28]

One of the most important on-campus influences on this generation of Tōdai academics was the pioneer social statistician Takano Iwasaburō (1871–1949). Professor Takano, born shortly after the Meiji Restoration, was the third son of a Nagasaki tailor and a daughter of a rice retailer—or as he put it in his autobiography, "in the house of a tradesman in the artisan quarter of a cosmopolitan free city."[29] The father's business was not very successful, and when Takano was seven, the family moved to Tokyo for a new start. Only two years later the father died. Nevertheless, Takano was able to continue his education beyond the compulsory public elementary level, attending private middle schools. In 1887 he entered the First Higher School, where among his friends were two other students who later joined the Tōdai law faculty—Onozuka Kiheiji and Yahagi Eizō, both also sons of commoners. After what his biographers describe as a brilliant senior thesis on the history of Japanese coinage, Takano was accepted at the Tōdai College of Law to major in economics under the tutelage of Kanai Noburu and Wadagaki Kenzō. Among his Tōdai classmates graduating in 1895 were a pair of future prime ministers and several privy councillors as well as his two friends from First Higher School, Onozuka and Yahagi. Despite Takano's poverty, he was able to continue his studies while supporting himself by lecturing at a private law school. In 1898 Tōdai sent him abroad to Mannheim for advanced training in the new field of social statistics.

28. Smith, *Japan's First Student Radicals*, pp. 145, 148. Hirano was an associate professor of law; Ōmori and Yamada were associate professors of economics. The suffix *-tarō* is frequently used in male names, and the coincidence was hardly uncommon; rather, the nickname was typical of a Japanese penchant for acronyms and other word plays. The original Rōnōha, not to be confused with the Rōnōtō (Labor-Farmer Party), included such veteran socialists as Yamakawa Hitoshi, Sakai Toshihiko, and Arahata Kanson—all among the founders of the first Japanese Communist Party of 1922. See Beckmann and Okubo, *The Japanese Communist Party*, pp. 48ff, 134–138, 145–148; and Totten, *The Social Democratic Movement in Prewar Japan*, pp. 151–157. Hoston, *Marxism and the Crisis of Development in Prewar Japan*, treated the intellectual history of Japanese Marxist thought in this period.

29. Ōshima, *Takano Iwasaburō den*, p. 4; see also the posthumous publication of Takano's writings, *Kappa no he*, edited by Suzuki Kōichirō.

Takano's deep involvement in the problems of the working classes had already begun during his Tōdai undergraduate years. His older brother, Fusatarō, had returned in 1896 from the United States, where he had worked as a laborer and had participated in the activities of a small group of Japanese in the San Francisco area who were enthusiastic about transplanting labor unions back into Japan. Takano had accompanied this elder brother to meetings in Tokyo and Yokohama in Japan's first serious union campaigns and had even published in the journal *Rōdō sekai* (*Labor World*). While Takano was studying in Europe he received news of the 1900 police laws outlawing union activity and of his brother's exile to China. Shortly thereafter the elder brother died. Takano later recalled these events as enormously important in strengthening his resolve to use his expertise as a scholar and his prestige as a Tōdai professor to support social reforms for the working classes.[30]

When Takano returned to an appointment as full professor in 1903, he also resumed his participation in the very influential Social Policy Study Association, whose first meetings he had attended as a student in 1896. Throughout his membership in the association Takano placed himself solidly on the left-wing, or "progressive," end of the spectrum.[31] He acted on these same convictions when, in addition to researching the conditions of urban poverty, he joined Yoshino Sakuzō in supporting the efforts of Suzuki's Yūaikai.[32] This strong commitment to put his academic discipline into the service of progressive social reforms involved him in some of the most critical Taishō controversies regarding the role of the imperial university and its faculty.

Ironically, one such controversy caught Takano between the Hara cabinet, which in 1919 sought to name him the Japanese representative

30. On the historical importance of Takano Iwasaburō's brother, see Ōshima, "Takano Fusatarō to rōdō kumiai no tanjō"; and Marsland, *The Birth of the Japanese Labor Union Movement.*

31. For a description of the political spectrum within the Shakai Seisaku Gakkai, and the parallels with the Verein für Sozialpolitik in Germany, see Pyle, "Advantages of Followership." One should be careful, however, not to attribute too much weight to the influence of German antecedents in assessing the origins of their concerns, even granted the fact that Kanai, Takano, and others in the association had studied in Germany. As has been noted, Takano's inclination toward progressive social positions predated both his membership in the Shakai Seisaku Gakkai and his study abroad. Most probably what German theorists provided to him was ammunition to be adapted for battles in which he had already chosen sides. See Minear's study of Hozumi Yatsuka, *Japanese Tradition and Western Law,* for a parallel example.

32. For Takano Iwasaburō's influence on Suzuki Bunji and the Yūaikai, see Large, *The Yūaikai,* pp. 19–24.

to the inaugural meeting of the International Labor Organization (ILO), and the leadership of the Yūaikai, which argued that the post should go to the head of a labor union. The Japanese government had agreed at Versailles to the creation of the ILO and had appointed Keiō University president Kamata Eiji as the official government envoy. The government's problem now was the absence of any legally recognized union from which a leader could be selected to represent the nation's labor movement. The minister of agriculture and commerce called a meeting to seek a modus vivendi, but the negotiations were broken off when Suzuki Bunji stormed out and the Yūaikai threatened to boycott the official delegation. Takano was strongly inclined to take the post, and this was what Professor Yoshino and other moderates associated with the Yūaikai urged him to do. In the end, however, Morito Tatsuo and others among his younger colleagues combined to convince him that he would find himself in an untenable position if he went against the opposition of the Yūaikai militants.[33]

Takano's agenda for social reform went beyond the Yūaikai, however, and an essential step in the direction of applying economic research to social practice, in Takano's view, was the freeing of the study of economics from the Law College. In this effort he had the support of both his more conservative senior colleague Kanai Noburu and the liberal political scientist Onozuka Kiheiji. Takano's intellectual rationale was grounded in methodological concerns for a new curriculum stressing empirical study rather than the deductive approach that characterized much of theorizing about constitutional law and training in jurisprudence. These men joined together in the early 1900s to lobby for recognition of economics as a separate discipline, and a rapid expansion of faculty and courses in that field took place at Tōdai. In 1907 a separate professorship in finance and a fourth chair in economics had been established in the Tōdai Law College. In 1909 a fifth professorship in the field of commerce (as opposed to commercial law) had been created, and economics had been recognized as a formal "section" (gakka) within the Law College. Commerce had been given the same status the following year. Between 1900 and 1915 the total number of seminars in economics had doubled, while the number of students

---

33. Suzuki Bunji, Rōdō undō nijūnen, pp. 209–210; Ōshima, Takano Iwasaburō den, pp. 146–148, 164; Takano, Kappa no he, pp. 306–315. Actually Takano had originally been named alternative to Honda Seiichi, the publisher of a periodical devoted to economics and business news, the Tōkyō zaisei keizai shinpō. Honda had withdrawn earlier.

graduating from the economics or commerce sections of the Law College had reached an average of seventy a year.[34]

In October 1913 Takano and Kanai had reason to believe they had won their case for a separate department when Tōdai president Yamakawa Kenjirō agreed to carry the proposal forward to the Educational Ministry with his endorsement. Ministry officials seemed receptive, and President Yamakawa proceeded to place the question on the agenda of the University Council for formal deliberation that same month. Much to the frustration of Takano, however, the matter dragged on through the winter and spring of 1914. It was apparently held up by the issue of the status of the Tokyo Higher School of Commerce, whose administration was seeking to have the school raised to the level of a full-fledged college. The Tōdai economists nevertheless persisted in their campaign, and by the summer of 1915 the University Council had given its endorsement to the proposal, which was then submitted again to the Education Ministry. Progress was once more stalled, this time by difficulties in getting the government to provide funds for the new department. In March 1917, because of these long delays, Takano took the dramatic step of handing in his resignation. He withdrew the letter once assurances had been won from both Tōdai and the ministry that they would make further efforts to expedite the matter.[35] Because the government had begun to act on plans for a general reform of higher education, however, it was not until the following year that plans for a Tōdai department of economics could actually be implemented.

The new Economics Department could not have been launched in a more turbulent season, for it was sailing into the most violent ideological storms experienced in Japan since the Meiji Restoration a half-century earlier. Research on social problems was now inextricably intertwined with the conflicts over political participation and social justice that erupted on the national scene in the wake of World War I. The unity maintained among the economists in their campaign for the

34. *Danshaku Yamakawa*, pp. 307–310; Ōshima, *Takano Iwasaburō den*, pp. 124–136; Tōdai, *Gojūnenshi*, vol. 2, pp. 181–198; Tōdai, *Gakujutsu taikan*, pp. 467ff; Tōdai, *Keizaigakubu*, pp. 3–23.

35. *Danshaku Yamakawa*, pp. 307–309; Ōshima, *Takano Iwasaburō den*, pp. 129–133; Takano, *Kappa no he*, pp. 296–306. These accounts do not mention any significant opposition within Tōdai and concur in blaming this early delay on the ambitions of higher school principal Hirano Keitarō and others at the Hitotsubashi school. Kanai Noburu also threatened to resign according to Kawai Eijirō's account, *Kyōdan seikatsu nijūnen*, p. 105.

independence of their discipline soon frayed under the strain as faculty members and graduate students began to divide between the opposing poles of the new political activism of Yoshino and Takano, on the one side, and the more conservative elitist orientations of the senior men in the department, on the other.

Even before the new department was formally established, Takano had attracted to himself a circle of younger economists. These included three of the six associate professors appointed in economics in 1919, four graduate assistants, and a number of undergraduates (some of whom were being groomed for future academic careers). Among those already on the regular faculty were Ueno Michisuke (b. 1888, Tōdai law 1912), who had returned from four years abroad to an associate professorship in 1918 and then had been promoted in 1919 to full professor; Maide Chōgorō (b. 1891, Tōdai law 1917), a student of Yahagi Eizō appointed an associate professor with Takano's support in 1919; Morito Tatsuo (b. 1888, Tōdai law 1914), appointed associate professor in 1916; and Ōuchi Hyōe (b. 1888, Tōdai law 1913).

Ōuchi, the self-described son of "the rural intelligentsia" in Hyōgo Prefecture, was one of several Tōdai graduates who, after having first entered other careers, returned to their alma mater in the expansion of 1918–1919. He had initially obtained a coveted post in the Finance Ministry following his graduation from the economics section of the Law College in 1913. In six years with the ministry he had visited the United States, had authored parts of the Carnegie Endowment for Peace Studies on Japanese armament expenditures, and in 1918 had been asked to lecture on finance part time at Tōdai. The following year he left the ministry for a full-time associate professorship in economics.

Also among the circle—indeed, described by Yanaihara Tadao as its "general [*taisho*]"—was Kushida Tamizō (1885–1934).[36] Although only a lecturer, Kushida was actually senior in age to all the associates as well as to some of the full professors in economics. The son of a farming family from rural Fukushima Prefecture, Kushida had done his undergraduate work at Kyoto University, where he was both student and sometime tutor to Professor Kawakami Hajime. Kawakami had emerged by 1919 as one of the more widely published academic critics of Japanese capitalism and a favorite author of radical students. Kushida

36. Yanaihara, *Watakushi*, p. 14.

had entered the Tōdai economics section of the Law College as a graduate assistant but had dropped his academic career in 1917 to work for
the liberal newspaper *Ōsaka Asahi shinbun*. After right-wing attacks had
forced the reorganization of the paper's editorial staff, Kushida first
took a teaching position at a private university in Kyoto but then
reentered Tōdai. At Tōdai he had considerable impact on the younger
staff as well as the students, in large part because he was one of the few
academics at the time in Japan who could be considered truly well read
on Marxism.[37]

At the time Professor Takano was the faculty member in charge of
the economics *kenkyūshitsu*, the reading room and meeting place
central to interaction among the department members. The Takano
circle often stayed far into the night discussing new ideas, especially
those of Karl Marx and Pyotr Kropotkin. Outsiders soon began to call
the room the "Lenin village." It also became the organizational base
for the publication of a departmental research journal, the *Keizaigaku
kenkyū* (Studies in the discipline of economics), edited at the outset by
Professor Ōuchi Hyōe. It was as a consequence of this publishing
venture that the Takano circle first found itself in the midst of a
political storm.

The inaugural issue of the Economics Department journal carried an
article by Associate Professor Morito entitled "A Study of the Social
Thought of Kropotkin." The article combined a scholarly analysis of
anarchism with a personal endorsement of Kropotkin's ideal society in
which each member enjoyed absolute freedom from economic as well as
political oppression. Morito did criticize some aspects of Kropotkin's
thought and expressed doubts about the likelihood of achieving such an
ideal in practice. Morito also entirely eschewed violent means to these
ends. Nevertheless, bureaucrats in charge of press censorship in the
Home Ministry ordered this issue of the journal withdrawn from circulation. Tōdai president Yamakawa Kenjirō, the same man who had
been at the helm during the Affair of the Seven Ph.D.s, was alerted to
the problem as soon as the Home Ministry order was given, and he
summoned three senior members of the Economics Department—
Chairman Kanai Noburu and two other full professors who had transferred to the department from the Law College, Yamazaki Kakujirō and

37. For a discussion of Kushida's influence on Kawakami, see Smith, *Japan's First
Student Radicals*, p. 240. For an analysis of Kushida's role in the public debates over
Marxian theory, see Sasaki Kyohei, "A Western Influence on Japanese Economic
Thought"; see also Hoston, *Marxism and the Crisis of Development in Prewar Japan*.

Yahagi Eizō. The four men agreed if all copies were recalled, then the matter could be be laid to rest with a public apology from Morito. The difficulty was that Morito refused to cooperate.[38] When the government proved determined to pursue the issue further, Yamakawa and the senior professors convened a special department meeting. There the full professors agreed to suspend both Morito (the author) and Ōuchi (the editor). Only Professor Ueno Michisuke is said to have cast a dissenting vote.[39]

The suspension and subsequent indictment of Mori and Ōuchi led to considerable protest among the faculties and student bodies of Tōdai and other Japanese universities. (The ideological defense of Morito and Ōuchi will be examined more closely in the next chapter.) The trials ended in convictions with a three-month jail sentence and a fine of ¥70 for Morito and a one-month suspended sentence with a year's probation and a fine of ¥20 for Ōuchi.[40] The important point here is that the incident marked a watershed in the course of polarization within the Economics Department.

38. I have found no references to any official written records of the discussions within the Economics Department, and the minutes of the University Council simply record the decision to suspend Morito (Tōdai, "Hyōgikai kirokushō" for January 20, 1919). As is typical of these emotionally charged events, there is disagreement in the sources on whether the proposal of a formal apology was ever put to Morito in such explicit terms; see Ōshima, *Takano Iwasaburō den*, pp. 168–169 and n3. Because Morito and Ōuchi are listed as *kanshū* (editorial supervisors) for this biography of Takano, I have taken it as representative of their views on the compromise question; but see also Ōuchi's earlier versions in *Watakushi*, pp. 161–163; and in *Keizaigaku gojūnen*, vol. 1, p. 114. Yamakawa's biographers describe the president as coming away from the meetings with Morito on January 9 and 10 convinced Morito would not back down (*Danshaku Yamakawa*, pp. 338–339). Presumably Morito's attitude toward any possible compromise would have been affected by Takano's assurances that Morito could count on a position at the Ōhara Institute as well as funds for study abroad should he lose his post at the university (Ōshima, *Takano Iwasaburō den*, pp. 168–169).

39. The result of the vote and Ueno's holdout are reported by Kawai Eijirō, who probably learned it from his father-in-law, Kanai Noburu (*Kyōdan seikatsu nijūnen*, p. 162). The full professors with authority to vote on personnel matters in January 1920 included, in addition to Ueno, Kanai, Yamazaki (b. 1868, Tōdai law, 1895), and Yahagi (b. 1870, Tōdai law, 1895), Kawazu Susumu (b. 1875, Tōdai law, 1899), Matsuoka Kinpei (b. 1867, Tōdai law, 1900), and perhaps Mori Shōsaburō (b. 1887, Tōdai law, 1913), who had recently been promoted. The vote is sometimes given as six to one, however.

40. The yen would have been worth somewhere between fifty cents and a dollar in U.S. currency at the time. See *Danshaku Yamakawa*, pp. 338–339; Minobe Ryōkichi, *Kumon suru demokurashī*, pp. 25–26; and Arisawa Hiromi, *Gakumon to shisō to ningen to*, pp. 21–22.

The Early Symptoms of Factionalism

The associate professors and graduate students who constituted the original Takano circle now began to form a more tightly knit and easily identifiable faction. On hearing of the suspensions and indictments, they initially decided to resign en masse to protest the failure of their seniors to protect their colleagues. Takano was not officially involved in the department deliberations because he had left his professorship prior to the incident for other reasons. But he prevailed on the group not to resign because such action would sway neither the Justice Ministry nor the university administration. All should remain in their posts within the department because, Takano argued, "the *goal* is the construction of a more rational [*goriteki*] society; the *method,* gradual [*zenshin*]; the *place,* the university as the agency for research into the truth; [but] the *time* [is] too early when the research is not yet accomplished and our colleagues are [too] few."[41]

The group was soon involved in further controversy within the department. Takano had continued to serve the department as a part-time lecturer in this period. Professor Yahagi Eizō, who had voted with the majority in ousting Morito, initiated a move to bring Takano back as a full-time professor. As a precondition to negotiations, Takano insisted on assurances that Ōuchi Hyōe would be reinstated within the department at the end of the year of probation, which Ōuchi was spending in study abroad. The question of reappointment of Takano thus became a point of major contention. Takano's younger supporters were accused of attempting to pressure others into joining their threat of mass resignations to ensure a favorable vote by the full professors. Opposition to the Takano group took shape and included two new actors on the departmental scene: Kawai Eijirō and Hijikata Seibi.

Professor Kawai was the second son of the owner of a liquor shop and a peasant's daughter. The father was originally from a region ruled by the Tokugawa House and is said to have harbored a lifelong hostility toward the political clique that had dominated the post-Restoration government. He was deeply interested in politics, although his greatest political achievement was election to his town council. These attitudes were transmitted to Eijirō, the only one of his children the father ed-

---

41. Quoted from Takano's diary in Ōshima, *Takano Iwasaburō den,* p. 183. See also Kawai, *Kyōdan seikatsu nijūnen,* p. 109.

ucated beyond elementary school. In 1908 Kawai Eijirō won entrance to the elite First Higher School, where he was an enthusiastic observer of political affairs, as were three of his schoolmates who also became Tōdai economics professors: Morito Tatsuo, Yanaihara Tadao, and Ebara Banri. Between 1911 and 1915 Kawai distinguished himself as a student at Tōdai, graduating at the top of his political science section class and attracting the attention of his professors, especially that of Onozuka Kiheiji and Kanai Noburu. Following graduation Kawai won a position in the Agriculture and Commerce Ministry; he also won the hand of the eldest daughter of Professor Kanai in marriage.[42]

In 1919, however, Kawai gave up his career in the civil bureaucracy, issuing a public statement of resignation—what he termed "a declaration of future war" in which he denounced his superiors in the government for their conservative approach to social problems and proclaimed his intention of working for social reform.[43] When the suspension of Morito and Ōuchi created an opening in the Economics Department, Kawai accepted an associate professorship. This surprised and antagonized the Takano faction because Kawai had previously been friends with Morito and had shared the group's attitude toward social reform, if not its interest in Marxism. Kawai is reported to have said he had been made to feel like a "strikebreaker [*sutoraiku bureeka*]."[44] A more charitable interpretation of Kawai's failure to take an outspoken stance on the Morito issue at the time has been suggested by some of Takano's biographers: that is, Kawai was bound by his sense of obligation to his father-in-law, who was then serving as department chairman. Kawai himself indirectly denied this interpretation but never publicly attempted to respond to these criticisms. He did, however, later

42. The information on Kawai's life is taken primarily from Shaikai Shisō Kenkyūkai, eds., *Kawai Eijirō denki to tsuisō;* Egami, *Kawai Eijirō den;* and Hirai's insightful intellectual biography, which I recommend in both its first version as a dissertation, "A Japanese Experiment in Individualism," as well as in its final published form, *Individualism and Socialism.*

43. Hirai, *Individualism and Socialism,* pp. 42–55; Hirai, "A Japanese Experiment in Individualism," pp. 91–96.

44. Hijikata recounted a conversation he claimed took place in the early spring of 1921 when Kawai paid a visit after Hijikata's return from Europe. Kawai reportedly told Hijikata of the hostility he felt directed at himself by the Takano group. Kawai's reminiscences made no mention of any such conversation, although he did discuss his opposition to Takano's reappointment and his alliance with Hijikata and Honiden over the issue (Kawai, *Kyōdan seikatsu nijūnen,* pp. 109–111, 123–126). Hijikata also claimed he and Honiden joined that alliance because Kawai told them Takano was insisting on the reinstatement of Morito as well as Ōuchi (Hijikata, *Gakkai shunjūki,* pp. 104–105).

praise Morito as "not merely a scholar but an educator [*kyōikusha*]" and stated, "Of the many men who were lost to the Economics Department, I think Professor Morito was the greatest of all."[45]

Whatever his motives, Kawai joined with Associate Professor Hijikata Seibi and others in opposing the reappointment of Takano. Their efforts at discouraging either senior professor Yamazaki, the new chairman, or Yahagi from pursuing the negotiations were not successful. Ultimately in July 1921 it was Takano himself who, despite assurances that Ōuchi would be reinstated, decided to decline the offer to accept the permanent full-time directorship of the privately funded Ōhara Institute for Social Problems in Osaka. By this time the dispute had continued for most of a year, causing the still open wound inflicted by the Morito-Ōuchi cases to fester in the process. The result was permanent scars as the divisions within the department hardened.

Among those most ardently opposed to the Takano group was Hijikata Seibi. Like Kawai, Hijikata was married to the daughter of one of his Tōdai professors, Hijikata Yasushi. Also like Kawai, Hijikata had grown up the son of a politically ambitious father in the merchant section of town.[46] A graduate of the somewhat less prestigious Sixth Higher School, Hijikata had entered Tōdai at the same time as Kawai and had also graduated first in his class, the economics section, in 1915. Unlike Kawai, however, Hijikata had chosen an academic career from the beginning and had entered graduate school directly after graduation. He received appointment as associate professor of economics in 1917.

During the Morito incident Hijikata was engaged in advanced study in the United States. Soon after his return in the spring of 1921, however, he emerged as a leading opponent of Marxism. As such he became a bête noire in later accounts of academic functionalism at Tōdai. Whether Hijikata can accurately be labeled a "fascist," he was without question a zealous anticommunist.[47] At the same time, like so many supporters of Japanese capitalism, he rejected the political liberalism that marked the writings of such anti-Marxists as Kawai Eijirō. Furthermore, although it is questionable whether he ever played the central role of the éminence grise attributed to him by his foes, it is quite evident from his autobiography that he did have a passion for

45. Kawai, *Kyōdan seikatsu nijūnen*, p. 109.
46. For autobiographical information, see Hijikata, *Gakkai shunjūki*.
47. See Ienaga, *Daigaku no jiyō no rekishi*, p. 63.

academic politics, incessantly maneuvering in the hallways and back-stairs to further one conservative cause or another.

In this latter respect at least, Hijikata seems to have been well matched by his chief antagonist, Ōuchi Hyōe. The original Takano circle had suffered serious attrition as Morito Tatsuo and Kushida Tamizō followed Takano to the Ōhara Institute, but there were new recruits as Marxism spread among Japanese university students despite concerted efforts by the authorities to discourage it. Ōuchi became the central figure in a revived left-wing faction after his reinstatement and promotion to full professor in 1923. Maide Chōgorō was promoted the same year, along with the Christian Yanaihara Tadao (b. 1893, Tōdai law 1917). Yanaihara had left a job with Sumitomo Mining Company to accept an associate professorship in 1920. A fourth professor, Ueno Michisuke, had been the lone holdout in the vote to suspend Morito.

As the senior men who had founded the department retired, these Marxist supporters became a powerful voting bloc in faculty meetings. By 1925 opponents were accusing the group of attempting to solidify its influence by seeking control over the department chairmanship. In the spring of 1925 Chairman Yahagi Eizō invited Professors Kawazu Susumu, Watanabe Tetsuzō, Mori Shōsaburō, Yamazaki Kakujirō, and Hijikata Seibi to dine at a Chinese restaurant. There he told them that Ōuchi, Ueno, and Maide had asked him not to stand for a third one-year term as chairman. The six men agreed to form what Hijikata insisted was a "purely defensive" pact to block the Marxists' initiative and reelect Yahagi. They soon received the support of their colleagues Kawai and Honiden.[48]

Ōuchi's otherwise detailed memoirs made no mention of the issue of the chairmanship, but he expressed quite vividly the exhilaration he felt when he first returned to the Tōdai campus from his sojourn abroad. The university had been shattered by the earthquake and fire of 1923, and Ōuchi considered the task of reconstructing the department, both literally and figuratively, a personal challenge. He also confirmed that by 1925 the department was irreconcilably polarized between the left-wing minority and the majority faction—a polarization that was to persist throughout the next decade and a half, as Table 4-6 indicates.[49]

---

48. Hijikata, *Gakkai shunjūki*, pp. 108–110. Hijikata claimed it had been the "custom" to serve three terms, but given that the department was only in its sixth year and had had three chairmen already, the "custom" could hardly have been firmly established at this time.

49. Ōuchi, *Keizaigaku*, pp. 229–230; Yamada Fumio, "Tōdai Keizaigakubu," pp.

It must not be overlooked that in these years many of these academics were engaged in a long-running public debate on the relative merits of various economic theories;[50] but our focus here is with their behavior as departmental colleagues. The issues over which the Tōdai economists fought most frequently within their department were the familiar, if by no means trivial, questions that give rise to contention in academic units within most modern universities: the recruitment of new faculty members, promotion of junior members, the content of the core curriculum, and standards of student achievement. Surprisingly, perhaps, the election of the chairman is not mentioned in the sources as an issue for open conflict after 1925. The majority faction had prevailed in the reelection of Yahagi and continued to control that office until 1938, although there are some references to political maneuvering and compromise regarding the office and the two seats the department selected for the University Council. There were also lesser posts within the department, but these, too, receive little mention except on one occasion in the late 1930s. During a heated exchange in a faculty meeting Ōuchi Hyōe was accused of abusing his position as faculty adviser to the economics student club by inviting only leftists as speakers.[51]

The evaluation of student achievement—grading senior theses, awarding prizes in essay competitions, and recommending graduate students—provided recurring opportunities for clashes over which faction had a monopoly on academic truth. So did department discussions of curricular matters. In one memorable instance of the latter in 1927, the choice of textbook for a core course in foreign language readings on economics precipitated a debate that lasted for two school terms. Yanaihara Tadao and Yamada Moritarō had sought departmental approval to use Marx's *Das Kapital* in German and met with determined

---

71–80. Because there are no available official records of how individuals voted in faculty meetings (and associate professors did not participate equally in all cases), the incidents listed here are limited to those on which there is sufficient detail in the various sources to permit at least a partial listing of how individuals sided. Given the type of partisan and often self-serving accounts one must use as sources, inaccuracies are quite probable; but the overall shape of the divisions is confirmed by a cross-check of the claims of the participants in the materials cited in the List of Works Consulted. The reader is warned again that the political issues and academic personalities involved here are still matters for partisan conflict, and postwar treatments are no less subject to question than are accounts published at the time.

50. See, for example, the account of the disagreements between Hijikata Seibi and Maide Chōgorō in Sasaki Kyohei, "A Western Influence on Japanese Economic Thought."

51. Hijikata, *Gakkai shunjūki*, pp. 173, 185.

Table 4-6 *Tōdai Economics Department, 1920–1930,*
Divisions over Selected Issues (full professors in italics)

Year	Issue	Ōuchi and His Allies	Opponents
1920	Morito-Ōuchi suspensions	*Ueno Michisuke* Maide Chōgorō Ōuchi Hyōe Morito Tatsuo	*Kanai Noburu* *Kawazu Susumu* *Mori Shosaburō* *Matsuoka Kinpei* *Yahagi Eizō* *Yamazaki Kakujirō*
1921	Takano reappointment	*Ueno Michisuke* *Yahagi Eizō*	*Hijikata Seibi* Honiden Yoshio Kawai Eijirō
1925	Replace chair	*Maide Chōgorō* *Ōuchi Hyōe* *Ueno Michisuke*	*Hijikata Seibi* *Kawazu Susumu* *Mori Shosaburō* *Yahagi Eizō* *Yamazaki Kakujirō* *Watanabe Tetsuzo* Honiden Yoshio Kawai Eijirō
1927	*Das Kapital* as textbook	*Ōuchi Hyōe* *Yanaihara Tadao* Yamada Moritarō	*Yahagi Eizō* *Yamazaki Kakujirō*
1928	Ōmori case	*Kawai Eijirō* *Maide Chōgorō* *Ōuchi Hyōe* *Yanaihara Tadao* Yamada Moritarō	*Hijikata Seibi* *Honiden Yoshio* *Yahagi Eizō* *Yamazaki Kakujirō*
1936	Sasaki promotion	*Hijikata Seibi* *Honiden Yoshio* *Maide Chōgorō* *Ōuchi Hyōe* *Yanaihara Tadao*	*Araki Kotarō* *Kawai Eijirō* *Nakanishi Torao* *Tanabe Chushi* Yamada Fumio
1938	Ōuchi case	*Baba Keiji* *Kawai Eijirō* *Maide Chōgorō* *Ueno Michisuke* Yamada Fumio	*Hijikata Seibi* *Honiden Yoshio* *Tanabe Chushi*

resistance from Professor Yamazaki on the grounds the outside world would think that Tōdai had gone completely "Red." A compromise textbook was eventually substituted.[52]

Just as the Marxists and their supporters believed Hijikata and the majority to be reactionary on such issues, their antagonists in turn

52. Ōuchi, *Keizaigaku,* pp. 232–234. Among those who voted against the use of Marx's work was the liberal Kawai (Hirai, *Individualism and Socialism,* p. 125).

accused them of a long list of sins against the spirit of collegiality as well as violations of "democratic" procedure. These included, according to the anti-Marxist critics, always voting in a bloc, spreading slander, and leaking privileged information from faculty meetings to discredit individual faculty members in the eyes of their students and other departments. Professor Yamada Fumio later succinctly summed up such charges: "The formation of [a majority faction] was made necessary by the Marxist tactics of disruption that the minority faction used against the department. . . . They continually opposed for the sake of opposition and caused strife for the sake of strife."[53] Whatever truth there was in such allegations, they reflected vividly and accurately the rancor that had become endemic to the department.

Some of the most bitter accusations were provoked by disagreements over staffing as the Tōdai Economics Department expanded rapidly in the 1920s. The Ōuchi faction was convinced it was the victim of a concerted "plan for suppressing Marxism" manifested in the refusal of the majority to recruit talented graduate students if they were too closely identified with one or another professor in the Ōuchi group. Thus, Ōuchi charged that a number of brilliant young men were "driven away" from Tōdai. Others were said to have heeded advice to avoid Ōuchi and the group rather than risk unfair discrimination in the allocation of graduate assistantships and the recruitment of new associate professors. Furthermore, Ōuchi claimed that those already on the faculty who were stigmatized as Marxists—for example, Ōmori Yoshitarō, Yamada Moritarō, and Arisawa Hiromi—were placed on a list of "perpetual [*mannen*] associate professors" and that to avoid promoting them the majority faction brought in Yamada Fumio, Tanabe Chūshi, and Araki Kōtarō from outside the department to fill vacancies.[54]

It would not be easy, if indeed possible, to reconstruct the details of the treatment of graduate students who, according to Ōuchi, would otherwise have gained faculty positions at Tōdai. Figure 4-5 does, however, reveal something about the charges regarding appointments and promotions.

53. Yamada Fumio, "Tōdai Keizaigakubu," p. 73.
54. See the lists Ōuchi offered in *Keizaigaku*, pp. 148–150, 230–234. See also the counter-charges in Yamada Fumio, "Tōdai keizaigakubu"; and in Hijikata, *Gakkai shunjūki*, pp. 107–171, 186. I have chosen to translate *jokyō* as "associate," rather than "assistant professor," because there were only two professorial ranks and the *jokyūju*, unlike U.S. assistant professors, normally had academic tenure.

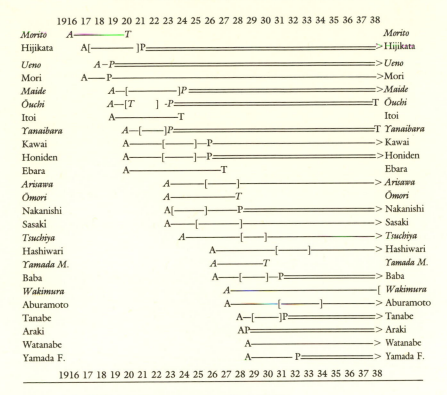

Figure 4-5 Tōdai Economics Faculty, 1916–1938

Italicized names = Ōuchi allies
A = appointments
P = promotions
[ ] = leaves
T = termination/suspension/resignation under duress
—— = years as associate professor
== = years as full professor

Of the total of eighteen appointments to associate professorships made after the Morito-Ōuchi suspensions of 1920, six were men identified with the Ōuchi faction. Five of those, however, were appointed prior to the hardening of factional lines in 1925. By contrast, five anti-Marxists were added between 1925 and 1932. The career patterns of those appointed prior to 1923 do not clearly indicate systematic bias against promotion of those within the Ōuchi faction. Ueno and Yanaihara spent the shortest time in rank before promotion to full professor, and both consistently sided with Ōuchi. Two of those who spent the longest years in rank, Kawai and Honiden, were counted as part of the anti-Ōuchi faction in the 1920s. In the cases of those appointed after 1932, the evidence for Ōuchi's charges, if not entirely consistent, is persuasive. None of the men Ōuchi or his opponents termed *Marxists* were promoted over these years, even though by 1939 four of the six had served at least ten years in the rank of associate professor. Four others did receive promotions during these years after shorter periods in rank. A fifth, Araki Kōtarō, was a joint appointment after being promoted to full professor in the Agriculture Department. All five were men considered by Ōuchi and others to be in the anti-Marxist camp.

Of course, such evidence is not entirely conclusive. It could be objected that of the fourteen individuals added to the faculty between 1923 and 1930, there were only five (including Araki Kōtarō) who were promoted at all prior to 1939; and in 1939 two of those whom Ōuchi said were treated unfairly were finally elevated in rank. Moreover, it is possible, if not necessarily plausible, to assume that Ōmori Yoshitarō and Yamada Moritarō might have attained senior rank had not the normal course of their careers been terminated by outside attacks on them. Yet it is precisely the record of the department's reaction to such outside intervention against those accused of radicalism that affords the clearest indication of how factionalism plagued the department when it and the university were faced with the need to defend academic autonomy.

The Bases of Academic Factionalism

Before examining more closely the series of challenges to these academics that began in the 1920s, we must consider further the nature of this factionalism. In the common rhetoric of Japanese political criticism and the conventional wisdom of many commentators on Japanese social values, factions, or *habatsu* (cliques), are often treated as the result of a lingering heritage of the "feudal" (*hōkenteki*) past. What is usually meant by such terms is that particularistic ties tend to form around common regional roots, shared school experiences, or relations to paternalistic mentors and that these personal ties then take precedence over adherence to transcendental values or the exercise of judgment based on universalistic standards. Academics are thus described in terms of the mentor-disciple (*sensei-deshi*) or patron-protégé (*oyabun-kobun, senpai-kohai*) relationships said to characterize other sectors of modern Japanese society.[55]

In fact, however, there is very little systematic study of such clique formation in the Japanese academic community or, indeed, in the world of academics elsewhere.[56] The absence of such studies makes it difficult to put the factionalism in the Tōdai Economics Department into a meaningful perspective. Yet it is possible to point out certain aspects that seem to run counter to these accepted notions regarding Japanese cliques, especially in the period prior to World War II.

In terms of regional roots and socioeconomic origins, the economics faculty members of the 1920s were as varied as their Meiji predecessors. Indeed, compared with their counterparts in the Meiji period, far fewer professors of the 1920s and the 1930s had fathers or brothers either on the Tōdai faculty or in the political elite.[57] Nor did school ties form any particular pattern. The members of the Ōuchi cluster had attended several different higher schools: Yanaihara and Ōmori graduated from First Higher School (which also produced Kawai); Arisawa was from the Second Higher School in Sendai; Ōuchi himself attended the Fifth Higher School in Kumamoto. All of the Economics Department faculty members were Tōdai graduates. At the pre-1919 Tōdai Law College most of the economists had majored in either the political science section (*seijika*) or the economics section (*keizaika*)—Kawai, Mori Shōsaburō, and Maide in the former; Hijikata, Morito, and Ōuchi in the latter.

Available information on mentor-disciple relations between students and professors reveals a more complex picture. Although Kawai married the daughter of Kanai Noboru, Kawai was a specialist in English

55. For those unfamiliar with this literature, there is a succinct introduction by Harumi Befu in the *Kodansha Encyclopedia of Japan,* vol. 1, pp. 46–147. For one example of how analysts have attempted to use these supposed "legacies of feudalism" to explain Japanese politics, see Yanaga, *Big Business in Japanese Politics,* pp. 12ff, 327–328.

56. Two outstanding exceptions are Bartholomew's study of Kitasato Shibasaburō and his circle in Japanese medical science, *The Formation of Science in Japan;* and Clark, *Prophets and Patrons,* which describes the "clustering" of the Durkheimians in France.

57. The major exception to this generalization in the Economics Department was Kawazu Susumu, who married the eldest daughter of former Tōdai agricultural professor Kanda Naibu and was therefore related to Law Professor Takagi Yasuka as well as to the ambassador to France. The father of Professor Matsuoka Kinpei, Matsuoka Yasutake, had been a cabinet minister in 1906 and a privy councillor before accepting the presidency of Nihon University; Kinpei, however, had retired early in 1921.

political theory from the political science section, whereas the father-in-law was a German-trained economic historian in the economics section. Moreover, Kawai apparently considered Onozuka Kiheiji (who served as a go-between in the marriage) his real mentor. Hijikata Seibi was the adopted heir of Hijikata Yasushi, but Seibi graduated from the economics section and taught public finance; the father-in-law was trained at Middle Temple and specialized in civil law in the political science section. Maide Chōgorō had been recommended originally for a graduate fellowship by Yahagi Eizō but gravitated to the group around Takano Iwasaburō, who then sponsored Maide for an associate professorship. Yanaihara considered Yoshino Sakuzō his mentor, although Yoshino was a constitutional theorist and Yanaihara replaced Nitobe Inazō as professor of international economics and colonial policy. Nitobe, a Christian who served as principal of the First Higher School between 1906 and 1913, was often mentioned as an early inspiration to a number of younger Christian converts on the faculty—Yanaihara, Ebara Banri, Tanaka Kōtarō, and Nanbara Shigeru—all of whom attended meetings of a campus Bible study group in the 1920s. But these ties were outside the factional alignment in the Economics Department.[58]

It is thus difficult to attribute the type of factionalism that plagued the Economics Department to regional origins, school ties, or even mentoring relations. Nor is it obvious that the vertical model of diffuse patron-protégé relations, where it did exist at Tōdai, was necessarily dysfunctional in the sense of being itself a primary cause of disruptive conflict. The reflections of Nanbara Shigeru, a law professor in this period, suggested the opposite may have been closer to reality—that it may well have been the absence of senior authority figures that exacerbated the situation in economics:

The Law Department was not without similar rivalry and alienation among colleagues, and there was an antagonism over theories and ideas. But [the law faculty] never reached the point of carrying the dispute outside the [Law] Department because there were many senior professors who by long tradition worked together to transcend all such disagreements and would put everything else aside to protect the autonomy of the university and the system as a whole.[59]

58. Yanaihara, *Watakushi*, p. 42.
59. Nanbara et al., *Onozuka Kiheiji*, p. 281. This, of course, greatly understates the disputes that did become public in 1939; see chapter 5.

Hijikata Seibi's own remarks on why he and his colleagues fought so bitterly and frequently in the 1920s are also revealing despite his unremitting anti-Marxist bias: "During the period personnel issues were continuously arising . . . because the Tōdai Economics Department had to recruit up-and-coming students to strengthen its lineup [in a department that] had been born prematurely."[60]

The circumstances Hijikata and Nanbara described existed not only in the initial phase of finding faculty to open the Economics Department in 1919 but also in the process that continued into the mid-1920s as the department experienced heavy attrition among older men such as Kanai Noburu and Takano Iwasaburō. These were replaced not by experienced associate professors who had long been waiting in the wings to take their places, as was true in the more established Department of Law, but by men very much their juniors. The average age of the full professors in Tōdai law after the division into two departments in 1919 was almost fifty years old. The median age of the ten full professors in economics in 1926 was in the midthirties. The only three economists older than forty were the three surviving founders, Yamazaki (fifty-eight), Yahagi Eizō (fifty-six), and Kawazu Susumu (fifty-one), none of whom seemed to fit well the model of *oyabun*-style patrons with intimate ties to loyal protégés.

Indeed, the "majority" or "anti-Marxist" faction was less a tightly knit clique or even a coalition of factions than a shifting alliance of individuals, each with at best a limited following. Nor was the opposition in the minority faction led by Ōuchi, Maide, and Ueno descended from a common mentor, despite membership in the original circle that revolved around Takano Iwasaburō before his departure.

It is true that during the 1920s patron-protégé relationships did develop between Marxists and some younger Tōdai graduate students. Ōuchi and others sponsored these men for faculty openings in both their own department or, more especially, at the newer imperial universities and expanding private colleges. Such ties, of course, were hardly peculiar to the Japanese academic world and seem to have had less to do with any lingering heritage of feudal values than with the Marxists' conscious attempt to institutionalize what in the Japan of the time was a still novel approach to their discipline. They thus acted as academic patrons in a manner closely resembling the clientage of "clus-

---

60. Hijikata, *Gakkai shunjūki*, p. 107.

tering" that marked, for instance, the establishment of Durkheimian sociology in early-twentieth-century France.[61]

It should also be noted that by the end of the 1920s these Marxists had split into two major intellectual camps with quite different views of how Marxist principles fit the Japanese case. These views divided them both in their study of the past and in their commitment to political action in the present. Ōuchi, Ōmori, and Tsuchiya Takao, for example, were associated with an interpretation that held Japanese capitalist society had already passed through a bourgeois revolution with the Meiji Restoration. Yamada Moritarō, like his friend in the Law Department, Hirano Yoshitarō, were equally committed to the contrary view—that Japanese society was still in a transitional stage of "absolutism" between feudalism and capitalism. These two camps exchanged numerous intellectual volleys in a prolonged and heated duel, known as the Rōnōha-Kōzaha Debates, in which almost as much ammunition was expended on each other as on the common adversaries, the anti-Marxists.[62]

More striking than distinctions between the Law and Economics departments were the generational differences in career patterns between the academic elite that had become prominent prior to 1920 and the professors appointed in the 1920s and 1930s. Although both groups included men who were passionately involved in the political and social issues of their times, those professors who began their careers prior to the Taishō Political Change of 1912–1913 were far more likely to sever voluntarily their official ties with the university to pursue their goals. Even if one counts those actually driven involuntarily from the university, there was nevertheless a greater tendency in the post–World War I generation to remain in academic posts. To put it in quantifiable terms, a far greater number of the pre-1920 generation—sixteen out of the thirty-five (or forty-three if one includes early deaths and transfers)—left their professorships than did the succeeding generation, even though the latter included at least six "forced" resignations.[63]

61. See Clark, *Prophets and Patrons*.

62. For Ōuchi's own description of these factions, see Tōdai, *Keizaigaku,* vol. 1, pp. 148ff. In English there are numerous brief summaries of this division, but one of the most informative is contained in the analytical descriptions of their major works in *An Outline of Japanese Economic History,* edited by Sumiya Mikio and Koji Taira. For greater detail, see Yasuba, "Anatomy of the Debate on Japanese Capitalism"; and Hoston, *Marxism and the Crisis of Development in Prewar Japan.*

63. The careers of professors and associate professors on the Tōdai faculties of law and economics (regular appointees) can be summarized as follows:

The point is clearer when the subsequent careers of the 1886–1912 group are examined. This group included at least nine whose departures were motivated by a desire to pursue politics in the public arena: Hozumi Nobushige and Tomii Masaaki became privy councillors; Ichiki Kitokurō and Okano Keijirō entered the civil bureaucracy; Terao Tōru and Okada Asatarō left to act as political advisers to the Chinese; Hatoyama Hideo, like Yoshino Sakuzō, entered electoral politics; and, of course, Takano Iwasaburō conformed to this pattern when he chose to exert his efforts outside the university.

In contrast, young scholars such as Hirano Yoshitarō, Ōmori Yoshitarō, and Yamada Moritarō took part in partisan debates and even in political activities without first giving up their academic bases. Professors Kawai, Yanaihara, and Ebara Banri in economics and Nanbara in law, men committed to working toward social change, returned to their alma mater as teachers only after a number of years of frustration in the bureaucratic or business worlds. For these intellectuals, academic appointment afforded them a second chance to make a mark on their times. Nor were there many cases in this generation of Tōdai faculty comparable to the voluntary shifts out of the university by their predecessors. Whereas the men of the 1920s and 1930s generation on the whole may not have been any more devoted to political causes, they were less likely to dissociate themselves from the university before becoming deeply involved in political action off campus. This increased the likelihood that the university would be even more subject to attempts at outside intervention in the 1920s and 1930s than in the Meiji decades. As we will see in more detail in the following chapter, it was

---

All appointed, 1866–1912 (law and economics combined)

Retired at 60 years or still on staff in 1939	19 (43%)
Transferred to another department or school	4 (9%)
Resigned	17 (39%)
Died or information not available	4 (9%)
	44 (100%)

Appointed in law, 1913–1938

Retired at 60 years or still on staff in 1939	17 (81%)
Transferred to another department or school	0 (0%)
Resigned	2 (10%)
Died or information not available	2 (10%)
	21 (100%)

Appointed in economics, 1913–1938

Retired at 60 years or still on staff in 1939	23 (74%)
Transferred to another department or school	0 (0%)
Resigned	6 (19%)
Died or information not available	2 (6%)
	31 (100%)

precisely this line between scholar-as-commentator on political issues and professor-as-participant in partisan activities that Tōdai presidents such as Yamakawa Kenjirō and Onozuka Kiheiji used to delineate what was proper faculty behavior from what might be subject to disciplinary action.

This suggests the Marxists' own claim that their persecution was initially provoked by their intellectual heresy was closer to the mark than discussions of the particularistic antagonism of group orientations peculiar to Japan. But this conclusion, too, requires some qualification. Certainly the materialist interpretation of history and the labor theory of value, when coupled with methodological insistence on empirical data on class conditions, constituted a central source of intellectual disputes within the department. As we saw in such early disputes as the Minobe-Uesugi controversy, it would be naive to underestimate the fervor with which such theoretical models were held or their potential for creating lasting antagonism among academic intellectuals. But a plausible argument can be made that the personal commitment of Ōuchi and his colleagues to radical Marxism was still quite tentative at the time of the 1920 Morito affair, deepening only as time passed. Moreover, some of the economists identified with the Left—for example, the Christian Yanaihara—never completely accepted either Marxism or Ōuchi's style of academic activism.

Two other related aspects must be taken into consideration: first, the inordinate zeal with which the Takano circle sought to overcome the conservative biases within the social sciences at Tōdai; and second, the conviction that the role of teacher-scholar had to be expanded to encompass the task of mobilizing Japan's students and workers behind the effort to reconstruct their society. This commitment and the fervor with which it was pursued threatened the distribution of power within the academic establishment and led to the acceptance of the view that the Left was made up of conspirators bent on seizing control of the Economics Department and, perhaps, of the university as a whole.[64] Although Ōuchi and others denied any such conspiracy, their own accounts nonetheless leave a vivid impression of the missionary enthusiasm that marked their group—a sense of shared personal calling that bound group members together and left little tolerance for the frustrations of coping with the obstructionism of their antiactivist colleagues.

---

64. For an example of how students harassed lecturers, see Hirai, *Individualism and Socialism*, p. 125.

It was actually this commitment to activism, rather than the attack on a theoretical orthodoxy, that plunged the department and the university into repeated open conflict with government authorities. And it was the heat of those conflicts that fixed the ideological coloring of the academic Left and hardened the original Takano circle into a unified faction perpetually on guard against external political attacks—attacks the Tōdai colleges all too frequently acquiesced to or even abetted.

5

The Maintenance of
University Autonomy,
1919–1932

The Japanese academic elite of the 1900s and 1910s, when faced with attacks on its collective interests, had displayed a remarkable capacity to put aside ideological differences, factional divisions, and interdisciplinary rivalries. During the 1920s, however, that capacity for solidarity eroded steadily. This was evident in the relations both within the faculty at Tokyo Imperial University and between it and the faculties at its sister institutions. In part, that erosion was due to internal processes that sapped the cohesive strength of the university from within, as described in the previous chapter. The other half of the story, of course, was the increasing pressure from outside. The changes in the nature of that external pressure were crucial, and this chapter will examine those changes in some detail. In the process it will become evident that even liberals among imperial university faculty members were often more concerned with maintaining the elite status of their institutions than with defending the academic freedom of individual colleagues.

The Initial Attempt to Reassert Control

World War I provided a powerful stimulant to the Japanese economy, drawing an unprecedented number of workers into the industrial workplace. The rapid pace of this hothouse growth and the series of sharp business downturns that followed it created new gaps both between the work force and industrial managers and between the developing urban sector and the now depressed rural sector of the economy. Consequently, serious class strife between labor and management as well as between tenant farmers and landlords seemed imminent to many observers. In 1918 riots over rice prices spread rapidly from region to region throughout the nation, leading to the resignation of the prime minister. The new Hara cabinet, the first in which party politicians held a majority of the portfolios, devoted its attention to new strategies for coping with this perceived threat to political and social stability, as did its successors over the next decade.[1]

Members of Hara's cabinet and other conservatives in high places in the Japanese political system were particularly sensitive to the growing popularity of liberal and socialist ideas that challenged the core values of Meiji conservatism, especially the principles of hierarchical authority and self-sacrifice in service to the state. The social democratic movement led by academics, student groups, labor organizers, and others called for the greater liberalization of politics and reform programs to equalize wealth and power. The leaders of the two major parliamentary parties, which had gathered to themselves much of the political power once held in the hands of a small circle of Meiji leaders, were now in their turn attacked as behind the times and as too responsive to the interests of the large business firms at the expense of the people. That some of the most vocal critics of the status quo came from the elite universities in Tokyo and Kyoto was particularly vexing, and the government soon took steps to strike back in an effort to reassert government control over Japan's elite universities.

Very often in the forefront of this effort was a network of current or former Justice Ministry officials linked to Hiranuma Kiichirō.[2]

1. The Rice Riots are treated in Lewis, *Rioters and Citizens*. For a recent reexamination of changes among urban workers, see Gordon, *Labor and Imperial Democracy*; for government reactions, see Garon, *State and Labor in Modern Japan*, pp. 39ff.

2. Hiranuma (1867–1952), a Tōdai law graduate (class of 1888) who held a doctorate in law (1907), moved up rapidly as the Justice Ministry became increasingly professionalized. He was vice minister in 1911 at the age of forty-four and became procurator-general the following year, chief of the High Court in 1921, justice minister in 1923, and then privy councillor. In 1937 he was selected to serve as prime minister (Hiranuma, *Kaikoroku*, pp. 339–357). For English accounts of Hiranuma's political views and especially the part played by the Hiranuma "clique," see Yasko, "Hiranuma Kiichiro"; and Mitchell, *Thought Control in Prewar Japan*.

Hiranuma was one of the most prominent of the conservatives of his day, a reputation that eventually led him to be selected prime minister in 1939 and then, following World War II, caused him to be designated a class A war criminal. He had emerged as a leader within the justice system as early as the 1910s, and as the procurator-general in 1919 Hiranuma was an influential advocate of stronger measures to deal with political agitators both on and off campus. Many parliamentary party leaders, including Hara Takashi (Kei), prime minister in 1919, shared this intolerance for academics who behaved "irresponsibly" and jeopardized "the nation's future" by advocating universal suffrage, legalization of labor unions, or other dangerous ideas imported from abroad.[3] For Hiranuma and Hara the primary issue regarding academic political activity was how best to suppress it.

The December 1919 issue of the Tōdai Economics Department journal, which included the article on Kropotkin, provided an excellent opportunity to strike a blow against academic activists. Home Ministry censors stepped in on December 27 to stop distribution of the journal on the grounds that the article threatened peace and order and thus violated the press law. On the same day the Education Ministry sent an official to alert Tōdai president Yamakawa of the problem. Yamakawa consulted with three senior members of the Economics Department and with the education vice minister. The Tōdai president apparently believed an agreement had been reached: the matter would be dropped if all copies of the journal were recalled, and the author, Morito Tatsuo, would issue an apology clarifying that he had not intended to embrace violent means to achieve the social ideals of anarchistic communism. While the Tōdai administration and senior economics faculty members were cooperating with the Education Ministry in an effort to defuse the situation, Procurator-General Hiranuma was pressing the attack.

Hiranuma proposed to bypass the administrative channels of the Education Ministry and file criminal indictments through the Justice Ministry, an unprecedented tactic in a case involving the writings of an imperial university professor. On January 9 Hiranuma visited Prime Minister Hara to describe the incident and to seek Hara's approval for legal action against Morito and Ōuchi Hyōe. Hara sent Hiranuma to consult with the education minister, ex-businessman and Seiyūkai Party

3. Entries in Hara Kei's diary during the 1918–1920 period reveal clearly his growing hostility toward Tōdai professors (*Nikki*, vol. 8, p. 458, entry for January 13, 1920); see also the entries regarding his earlier discussions with Yamagata Aritomo (*Nikki*, vol. 8, p. 75, entry for June 17, 1918; vol. 8, p. 254, entry for November 3, 1918.)

stalwart Nakahashi Tokugorō. But Nakahashi, reflecting the mood of Education Ministry bureaucrats, proved cool to Hiranuma's plan. Undaunted, Hiranuma persisted in his efforts to discipline the Tōdai faculty. When the Tōdai administration failed to reach a compromise with Morito, Hiranuma was able to return to the prime minister and report the young scholar "gave no sign of being penitent." Prime Minister Hara subsequently recorded in his diary, "I told [Hiranuma] that recently university professors had become a gang of publicity seekers and that we could not sit idly by and ignore it while the abuses of publishing such absurd opinions were going on."[4] The following day, January 13, Hara overrode whatever qualms his education minister still might have had, and the cabinet gave its formal endorsement to legal proceedings.[5]

While the government was still in the process of reaching its decision, President Yamakawa and the senior economics professors had been pursuing their own course. Apparently at the suggestion of economics chairman Kanai, President Yamakawa attended a special meeting with the full professors of that department. Even though at that time no formal indictments against Mori or Ōuchi had been handed down from the Justice Ministry, all but one of the eight professors present voted to suspend both associate professors until the government's investigation was concluded.[6] This action by their colleagues caused great bitterness among the supporters of Morito and Ōuchi even though once the Justice Ministry did bring indictments, the two were automatically suspended under civil service regulations for the duration of any legal proceedings.

The Defense of Academic Freedom in the Morito Case

The unprecedented indictment of an imperial university professor for violating the press laws stirred the Left and Center of the Japanese intellectual spectrum into an impassioned defense of academic freedom. Protest began to spread among Tōdai students as soon as they

4. Hara Kei, *Nikki,* vol. 8, p. 457, entry for January 12, 1920.
5. Ibid., p. 458. President Yamakawa had visited Minister Nakahashi on January 13, presumably before the cabinet meeting, and had come away believing he had the minister's support (*Danshaku Yamakawa,* p. 338).
6. For details, see chapter 4.

learned that the department faculty had voted to suspend Mori and Ōuchi. Close to four hundred individuals are said to have attended a rally called by the Economics Department student club, Keiyūkai. A reported one thousand people gathered in another open demonstration against the capitulation of the senior faculty in the face of the government's attack. Tōdai faculty leaders sought to discourage student demonstrations of support, warning those in the Economics Department they might threaten the very survival of the new department. As a result, the defense of Morito and Ōuchi took place largely off campus and in the courtrooms.[7]

The administration's admonitions did not deter faculty members as individuals or as members of off-campus groups from expressing their opposition to these unprecedented indictments. When the prosecution formally requested jail terms for Morito and Ōuchi, various student and intellectual groups, including the still prestigious Social Policy Study Association, sponsored a mass rally at the YMCA in the Kanda district. There speakers castigated President Yamakawa and the Education Ministry for abandoning the principles of academic freedom in not standing firm against the suppression of the Economics Department journal.[8] This opposition to the government cut across departmental lines, although it is true that the natural and applied sciences were underrepresented among opposition leaders. Tōdai law professors Yoshino Sakuzō and Minobe Tatsukichi joined with Anesaki Masaharu, the Buddhist scholar in the Department of Letters, Sasaki Sōichi of Kyoto University Law Department, and Waseda University professors Abe Isoo and Miyake Setsurei as special consultants to the team of defense lawyers in court. Still other professors used the pages of national opinion magazines and interviews to popular newspapers to ridicule the government's case.

The basic defense was articulated publicly by Professor Sasaki Sōichi in the Kyoto law review of March 1920.[9] Two fundamental questions were raised: Was the publication of the article on Kropotkin a criminal violation of the laws that gave the government the power to control the

---

7. Arisawa, *Gakumon to shisō to ningen to,* pp. 21–22. Arisawa, a student on campus at the time, also recalled that President Yamakawa, when rejecting a student petition, scolded the authors for being "stupid."

8. See the lists of individuals and groups, for example, in Ōshima, *Takano Iwasaburō den,* pp. 191–195.

9. Sasaki Sōichi, "Daigaku kyōju no kenkyū no genkai"; see also Niho, "Shisō mondai oyobi Morito jiken to Uesugi kyōju no ronsetsu ni tsuite."

press? Did the actions of Morito and Ōuchi constitute a breach of their official responsibilities as university professors? Although Sasaki argued no to both, he also took great pains to make clear that he was not defending the validity of anarchism as a system of ideas: "I am one who advocates a nationalism [*kokka shugi*] that endorses the existence of the state [*kokka*]."[10] At the same time, he emphatically denied that either defendant had advocated the overthrow of the constitution as charged under Article 41 of the press law. If there was any criminal case at all, therefore, it rested on the lesser charge under Article 23—publishing material that disturbed the peace and order.

Professor Sasaki did not dispute the constitutionality of the 1909 press law or the authority it granted the Home Ministry to control publications dangerous to the political order.[11] Instead, Sasaki based his case on the narrower grounds of the need to make certain distinctions. First, the determination of whether an article was indeed dangerous to peace and order had to be based on its actual influence on society, not merely on the text. Second, even if it were reasonable for the Home Ministry to take steps to protect society from a dangerous influence, this did not necessarily mean the Justice Ministry was correct in bringing criminal indictments against the author or editor:

In cases where there is a danger in an article . . . it must be controlled. The only way to control such an article is to isolate it from the society where it is expected to disturb the peace and order. But legally the means to do this are limited to prohibiting the sale and distribution of the newspaper in which the article appears. . . . . They definitely do not extend to imposing disciplinary punishment.[12]

The question of the role of the university professor was closer to the heart of the problem, and Sasaki therefore attempted to come to grips with the section of the 1918 ordinance that defined the functions of the university in terms that could be used against Morito and Ōuchi:

According to the first article of the university ordinance, the essential functions of the university are to be found in scholarly inquiry and scholarly instruction combined with attention to nurturing the thought of the nation [*kokka shisō no*

10. Sasaki Sōichi, "Daigaku kyōju no kenkyū no genkai," p. 41.
11. Article 29 of the 1889 constitution permitted the Diet to legislate limits on freedom of speech and the press, which it did in the publication law of 1893 and the press law of 1909, the statutes in effect during the Morito Case. For more details on government censorship, see Mitchell, *Censorship in Imperial Japan;* and Kasza, *The State and Mass Media.*
12. Sasaki Sōichi, "Daigaku kyōju no kenkyū no genkai," p. 22.

kan'yō]. What does it mean to say, "Nurture the thought of the nation"? This phrase appears for the first time in the new university ordinance of 1918 . . . and one cannot find it used in [the regulations regarding] the university system before this. Actually the meaning of this phrase is unclear. . . . It may be thought that it is clear when considered [in some other context] separate from the university ordinance, but as used in the university ordinance regarding the responsibilities of university professors, it definitely cannot be said to be clear.[13]

On the one hand, Sasaki asserted that the inclusion of the phrase was done carelessly without any intent that it be used as a standard to judge behavior in specific cases. Whatever the words *kan'yō* (nurturing, fostering, cultivating) or *kokka shisō* (the thought of the nation/state) might connote subjectively to the general public, their meaning was ambiguous in this legal context. On the other hand, Sasaki sought to use the ordinance's call for scholarly inquiry as the basis for a logical defense of the freedom to publish the results of scholarly research. The words *gakumon no kenkyū* (scholarly inquiry) had objective meaning.

Here Sasaki's reasoning echoed one of the key arguments used fifteen years earlier in the defense of Tomizu Hiroto and the others in his group. That is, the university ordinance and the civil service regulations imposed on the professor the obligation to conduct research. For him to do so, he had to be able to examine controversial political subjects in a scientific manner. Anarchism was concerned with "the reasons for the existence of the state, a question which is a fundamental prerequisite for the study of the state." Therefore, by carrying out research on anarchism, Professor Morito was performing his duties as a scholar as provided for in the ordinance. That he and Ōuchi were higher civil servants assigned as professors to an imperial university, rather than being employed at a private university, did not alter their obligations as scholars.[14]

During the first trial of Morito and Ōuchi these denials that the two economists had committed any seditious act were well received in court. In early March 1920 the presiding judge, himself a sometime lecturer at Tōdai, ruled that the prosecution had failed to make its case for a violation of Article 42 of the press law. But the argument that in publishing an article on anarchism the two defendants were faithfully carrying out their legal responsibilities as university professors was not upheld. Instead, the judge found the defendants guilty of the lesser charge under Article 23 of disturbing the public peace by spreading

13. Ibid., pp. 27–28.
14. Ibid., pp. 37, 40.

doubts about the legitimacy of the state. Morito as author was fined ¥70 and sentenced to two months of imprisonment; Ōuchi as editor was fined ¥20 and given a one-month sentence.

This, however, was not the end of the legal process. As was possible under Japanese law, the Justice Ministry appealed the verdict as too lenient. Ultimately, in October 1920 the Supreme Court upheld a reversal of the lower court decision, convicting the two Tōdai faculty of charges under Article 42 of acts in defiance of the imperial constitution. Morito's jail sentence was increased from two to three months. Ōuchi was given a year of probation in lieu of jail.[15]

The Morito Case, as it came to be known, was a clear contest between two incompatible views of the function of the university. Among those who applauded the verdict, if not necessarily the light sentence, was Takeuchi Kakuji, a lawyer close to Hiranuma and his conservative circle. In his view,

Tokyo Imperial University should become the quarantine office for imported [ideologies]. If a thought is harmful, it should be treated as a harmful thought. For an ideology which is both harmful and harmless, the university should remove the harmful portion, and import the profitable part. . . . Mr. Morito has not only forgotten the duty of the quarantiner, but himself has become the importer of the harmful germ.[16]

The other side was represented by an editorial in the influential opinion monthly *Kaizō* that viewed the jailing of Morito as positive proof bureaucrats were still incapable of understanding the simple truth that academic freedom was "necessary to the progress of the state [*kokka*] . . . even if it sometimes opposed the interests of the state or rejected the state."[17]

Despite the clarity of the opposing sides, any analysis of the outcome of the Morito Case must not overlook the considerable ambiguity in its portents for the future. This ambiguity was evident both from the limited perspective of 1920 and from the later vantage point of the

---

15. The court proceedings are analyzed at length in Miyaji, "Morito jiken." It should be understood there were no jury trials in Japan at the time—as was typical on the continent of Europe, the judge determined the verdict as well as passed sentence. "Supreme Court" here refers to the Daishin'in, which is often translated as the "Great Court of Cassation" to distinguish it from its successor, the Saikō Saibansho, or "Supreme Court," under the 1947 constitution.

16. Takeuchi Kakuji, "Morito mondai no kenkyū," *Hōritsu shinbun;* as quoted in Mitchell, *Thought Control in Prewar Japan,* p. 41.

17. "Daigaku oyobi seifu no kokkakan ni tsuite," p. 1.

1930s. On the one hand, Procurator-General Hiranuma and his fellow conservatives seemed to have found an effective new tool for bending the faculties of the imperial universities to their will. Whereas the Education Ministry had been unsuccessful in its attempts to pressure the faculty with the threat of administrative discipline on a series of occasions following the Tomizu affair of 1905, the Justice Ministry had removed Morito and Ōuchi from their classrooms by the relatively expeditious means of formal criminal indictments.[18] Morito had been jailed, and he had subsequently left the university in disgust; Ōuchi had been automatically suspended from the faculty during the term of his probationary sentence and thus had been effectively barred from the classroom for one year.

The champions of academic freedom then and later have remarked on the damage done to their cause by the decision of President Yamakawa and the senior economics professors to suspend Morito and Ōuchi even before the indictments were drawn. Less attention is focused on the provisions in the civil service regulation that made suspension automatic once the indictments were handed down. Surely one of the more puzzling aspects of this and subsequent confrontations was the reluctance of the faculties at the imperial universities to challenge this automatic suspension provision in the civil service rules. Even if they were loath to consider giving up entirely the status as higher civil servants of the throne, quite different provisions for academics, specific to the imperial universities if necessary, could have been sought and obtained. It is reported that President Yamakawa did attempt to get an exemption from those regulations in the case of Ōuchi's probation. He argued that Ōuchi was treated with undue harshness in light of his lesser role as editor. These exploratory talks with officials in the Justice and Education ministries were dropped, however, when senior members of the Tōdai faculty allegedly sided with bureaucrats in the Education Ministry who opposed further negotiations.[19] (When such crim-

18. Although Barshay's study of intellectuals in this period, *State and the Intellectual in Imperial Japan*, is as a whole extraordinarily interesting, his comment (on p. 44) that the use of indictments "required (and enjoyed) the cooperation between the Justice and Education Ministries is of course the key point" misses the mark. This initial use of formal indictments seemed to have taken place precisely because such cooperation from the Education Ministry was not forthcoming and the Justice Ministry was determined to move against Morito and Ōuchi even without the support of the Education Ministry.

19. The economist Matsuoka Kinpei is identified as one who urged President Yamakawa to make the plea, but Yamakawa's biographers do not identify those who opposed the continuation of the negotiations (*Danshaku Yamakawa*, p. 339).

inal indictments were once again used in the 1930s, faculty leaders again acquiesced in the application of the automatic suspension provision.)

On the other hand, Procurator-General's Hiranuma's success in prosecuting the cases, as significant as it was in terms of legal precedents, had far less immediate influence on government-university relations than a superficial reading might predict. Certainly the trials had little, if any, negative effect on the spread of radical ideas among students or future faculty. Quite the contrary, the press coverage of the trials had an impact far beyond that of any junior economist writing in an academic magazine: it made the name *Kropotkin* and the term *anarchism* meaningful to a much broader public.[20] Moreover, the politicization of the campus continued apace over the next decade, and there were few signs of negative impact on the increasing student and faculty involvement in off-campus radicalism.

Nor were either Morito or Ōuchi silenced for long. Morito took a position with his mentor Takano Iwasaburō at the Ōhara Institute for Social Research. Morito soon became a respected political commentator and a hero to Tōdai students, who invited him regularly to speak at their gatherings. In the case of Ōuchi, the vigorous defense during the trials smoothed the way for him not only to be reinstated but also to be promoted to full professor after he had spent his year on probation doing research in a forced sabbatical abroad. Once back on campus he resumed the use of his prestigious position as an imperial university professor to criticize the political establishment. Given these facts, the 1920 confrontation was closer to a standoff than an overwhelming victory for the government. Indeed, no cabinet in the next ten years used the weapon of criminal indictments against an imperial university faculty member.

This is not to say that the enemies of academic freedom became dormant. On the contrary, in an attempt to find more effective means of controlling this radical dissent, the mainstream Hiranuma faction within the Justice Ministry redoubled its efforts. It secured from the dominant party in the Diet, the Seiyūkai, support for new laws with more severe penalties. Consequently, these conservatives were success-

20. For instance, Arisawa Hiromi, who later became a faculty member and eventually a prominent economic adviser to postwar cabinets, was a student at the time and recalled how he and others rushed out to buy any available copy of Kropotkin's *Mutual Aid* in their eagerness to discover what the conflict was all about (Arisawa, *Gakumon to shisō to ningen to,* pp. 21–22).

ful in enacting a new peace preservation law in 1925. Yet, much to their frustration, this turned out to have a new loophole for somewhat greater academic freedom, for it passed the Diet only with explicit assurances by the more tolerant Minseitō Party leaders that academics would be allowed to conduct and publish research even on Marxism so long as they did not actually engage in political behavior deemed illegal.

Thus, paradoxically in light of the precedents of the 1920 Morito Case and the intentions of the chief sponsors of the 1925 law, neither served well the purposes of those seeking to reassert control over the imperial universities. Scholarly publication was subjected to greater surveillance once again, but no indictments were brought against authors or editors of such scholarly works for their contents until after war broke out in China in the mid-1930s.[21] This does not mean there was no other official action against faculty dissenters in the late 1920s or early 1930s. Rather, because the use of the indictment weapon by the Justice Ministry was circumscribed by the need to produce admissible evidence of actual complicity in an illegal political act, the government's search for effective means of suppressing radical academics was forced into other avenues, as we can see from the events of the period 1925–1933.

The Campaign Against Student Radicalism, 1925–1930

The reluctance to attack faculty did not extend to students. In late 1925 and early 1926 the government moved against the Student Federation of Social Science (Gakusei Shakai Kagaku Rengōkai), a nationwide network of radical study groups in universities and higher schools. Between December 1 and January 15 police arrested several dozen students for alleged violation of the new peace preservation law. Kyoto law professor Kawakami Hajime's home was searched in connection with these student radicals, but no further ac-

21. For English-language studies of the 1925 law and the political circumstances of its passage, see Mitchell's informative, if at times argumentative, analysis in *Thought Control in Prewar Japan*, which notes that academics did not mount an attack on the law (pp. 65–73). Garon presented a stimulating treatment of the contrasting views of the two parties, *State and Labor in Modern Japan*, Chapter 3.

tion was taken against him or any other imperial university faculty member at that time.[22]

Faculties on the campuses of the imperial universities in this period seemed either in agreement about the danger of student radicalism or unwilling to confront the government directly in defense of students who were engaged in radical activities. At Tōdai, University Council representatives bemoaned the politicization of the student organizations (*gakuyūkai*), which had been intended for educational (*gakujutsu*) purposes, and talked indecisively about the need to keep outsiders from entering the classrooms. Some concern was expressed about the stigma of the suspensions being noted on student records, but the problem was left largely in the hands of the school administrators and regular staff that dealt with student affairs.[23]

Meanwhile, in 1927 the Seiyūkai Party was returned to power, and the new cabinet included Tanaka Giichi as prime minister, Suzuki Kisaburō as home minister, Hara Yoshimichi as justice minister, and Ogawa Heiji as railroad minister. These were not men likely to remain passive about subversive ideas. Ogawa had built his political career as a strident nationalist and had served as justice minister in 1925. Suzuki and Hara were former lieutenants of Hiranuma Kiichirō, who was now vice president of the Privy Council. All four men had pushed hard for the passage of the 1925 peace preservation law and fully intended to find ways to exterminate radicalism on as well as off campus. On March 15, 1928, a nationwide roundup began of some sixteen hundred individuals suspected of planning, in the language of the official charges, "to overthrow the present organization of our country, and by a proletarian dictatorship to realize a communist society. [They have] organized a Japanese Communist Party, . . . infiltrated into the various kinds of labor and farmer groups to recruit new members for the party and . . . broadcast handbills with inflammatory contents."[24]

This mass arrest of suspected subversives triggered the first truly concerted effort to purge the imperial universities of radical faculty. When large numbers of students turned up among those arrested, the Education Ministry stepped up its campaigns against campus radical-

---

22. Smith, *Japan's First Student Radicals;* Bernstein, *Japanese Marxist,* p. 142.

23. See *Tōdai, Hyōgikai kirokushō,* September 28, October 12, and the month of November 1926, especially the comments by Professors Watanabe and Minobe Tatsukichi.

24. Quoted from arrest warrants in Mitchell, *Thought Control in Prewar Japan,* p. 84. This is the most detailed account in English of the March 15 Incident.

ism, broadening the target area to include those teachers who in its view were responsible for misguiding their pupils. On April 13, 1928, the cabinet gave Education Minister Mizuno Rentarō approval for punitive measures against a list of faculty members at the imperial universities in Tokyo, Kyoto, and Kyushu. Minister Mizuno summoned the presidents of each of the imperial universities to inform them personally that, in addition to the disbanding of radical student groups on their campuses, they also had to take steps to remove leftist professors.[25]

Apparently, the precise manner of dealing with them was left to the university presidents, although actions at Kyoto and Kyushu universities bore a strong resemblance to each other. At Kyoto the key figure on the ministry's list was the celebrated author and patron of radical student groups, economics professor Kawakami Hajime.[26] Kyoto president Torasaburō took the first steps to deal with the problem while still in Tokyo for the meeting at the Education Ministry. He conferred with the Kyoto economics chairman Takarabe Seiji and Kawakami's senior colleague, Professor Kambe Masao, who were also present in Tokyo.[27] The three are said to have reached an agreement to demand Kawakami's resignation on three grounds: Kawakami had taken an active part in the election campaign of Waseda University professor Ōyama Ikuo, the leader of the leftist Farmer-Labor Party (Rōnōtō); Kawakami had preached Marxism in his lectures as well as his writings; and his influence as faculty adviser had incited students to acts of violence. (In 1928 only the last violated the letter of any Japanese law, and whatever admissible evidence may have existed on this count had not been uncovered by the police during the March roundups.)

When a formal faculty meeting of the Economics Department was called to deliberate on the case, Professors Takarabe and Kambe were

25. Monbushō, *Meiji ikō*, vol. 7, pp. 10–11. For a partial translation of the minister's instruction to administrators at state schools, see Suh, "The Struggle for Academic Freedom," pp. 159–162; but it should be noted that Suh confused the March 15, 1928, arrests with the Young Officers' Revolt of March 15, 1932, which of course had no direct bearing on these events. See also Nanbara et al., *Onozuka Kiheiji*, p. 159; and Smith, *Japan's First Student Radicals*, pp. 200–205.

26. For more on Kawakami, see Bernstein, *Japanese Marxist*.

27. President Araki Torasaburō is not to be confused with either the Tōdai economics professor Araki Kōtarō or with General Baron Araki Sadao, who served as education minister in the late 1930s. Araki Torasaburō (1866–1942) was an alumnus of Tōdai, held a doctorate in medicine, and had served as dean of the Kyoto Medical College for twelve years before being named president in 1915. In 1937 he was elevated to the Privy Council. Professor Kanbe was a Tōdai law graduate and a former dean of the Kyoto Law College.

unable to secure a majority vote for outright dismissal. Instead, they had to content themselves with a seemingly ambiguous compromise motion stating that if Kawakami himself were to offer his resignation, then the department should accept it. President Araki, armed with this resolution, confronted Kawakami. The president may have misrepresented the department action as a formal motion of censure calling for resignation, thereby inducing Kawakami to resign thinking his colleagues had explicitly repudiated him.[28]

The task proved even simpler for President Daikubara Gintarō at Kyushu Imperial University, where a number of associate professors had been targeted for removal. The faculty had been newly expanded within a joint Department of Law and Letters, and there apparently was considerable animosity toward the radical newcomers. The department chairman, Kazuga Masaji, was easily convinced that the future of the department and the best interests of the university required a positive response to the Education Ministry's desire to remove Sakisaka Itsurō, Ishihama Tomoyuki, and Sasa Hiroo. These three were maneuvered into submitting their resignations despite their denials of having been involved in communist activities.[29]

At Tōdai the ministry's blacklist included the so-called three Tarōs—Ōmori Yoshitarō, Yamada Moritarō, and Hirano Yoshitarō. But here things proved much more difficult. Tōdai's interim president, Onozuka Kiheiji, unlike his counterparts at Kyoto and Kyushu, had a reputation as a staunch advocate of university autonomy reaching back to his days as one of the Seven Ph.D.s in 1905. He had subsequently taken a leading role in the 1913 clash with the Education Ministry over the administration of Kyoto University. Now he let it be known again that

28. See the reminiscences of former Kyoto professor Suegawa Hiroshi in Tanaka Kōtarō et al., *Daigaku no jiji,* pp. 55–59. Also see Ienaga, *Daigaku no jiyū no rekishi,* p. 53; and Kawakami, *Jijoden,* pp. 157–159, 243. The account given here differs from the brief account in Bernstein's otherwise excellent biography, which implies a vote of the economics faculty as a whole—rather than President Araki and a minority of the faculty—had demanded Kawakami's resignation (*Japanese Marxist,* p. 145).

29. Actually Sakisaka later claimed someone else must have submitted a letter of resignation for him because he had not (Sakisaka, *Arashi,* pp. 170–171, 191). See also "Kubi kirareta daigaku kyōju retsuden"; and Ikazaki, *Daigaku no jisei,* pp. 57–58. Kyushu president Daikubara was a Tōdai graduate and former official in the Ministry of Agriculture and Commerce who had long served as a professor of agriculture before becoming president in 1926. He later served as president of Dōshisha University, the Christian college in Kyoto. The opposition to radicalism in the Department of Law and Letters is said to have been led by Professor Kanokogi Kazunobu (1884–1949), who was eventually purged by the U.S. Occupation for his wartime role as a censor.

he would not yield easily to outside pressure. His response to Education Minister Mizuno, whom he knew personally quite well, was that Tōdai would take care of its own internal housekeeping.

Nonetheless, Onozuka himself took a dim view of radical activism. Through former Tōdai president Yamakawa Kenjirō, who now served on the Privy Council, Onozuka assured that august body he did not intend to permit Tōdai to continue being torn asunder by political conflict, and he quickly carried out the Education Ministry's order to disband the offensive student organization. Onozuka also summoned two of his young radical faculty members, Ōmori and Hirano, to question them about the ministry's allegations that they were implicated in the illegal Communist Party. Onozuka particularly chastised Ōmori for articles published under a pseudonym in the *Rōnō* journal and for excessive extramural political activity. But Onozuka took no action against them. Instead, the president reminded the University Council that the Economics Department had jurisdiction in its own personnel matters and should not be coerced in these cases.

The next step was taken by Ōmori himself. Despite the urgings of Professors Ōuchi Hyōe and Kawai Eijirō that he not bend to outside pressure, Ōmori apparently decided to resign. In Ōuchi's account of the incident, Ōmori had the temperament of an impetuous "Edokko" (a child of old Tokyo) and was typically unwilling to listen to advice. Ōmori is also said to have believed his own sacrifice would spare his fellow activists on the Tōdai faculty. It is quite possible, in light of the continuing arrests of those suspected of communist ties, that Ōmori may have feared that if more of his political activities should come to light, then Onozuka and his other non-Marxist supporters would back down from further confrontation with the government. Whatever Ōmori's reasons, he tendered his resignation. President Onozuka accepted it without waiting for either the Economics Department or the Education Ministry to take any formal steps.[30]

As it turned out, Ōmori's resignation gave his fellow activists at Tōdai only a two-year reprieve. In April 1929 there was yet another nationwide dragnet that arrested more than six hundred communist suspects. By early 1930 Associate Professors Hirano Yoshitarō and Yamada Moritarō had been targeted again for removal. This time the

30. Nanbara et al., *Onozuka Kiheiji*, pp. 159–167; Ōuchi, *Keizaigaku gojūnen*, pp. 201–203; Ōuchi, *Watakushi*, pp. 256–258; Tanaka Kōtarō et al., *Daigaku no jiji*, pp. 60–65. Hirai gave a somewhat different account in *Individualism and Socialism*, pp. 122–123.

circumstances were such that a defense from within the university was much more difficult than it had been in 1928. In the intervening years both Hirano and Yamada had been involved in efforts to rebuild the outlawed Japanese Communist Party after the shattering blows it had been dealt by the 1928 arrests. Specifically, it was discovered that the two had been raising money for a publication of the Communist Youth League (Kyōsan Seinen Dōmei).[31] Previously successful tests of the 1925 peace preservation law against communist political activity of this sort had given the government procurators all too solid grounds for moving against Hirano and Yamada in court. In 1930 officials of the Justice Ministry told President Onozuka that they would indict the two unless they resigned from the Tōdai faculty. Both did so, only to be indicted and convicted anyway.[32]

The Defense of Marxists in the University

The three Tarōs and the other young academic radicals had supporters off as well as on campus. Ōmori Yoshitarō himself had access to the pages of some of the most influential opinion magazines of the day. In the August 1930 issue of *Chūōkōron* Ōmori wrote that the true causes of student unrest were to be found in a combination of poor educational facilities and an absence of jobs for graduates. University professors today, he asserted, no longer did serious research and were being rewarded primarily according to the "litmus test" of anti-Marxism.[33] Morito Tatsuo, the former economics professor now based in the Ōhara Institute for Social Research, addressed these issues in a speech to students at Kyoto University in June 1929. For Morito the

31. Tanaka Kōtarō et al., *Daigaku no jiji*, p. 65. For details in English on the Communist Youth League, see Smith, *Japan's First Student Radicals*, pp. 209–212; and Beckmann and Okubo, *The Japanese Communist Party*, pp. 188, 193–195.

32. Nanbara, *Onozuka Kiheiji*, pp. 171–172; Tanaka Kōtarō et al., *Daigaku no jiji*, pp. 63–65. Onozuka himself, although perhaps believing the resignation would prevent criminal charges, is said to have lost sympathy for the two because they had broken what he considered their pledge in 1928 to abstain from political activism and concentrate on scholarly production. The law faculty, in its consideration of Hirano's resignation, voted to accept it without protest.

33. Ōmori Yoshitarō, "Gakkō sōdō uramote"; see also Sakisaka, "Ishihama, Ōmori, Arisawa, Yamada, Hirano."

loss of the radical students and professors at the imperial universities constituted a turning point in the history of the nation: it marked the "fall of the university." Whereas once the imperial universities had provided the leadership essential to the capitalist stage of Japan's development, now these schools had become reactionary, opposing progress toward "the new world, new culture, and new science" of the socialist stage of development. Although "there are a good many so-called liberal professors who proclaim they stand between both capitalism and socialism or even declare they are at war with both," Morito warned, most were the "new type of liberals" who actually were allied with the ruling classes in the suppression of progressive thought. The influence of the "old-type liberal," whose sincerity and sense of justice Morito professed to admire, was limited by the weakness of the bourgeois class in Japanese capitalist development. Therefore, liberal influence in higher education, while once strong in such private universities as Keiō, Waseda, or the Christian school Dōshisha, remained weak in the face of the "transcendental nationalism [*chōzenteki kokkashugi*]" within the imperial universities.[34]

Despite Morito's pessimism, many of the leading liberals of the day did respond to the challenge, at least in print. The major opinion magazines carried numerous articles chastising the government for its high-handed tactics.[35] Off campus noted essayist Hasegawa Nyozekan posed the questions, "Is the university an organ of the state? Of the society?" and criticized the suppression of academic freedom.[36] On campus economist Kawai Eijirō was the most energetic liberal spokesman in the debate. Kawai had once viewed Ōmori as something of a protégé despite the younger man's radicalism. Although rejecting Ōmori's argument that Kawai, too, should resign from the university, he did publish a large number of articles and at least one book defending Marxists on campus. Kawai had thus become one of Japan's better-known academic advocates of political liberalism, and his well-reasoned case for academic freedom was of considerable importance then and later in Japan.

In an argument based on social utility, Kawai called for a recognition

34. Morito, "Daigaku no tenraku," pp. 19–20; also see Hirai, *Individualism and Socialism*, pp. 131–132.

35. In addition to the specific references, see, for example, the February 1925 and June 1928 issues of *Chūōkōron*; the January 1925 and September 1928 issues of *Kaizō*; and the pages of the *Keizai ōrai*.

36. Hasegawa, "Daigaku = kokka no kikan? shakai no kikan?"

of the importance of diversity in both personalities and ideas. Social progress depended on such diversity: "Each man's progress is possible only if each individual serves the mutual benefit with his different personality [*kosei*]. Accordingly, I give my unreserved blessing to the vigorous clash of diverse ideologies taking place in present-day society, for it is both a sign of the differentiation of personalities and a contribution to the maturation of personality." The clash of ideas was especially essential within the university, where "we should rejoice at the profusion of a hundred flowers blooming." Most faculty and students might be conservatives, but in intellectual debates the general principle of majority rule could not be applied. The rights of those in the minority had to be protected because "the majority does not necessarily represent righteousness; no one can guarantee that the decision of the majority necessarily corresponds to the truth." If the freedom of such intellectual debates was not protected, Kawai asserted, then new ideas could not come forth, and society would be bound by past practices.[37]

Not only should the university be free from the external interference of government, Kawai went on to say; there must also be internal freedom within the campus. Too often academic officers adopted the same attitudes as political officials and attempted to suppress minority views. Tolerance of unpopular ideas should govern relations within the faculty and between students as well. For Kawai the principle of intellectual freedom meant that the advocates of all ideologies had to be guaranteed freedom of speech, and he explicitly included Marxists. There were two reasons Marxists were in special need of protection, he argued. On the one hand, Marxists had important contributions to make to academic debates. On the other hand, present-day conservatives were targeting Marxists. To prevent Marxists from being suppressed, Kawai called for a "united front" between Marxists and liberals.[38]

Kawai's view of the problem of student thought was far more tolerant than that of the majority of his non-Marxist colleagues. In 1932, when the report of the Education Ministry special committee on the causes of student radicalism was released, Kawai and his friend, law professor Rōyama Masamichi, published their own "minority report"

37. Kawai, "Ken'o subeki gakkai no ichi keikō," pp. 37–38. For more on Kawai's philosophical commitment to individualism, see Hirai, *Individualism and Socialism*, especially pp. 57–60, 95, 195–196.

38. Kawai, "Daigaku gakuen ni okeru jiyūshugi no shimei to omou," pp. 6, 37; see also Hirai, *Individualism and Socialism*, pp. 120ff.

in rebuttal.[39] They attacked the government for reliance on police power in an ineffectual attempt to impose a narrow version of nationalism (*kokkashugi* or *kokutai shisō*). The commission had failed, in the eyes of Kawai and Rōyama, to comprehend the true nature of Marxism and the real reasons for its spread among Japanese students. Marxism was composed of a commitment to four separate elements: historical materialism, the labor theory of value, violent revolution, and the dictatorship of the proletariat.[40] It was only on the latter two grounds that Marxism could be viewed as "evil." Even here, however, the two authors contended that conservative arguments about Marxism contradicting the national polity were not only irrelevant but also false: "Marxism and the ideas of national polity are not totally antagonistic. The philosophy of dialectic materialism is, in part, perhaps antagonistic, but violent revolution, socialism, dictatorship [*dokusaishugi*], and the [Marxist] analysis of capitalism are not ideas directly antagonistic [to the ideas of the national polity]." Indeed, the real evil political ideologies were fascism and right-wing radicalism. The dangers from the Right and the Left needed to be countered by stimulating faith in parliamentarianism (*gikai shugi*), which meant strengthening the constitutional right of freedom of speech so necessary to public debate.[41]

While thus arguing for protection of the rights of Marxists, Kawai also criticized Marxists who themselves sometimes violated the academic freedom of others: "It is by no means only conservatives who oppose the principle of freedom of speech. There are Marxists who, because they are right now in the minority, advocate freedom of inquiry and publication but in their minds despise opposing views and tend easily toward suppression of them."[42] There should be certain limitations on the freedom of speech that Marxists must also abide by, Kawai asserted. Libel and blasphemy were not protected by the right to free speech. Furthermore, "because the university is the organ of scholarly inquiry, propagandizing, intimidation, or struggle is not permitted."[43]

Kawai was a specialist in British political philosophy, and he based his argument for academic freedom in part on the writings of John

---

39. Kawai and Rōyama, *Gakusei shisō mondai.* See also Smith, *Japan's First Student Radicals,* pp. 204–205; and Suh, "The Struggle for Academic Freedom," pp. 283–302.

40. Kawai and Rōyama, *Gakusei shisō mondai,* pp. 1–4.

41. Ibid., pp. 36–45.

42. Kawai, "Daigaku no jiyū to wa nani ka," pp. 119–120; see also Kawai, "Daigaku no unmei to shimei," p. 79.

43. Kawai, "Daigaku no unmei to shimei," p. 67; Hirai, *Individualism and Socialism,* p. 133.

Stuart Mill. Like Mill, Kawai made a critical distinction between speech and action.[44] He also, however, made a crucial distinction between the university and other social institutions: "The university is both the organ [*kikan*] of scholarly inquiry and the organ of scholarly education. In this lies the special character of the subsociety [*bubun shakai*] that is the university, as opposed to such other subsocieties as the state [*kokka*] or the church."[45]

Here Kawai's argument rested on a particular definition of the key term *kokka*: "People may find it strange to hear the *kokka* is a subsociety, having the same status as the university or the church. But that is because they forget that the single word *kokka* has two meanings." In one sense the term was synonymous with "'the nation [*kokumin*]' or society [*shakai*] having a common history, culture, sentiments, and concerns." In another sense, *kokka* simply referred to the state: the "organ that has the coercive power to maintain peace and order." But just as the state had its special purpose, so, too, did the church and the university: for the church it was religion; for the university it was "scholarly inquiry and education."[46]

This fundamental premise regarding the separate sphere of the university led Kawai in 1928 to argue that freedom for the university community and freedom for the ordinary populace were not necessarily the same thing. It was not merely that students should not take an active part in social movements while being trained in the search for truth. Such participation might also be properly limited for faculty:

The university is the organ for academic inquiry and education [*gakumon kenkyū to kyōiku to no kikan*]. Consequently, within academe [*gakuen ni oite*] it is necessary, in keeping with the basic character [*honshitsu*] of academe, to have a freedom of inquiry beyond that possessed by the general citizenry [*ippan shimin*] outside the university; and, at the same time, it is necessary to have a freedom of action less than that of the general citizenry.[47]

This view that academics should not play political roles in the larger society was by no means uniquely Kawai's. When Professor Ōyama

44. Kawai, "Daigaku gakuen ni okeru jiyūshugi no shimei to omou," pp. 5ff.
45. Kawai, "Daigaku no unmei to shimei," p. 67. Hirai translated *bubun shakai* as "partial society" (*Individualism and Socialism,* p. 133).
46. Kawai, "Kokka, daigaku, daigakurei," p. 218. For a more extensive treatment of Kawai's theory of the state, see also Hirai, *Individualism and Socialism.*
47. Kawai, "Daigaku no unmei to shimei," p. 79. See also Kawai, "Daigaku gakuen ni okeru jiyūshugi no shimei to omou," pp. 7–8; and Hirai, *Individualism and Socialism,* pp. 132–133.

Ikuo (1880–1955) was forced out of Waseda University in the mid-1920s because of Ōyama's chairmanship of the Labor-Farmer Party, his erstwhile political ally, Professor Yoshino Sakuzō, refused to defend him. Writing in 1927 Yoshino pointed out that it was illegal for either schoolteachers or students, whether in public or private schools, to belong to political organizations. Although the law was not then being strictly enforced, in Yoshino's opinion it should be observed until it was changed. But Yoshino was not merely arguing for respect for the law, even if it was flawed. More significantly, Yoshino stated that he could not perform adequately as a professor *and* serve as an active member of a political party. The demands on the energies and abilities were simply too great for "an ordinary person such as myself."[48] In his view, therefore, Ōyama should choose one or the other of the two roles. As Tōdai law professor Rōyama Masamichi put it more succinctly in an appeal to students published in 1933: "It is absolutely impermissible in a nation such as Japan for university professors or students to be in movements colored by politics. Perhaps in China or South America, but it is impermissible in a civilized country [*bunmeikoku*]."[49]

Kawai Eijirō was also concerned with another type of special status shared by the faculty of the imperial universities: the fact that as government officials they were subject to the personnel regulations of the Ministry of Education. This, of course, had been the legal grounds for suspending Professor Morito Tatsuo in 1920 when he had been indicted for violating the press laws. Yoshino Sakuzō had argued in 1928 that it was a mistake to confuse the status of university professors with that of teachers in ordinary schools. Even though Education Ministry inspectors did oversee the content of courses in lower schools, "the university was the place where the ultimate in scholarship [*gakujutsu no un'o*] was pursued, and therefore it is impossible to have others critique the content of university research or lectures."[50] Writing in 1930 Kawai Eijirō was still quite sanguine about these problems:

In practice, because the imperial universities of today possess a type of autonomy [*isshu no jijiken*], this cannot give rise to legal problems regarding such matters as courses, lectures on campus, or the publication of research

48. Yoshino, "Kyōju to seitōin to no ryōritsu furyōritsu," p. 124. Ōyama subsequently went into exile in the United States at Northwestern University; he returned to Japan in 1947 to be elected to the House of Councillors and receive the Stalin Peace Prize for his part in postwar left-wing movements.
49. Rōyama, "Kyōdai gakusei ni ataruru no gaki," p. 52.
50. Yoshino, "Daigaku ni taisuru shisō dan'atsu," p. 60.

through [campus] research organizations. Accordingly, the issue is limited to cases where university professors publish their research in newspapers or magazines read by the general public. Even in these cases it is the established practice for the procurator office to exercise great caution.

Kawai saw more of a contradiction between this civil service status and the principle of academic freedom, but he dismissed as impractical any talk of a change in legal status. Instead, he proposed that "university professors unite as one [*itchi kessoku shite*]" to convince the government "there would be a threat of causing very serious social consequences [*jūdai naru shakaiteki kekka*]" if it should again attempt to indict a professor for exercising the right of free speech.[51]

The 1920s in Retrospect

In light of the events of the following decade, Kawai's call for unity in the face of government suppression of academic freedom can only strike one as naive and myopic. The crucial contradictions in his and others' arguments for academic freedom were soon exposed in the political turbulence of the 1930s. First and foremost among these confusions was the conflation of university autonomy and academic freedom. By the end of the 1920s university officers and the majority of the faculties at the imperial universities were all too frequently willing to sacrifice freedoms of speech and press to avoid a threat to their control of their elite institutions. To prevent external authorities from intervening on campus, leftist study groups were disbanded, militant students were suspended, and radical professors were persuaded to resign. Thus, university autonomy came to be identified with such compromises with external enemies.

In this struggle, moreover, even such staunch liberals as Kawai Eijirō acquiesced in an elitist defense of freedom of dissent, attempting to justify academic freedom at the expense of freedom for the wider populace. This conception of the university as separate and apart from the other institutions of society was even taken to mean professors had relinquished rights to political roles possessed by ordinary citizens. Neither Kawai's writings nor Yoshino Sakuzō's article on the incom-

51. Kawai, "Daigaku no jiyū to wa nani ka," pp. 120–121.

patibility of being both professor and party member placed any parallel restrictions on journalists, businessmen, or members of other civil occupations. But perhaps most critical for the future was the reluctance of the faculties at the imperial universities to seriously consider relinquishing their status as government officials even while recognizing the legal difficulties this placed on them.

6

The Purge of the Imperial Universities, 1933–1939

The ouster of radical social scientists from imperial universities during 1928–1930 was only a prelude to even greater losses in the 1930s. Beginning with the onset of the Depression in 1929, the controversy over naval disarmament in 1930, and the military seizure of Manchuria in 1931, anti-Western sentiments and nationalist passions against "subversive influences" and "dangerous thoughts" grew steadily more intense within Japan. Between 1930 and 1937 there was a series of political assassinations and attempts at coups by the radical Right. Political pressures on leftist activists and liberal writers grew apace. The most celebrated case of attacks on academic intellectuals in this period was the political persecution of Tōdai law professor Minobe Tatsukichi.[1] His case is often seen as emblematic of the process by which academic intellectuals were hounded out of public life as fascists took power in Japan. But these generalizations need amending in two important respects.

First, there is a question of periodization. The Minobe affair took place in 1935, and general histories of the period tend to date the initial peak in the mounting pressure against liberal academics from that year. Although political historians differ on how useful it is to categorize the Japanese state as "fascist," even those who believe the label accurate

---

1. See Miller's exhaustive account, *Minobe Tatsukichi*.

would hesitate to apply it until sometime in the mid-1930s.[2] In reality, the first full-scale confrontation between the Japanese state and its imperial universities in the 1930s came not at Tōdai in 1935 but at Kyōdai almost three years earlier. It is this so-called second Kyōdai Incident, or Takigawa Case, that affords the clearest picture of the possibilities for academic resistance to government intervention after the Manchurian invasion of 1931. And by the same token it was this incident, rather than the Minobe affair, that provided the precedents for the subsequent purge of the Tōdai Economics Department.[3]

Second, more careful attention needs to be given to the processes by which academic dissenters were silenced. The term *fascist* conjures up images of intellectuals forced to flee into exile to escape Gestapo raids and forced labor camps. Such dramatic images do not accurately reflect the experiences of the Japanese academic elite.[4] It was a rare exception for anyone with faculty status at an imperial university to be imprisoned for any length of time.[5] There was no flight of imperial university professors into exile, and none was ever executed. Instead, there were three distinct scenarios, albeit sometimes all played out within the course of the same "incident." In one, the Justice Ministry would indict an academic, who would then be automatically suspended until such time as his court case was concluded. In another scenario, the professor, on being denounced in public and threatened by government investigations, would be removed from the classroom when his colleagues voted to suspend him. In yet another scenario, he would simply leave

2. See the recent call for a renewed debate in Gordon, *Labor and Imperial Democracy,* pp. 333ff.

3. In addition to the secondary descriptions contained in the histories of academic freedom and biographical material already cited in previous footnotes, the following summary of the 1933 confrontation at Kyoto University relies heavily on the narratives of participants, some of which appear in Sasaki Sōichi et al., *Kyōdai jiken;* and Gakugei Jiyū Dōmei, eds., *Kyōdai mondai hihan.* The latter account includes sections by victims of earlier government attacks on academic freedom and some well-known liberals of the period. For the only lengthy account in English, see Suh, "The Struggle for Academic Freedom," pp. 168ff, but note there are a number of discrepancies between his and my reading of the sources.

4. This generalization is made more broadly by Mitchell, *Thought Control in Prewar Japan,* p. 190; and by Tipton, "The Civil Police in the Suppression of the Prewar Japanese Left," p. 328.

5. Neither the case of Ōmori Yoshitarō nor that of Kawakami Hajime is an exception to this generalization. Ōmori, charged in the 1938 Popular Front affair, had been forced out of Tōdai ten years earlier. Kawakami, who served four years in prison between 1933 and 1937, was convicted as a member of the illegal Communist Party five years after he had been driven from Kyoto University.

when advised to resign. Although we have already seen individual examples of each of these, the wholesale purgings of the Kyoto Law Department and the Tōdai economics faculty in the 1930s were nonetheless unprecedented. The main task of this chapter will be to describe those purges in greater detail.

The Frontal Assault on Kyoto University

There is some confusion over what was the proximate cause of the second Kyōdai Incident. According to the postwar memoirs of the central figure, Kyoto law professor Takigawa Yukitoki (1891–1962), it began in October 1932 when he delivered a guest lecture at a private university that offended top officials in the Justice Ministry. Takigawa, who had served briefly in the judiciary before becoming an academic, was in Tokyo to discharge his occasional duties as a civil service examiner on the penal code. He had been invited to Chūō University to speak on a panel that included a Tōdai professor and a procurator from the High Court. The topic Takigawa had chosen was one on which he had often spoken previously, even to audiences that included Justice Ministry personnel: the need for the judiciary to understand the social roots of crime in dealing with the criminal. He illustrated his theme with references to the trial in Leo Tolstoy's 1899 novel *Resurrection* (*Voskresen'e*). Takigawa speculated in his memoirs that some ministry officials considered the novel's depiction of judicial incompetence insulting; they reacted by accusing Takigawa of communist tendencies for his emphasis on crime as a product of social forces.[6]

In testimony at the Tokyo War Crimes Trial in 1946, Takigawa gave several other reasons he might have been singled out for attention by the government. Specifically he cited a 1932 book in which he had argued against the use of the peace preservation law "for the criminal prosecution of students for liberal thoughts and expressions." Takigawa

6. In his autobiography (*Gekiryū*) Takigawa said he was never quite certain what in his lecture had given offense or to whom and that it was six months later before he became aware of how serious a reaction his remarks had triggered. Much later still he was told by a colleague with connections in the Justice Ministry that the real instigator was the Army Ministry, which viewed Takigawa as an opponent of the Japanese seizure of Manchuria in late 1931 and early 1932. Takigawa disclaimed having made any antimilitary statements, although members of the Trinational Student Club (Sankoku Gakuseikai), to which he was a faculty adviser, may have done so.

also cited "other transgressions, that is, my article in opposition to the Manchurian Incident and article in opposition to the Nazi form of government."[7] Commentators have also speculated that "Takigawa was picked as a scapegoat. If somebody of Tokyo Imperial University had been victimized, repercussions might have been serious enough to damage the government; yet if someone from local universities such as Tōhoku or Kyushu had been picked, the rightist forces might have considered the government too lenient with liberal scholars."[8]

In any case, some weeks after the Chūō University lecture, Justice Minister Koyama Matsukichi—the procurator-general during the 1925 and 1928 raids on student organizations—communicated his displeasure with Takigawa to Education Minister Hatoyama Ichirō. Minister Hatoyama was the son of a onetime Tōdai law professor and had followed his father into the leadership ranks of the Seiyūkai Party. Hatoyama apparently was not stirred to any immediate action. But he was soon pressured to pay more attention to the case. Public accusations were made that "Red" judges were serving on the Tokyo District Court and among civil service examiners. Formal questions were soon raised on the floor of the Diet.[9] To prepare a response, the chief of the Bureau of Professional Education sought a clarification from Kyoto president Araki Torasaburō, who in turn passed the inquiry on to law chairman Miyamoto Hideo. Chairman Miyamoto, after consulting with another of his specialists on penal law, satisfied himself that neither Tolstoy's novel nor the version of the speech Takigawa had published in the Kyoto University law review gave any cause for alarm. Miyamoto conveyed that opinion to the Education Ministry in December 1932.

The matter was far from over, however. It was kept alive in the public arena by the right-wing press and like-minded members of the national Diet. In January 1933 a member of the House of Representatives used his seat on the Diet Budget Committee to denounce Takigawa-authored textbooks as examples of the type of material being taught by "Red professors" at Kyoto and elsewhere. Nevertheless, it was not until April 1933 that the government took formal action. First

7. Takigawa's "Affidavit" introduced June 19, 1946, as Exhibit No. 131, International Military Tribunal for the Far East; reproduced in Pritchard and Zaide, eds., *The Tokyo War Crimes Trial*, vol. 1, pp. 990–993, 1004. In a book published in 1947 Takigawa added yet other possible reasons for the attack on him (*Kenkyū no jiyū*, pp. 107–109).

8. Gotoda, *The Local Politics of Kyoto*, p. 75.

9. Hirai, *Individualism and Socialism*, p. 153.

the government banned the sale of the Takigawa-authored textbooks. This action may have come after a request from the Education Ministry Student Bureau—a unit created as a part of a reorganization in 1928 aimed at more effectively combating student radicalism. Then the newly appointed Kyoto president, Professor Konishi Shigenao (1875–1948), was called to Tokyo for a meeting with Education Minister Hatoyama and the vice minister of home affairs. Following more meetings with other Education Ministry officials, the Kyoto administrator returned to campus to confer with faculty leaders. Before the end of the month the Education Ministry again summoned President Konishi to the capital. This time the education vice minister told him that Takigawa was now viewed as "an evil influence on students and on society in general." Therefore, the ministry had to insist on his removal, preferably through his resignation but by official suspension if necessary.[10]

President Konishi protested, arguing that Takigawa's work was "objective" and "moderate" and that in any case it could be evaluated only by his peers in his academic discipline. Konishi further warned that unilateral action to remove the professor would produce "serious complications" on his campus. The official is said to have replied that in the view of the Education Ministry, "the preservation of university self-government and academic freedom" could best be assured by expediting Takigawa's resignation. The involvement of the university and the ministry in public squabbles, given "the situation in the world today," the vice minister cautioned, "could cause difficulties for research and harm to the progress of scholarship and could even result in demands for closing the universities."[11] President Konishi recorded that he nevertheless returned to Kyoto determined to resist such pressure, a determination strengthened by the resolve of the Kyoto law faculty not to abandon Takigawa.

Up to this point there was still little that was novel in these events. Since the founding of the imperial university system, as we have seen, there had been a number of instances in which the Education Ministry had attempted to oust faculty members by convincing university administrators to prevail on troublesome professors to resign. Indeed, this

10. Miyamoto, "Kyōdai mondai no shinsō," pp. 309–326; see also Tōyama et al., *Shōwashi,* pp. 108–109.

11. Miyamoto, "Kyōdai mondai no shinsō," pp. 326–328. It should be noted that the ministry's point of view expressed at this meeting is here reported third hand: i.e., Miyamoto quoting Konishi's description.

was precisely the manner in which five years earlier the government had moved against left-wing activists at the imperial universities at Kyoto, Tokyo, and Kyushu. Absolutely without precedent, however, was the reaction of the education minister when it became clear that Kyoto University faculty members were not swayed by his earlier warnings. After waiting only two weeks, Minister Hatoyama again summoned President Konishi to Tokyo. The minister brushed aside Konishi's objections and informed him that the ministry had decided to convene a personnel regulations review board (bunkan kōtō bungen iinkai) to determine Takigawa's fate. This was a long-standing procedure for civil service disciplinary cases, but it had never before been applied against an imperial university professor. Clearly the ambiguity of the civil service status of the faculty was now to be used to counter its attempts to maintain independence from the bureaucracy.

The Kyoto campus was soon alert to the potential for a full-scale confrontation. The law faculty collectively issued a formal protest, denying the Education Ministry was qualified to judge Takigawa's scholarship and accusing the government of obstructing research. The ministry replied it was legitimately concerned with "the social influence of academic theory [gakusetsu]." These exchanges continued through mid-May, with the Kyoto spokesman asserting three principles common to the tradition of such conflicts since the Tomizu affair of 1905: freedom was necessary to disseminate research findings through publication, peer judgments were the only acceptable form of evaluating research, and by long-standing custom university personnel decisions were made by the president in consultation with the faculty members in the appropriate department.

Noteworthy in the exchanges with the Education Ministry at this stage was the explicit acceptance by the Kyoto law faculty of the ministry's insistence on a distinction being drawn between dissemination of scholarship among the general public as opposed to dissemination within the academic community. On the one hand, the faculty followed precedent in avoiding any direct challenge to the authority of the Home Ministry to ban a book on the basis of its being, in the Education Ministry's words, "contrary to public order and good customs [kōkyō ryōsoku]." On the other hand, Professor Takigawa's supporters insisted the authoring of a subsequently banned book did not disqualify a scholar from teaching in the university. To prevent Takigawa from lecturing would therefore be an unwarranted restriction of his "freedom to teach [kyōju no jiyū]."

The Education Ministry, for its part, claimed to be willing to recognize the scholar's right to "freedom of research [*kenkyū no jiyū*]" and even conceded that authorship of a banned book did not automatically disqualify a teacher. Nevertheless, the ministry rejected the notion that "the freedom to teach" permitted the dissemination of socially harmful ideas even if restricted to classroom lectures. To do so would be inconsistent with "the proper role [*honbun*]" and the "responsibility [*sekinin*]" of a teacher, whose "attitude in the university [should be] scholarly."[12]

By mid-May 1933 the national press was giving major attention to the controversy. On May 20 a reporter, who obtained an exclusive interview with the education minister by simply following him aboard a train, quoted Hatoyama as saying Takigawa was guilty of "dangerous thoughts" and that "it won't do to have someone embracing those kinds of theories going around giving speeches and calling himself an imperial university professor."[13] That same day the Kyoto University Council held a formal meeting in which the various department chairmen and the elected faculty representatives in attendance agreed to sanction whatever action the Law Department chose to take, invoking the principle that each department had jurisdiction over its own personnel matters. On May 23 law chairman Miyamoto met with his faculty members and received their personal seals on a formal letter of joint resignation. The faculty empowered the chairman to submit the letter should the education minister actually follow up on his threat to suspend Takigawa. Meanwhile, the seven-man Personnel Regulations Review Board had been impaneled. The importance given to it by the government was reflected in its membership, which included the chief of the High Court, a privy councillor, and two civil service vice ministers. On May 26 this panel announced its recommendation in favor of suspension.

Professor Miyamoto reacted as Law Department chairman by convening a general assembly of law students to announce the cancellation of all classes. He explained this was necessary because the entire teaching staff of the department, from the chairman down to the most junior

---

12. See ibid., pp. 332–334. Longer excerpts translated into English can be found in Suh, "The Struggle for Academic Freedom," pp. 177–179. For a reference to an earlier Home Ministry statement making a distinction between mature scholars and impressionable students, see Mitchell, *Thought Control in Prewar Japan*, pp. 69–70.

13. Takigawa, *Gekiryū*, p. 20.

graduate assistant, was resigning in protest.[14] This pitched the campus into turmoil as right-wing, self-styled patriotic student groups clashed with student supporters of Takigawa. Attempts were made to rally support off campus through Kyoto alumni groups, and pro-Takigawa speakers publicly invoked the precedents of the victory over the Education Ministry in the Sawayanagi Affair of twenty years earlier.

Faced with President Konishi's own resignation as well as the firmness of the resolve of both the Law Department and the University Council, the Education Ministry now sought to negotiate. It persuaded President Konishi to remain at his post at least temporarily and appealed to a number of Kyoto emeritus professors to mediate the dispute. Konishi spent much of his time traveling to and from Tokyo, and the nation's newspapers reported conflicting stories of compromise proposals as the stalemate dragged on into June. At least one senior Kyoto professor explored with Takigawa the possibility of his accepting a two-year suspension to be spent in research abroad with assurances of reinstatement on his return—in effect a paid leave. This would have been similar to the resolution of the 1920 Ōuchi case when Ōuchi spent a year abroad before being reinstated at Tōdai. The important differences, of course, were that Ōuchi was then serving a suspended sentence for violation of the press laws and his suspension had been by vote of his own department. Takigawa had not been indicted, much less convicted of any crime; nor had his department voted to suspend him. Instead, Takigawa had submitted his own resignation in concert with his law colleagues and was unwilling to back down even to accept a compromise.[15]

Newspaper accounts at the time attributed the proposal for a one-year leave of absence to President Konishi. It is unclear what Konishi proposed to the Education Ministry, but he did return to Kyoto on June 15 to express optimism that a breakthrough was imminent. At a closed meeting of the law faculty the president reported that Minister Hatoyama was willing to affirm the president's authority in personnel matters, to consult with the faculty in the future, and to reiterate publicly the ministry's dedication to academic freedom. In response, Chairman Miyamoto disdained such talk as meaningless. These long-

14. The declaration of mass resignation was printed in the Kyoto law review, *Hōgaku ronsō* 29, no. 6 (June 1933): 1–9.

15. Takigawa, in his postwar memoirs, expressed doubts about the accuracy of these news stories and stated he was uncertain whether the president ever even considered the proposal (*Gekiryū*, pp. 161–163).

standing practices could be protected only by the immediate reinstatement of Takigawa. This view was supported by the other leaders of
what was in essence, if not in name, a strike.

President Konishi now informed the University Council that, having
done all he could, he was resigning. A faculty vote was soon held to
nominate his successor. The first vote failed to give any candidate a clear
mandate and forced an uncommon runoff election. The front-runners
were law professor Sasaki Sōichi, long an outspoken advocate of academic freedom who had been active in the 1919 Morito Case and was
now one of Takigawa's most staunch defenders, and Professor Matsui
Motooki, a former Science Department chairman. The faculty chose
Matsui. This defeat of Sasaki may have been the first overt sign of
weakening in the faculty will to face down the government. President
Matsui announced shortly after taking office that he viewed the situation ripe for a solution if only those "outside" the dispute would cease
meddling in it.[16] His remarks seemed to refer to agitators on both sides,
but his subsequent actions indicate the warning was aimed especially at
the liberal and leftist intellectuals who were urging the university not to
succumb.

The affair reached its climax on July 10, 1933, when President
Matsui returned to Kyoto after his meeting with the Education Ministry and announced the minister was formally accepting the resignations of Takigawa, Sasaki, Miyamoto Hideo, and three other law professors. The remaining members of the law faculty were asked to
continue at their posts. This attempt to split the opposition was quickly
rejected by two of the remaining nine full professors. Their resignations
were accepted on July 26. The confrontation had now run its course.
When the remaining seven full professors showed no sign of following
their lead, Professors Sasaki, Tamura, and Tsunetō, and the others who
were leaving now appealed to their junior colleagues to stay at their
post "to work toward the rebuilding of the department." In the end
exactly half of the associate professors (four of eight) chose to ignore
this advice and also left the university. The final count showed twenty
teachers lost to a department that had previously numbered thirty-
one.[17]

16. Ibid., pp. 175–176. Some claim the Economics Department was particularly
eager to abandon the struggle (Gakugei Jiyū Dōmei, eds., *Kyōdai mondai hihan*, p. 25).

17. The final losses to the department totaled eight of the fourteen full professors,
four of the eight associate professors, and eight of the nine lecturers and graduate assistants. Two other law faculty members died in 1933. For faculty lists, see Kyōto Daigaku,

Reaction to these events in the other imperial universities was sur-prisingly mild. The failure of Tōdai leaders to offer more than nominal support to Kyōdai was especially noteworthy. The student clubs of the Tōdai Law and Economics departments did stage a rally on June 21, and this was attended by student representatives from Tōhoku Imperial University and some higher schools as well as from Kyoto. The student speakers' denunciation of the Education Ministry led to a struggle with the police, and as a result of the ensuing melee, seventeen students were suspended from school. Threats of violence by right-wing groups in-duced President Onozuka Kiheiji to employ a judo expert as his private secretary. But the student demands for faculty action in support of academic freedom ultimately had little effect. A general faculty meeting was called by concerned professors, and President Onozuka agreed to convene a special meeting of the Tōdai University Council on July 21. Despite expressions of great sympathy for colleagues in Kyoto, the University Council limited its protest to formal statements of concern sent to the prime minister and the education minister. Calls for stronger faculty action were turned aside by the voices of caution among the senior professors.[18]

Kyoto participants and contemporary commentators were quick to note the contrast between the present role of Tōdai professors and earlier conflicts over academic freedom, asking, "What has happened at the other imperial universities? . . . In particular what have the Eco-nomics and Law departments at Tokyo Imperial University done?" The answer was little or nothing, according to one commentator who re-proached the Tōdai law professors by name:

Are there not numerous prestigious scholars at Tōdai who proclaim themselves to be liberals? Is not the president at the top, Onozuka Kiheiji, acknowledged by himself as well as by others to be a liberal? There is also Minobe Tatsukichi and Makino Eiichi. And shouldn't we also include Suehiro Izutarō and, when younger, Rōyama Masamichi? The chairman of the Law Department, Hozumi Shigetō, is also supposed to be a famous liberal.

Kyōto Daigaku shichijūnenshi, pp. 357–359; for Sasaki's plea, see Sasaki et al., *Kyōdai jiken,* pp. 369ff.

18. The summary minutes (*kirokushō*) of the July 21 University Council meeting seemed to indicate that, even though the Takigawa affair was clearly seen as part of a larger attack on the autonomy of the university, those in attendance spent more time focused on the question of the military's insistence it be permitted to increase from four to five the officers assigned to conduct student drills at Tōdai. The issue was less the drills themselves, which were being held only sporadically, but the army's failure to consult with the university administration before pressuring the Education Ministry. For more on this, see Tanaka Kōtarō, *Ikite kita michi,* pp. 83–85, 95–96.

Economics faculty members were also faulted for not living up to their own ideals: "There are supposed to be liberals and Marxists in the Tōdai Economics Department. What have they done?"[19]

The September 1933 issue of the influential opinion magazine *Kaizō* carried an article highlighting the alleged change on the part of Tōdai president Onozuka Kiheiji. It claimed that, although Onozuka had stood up to the government in 1905 and again as a leader in the first Kyōdai affair of 1913, in this latest conflict Onozuka had actually helped to stifle faculty protest.[20]

Bad blood between Takigawa and Tōdai faculty was also cited as a reason for the lack of support. But perhaps closest to the heart of the matter was the observation that the two schools had developed separate identities over the intervening decades and that relations between the two law faculties were no longer close enough to facilitate sustained cooperation:

If one compares the scholarly journals . . . of the [two] law departments it is easy to see. The [Kyoto law review] is bright, lively, radical. In the [Tōdai journal] there has long been a kind of stagnation, and it does not impress one as having any underlying strength below that surface. [Yet] the Tōdai Law Department considers itself the most outstanding and looks down on Kyoto men as their juniors, while Kyoto regards them as being senile.[21]

This rivalry was thus blamed for the fact that an attack on one was no longer necessarily perceived by the two universities, as it had been in 1913, as an attack on both.

There were exceptions to this apparent lack of response. One Tōdai faculty member who did see the fate of the two schools as clearly interlocked was economics professor Kawai Eijirō. For him the Takigawa case was clearly a continuation of the attacks on imperial universities of the late 1920s. Kawai was again willing, as he had been in the 1920s, to concede that "in cases where a university professor has committed illegal acts, then his status cannot be protected."[22] Indeed, the

19. Takimoto, "Tōdai hōgakubu to Kyōdai hōgakubu," pp. 161–162. Takimoto did quote a statement issued by the faculty of the Kyūshū Imperial University Department of Law and Letters.

20. Sasa, "Daigaku no sōchō ron." Writing in 1950 Tanaka Kōtarō also remembers Onozuka as having a great influence over his law colleagues on this issue (*Ikite kita michi*, p. 83).

21. Takimoto, "Tōdai hōgakubu to Kyōdai hōgakubu," p. 165. Tanaka Kōtarō also suggested "differences in theory and in Takigawa's approach" as one factor that explains the unwillingness of some to support him (*Ikite kita michi*, p. 83).

22. Kawai, "Kokka, daigaku, daigakurei," p. 225.

state might appropriately censor certain types of publications by a university professor:

> Suppose a university professor writes for the edification of the general public [*ippan seijō no keimō*]. If that threatens to disturb the peace and order, then the state can ban its publication or proceed to mete out appropriate punishment. This is the natural function of the state [*kokka tōzen no ninmu*]. Writing for general edification is not naturally inherent in the mission of *shokunō* the university professor. The person is merely presenting himself in his capacity as a writer, not in that of a professor. There would be no reason for him in this capacity to receive special privileges above other writers.[23]

The key point in this argument as applied to Takigawa was that any punishment resulting from such acts "must stop with punishment in his capacity as a citizen [*shimin*] and not extend to his status as a professor."[24] Thus, although the state always had jurisdiction over citizens, only the university had jurisdiction over professors in such cases. Kawai was not denying that certain behavior on the part of a professor, regardless of whether it was illegal in the eyes of the state, might be grounds for dismissal if it was injurious to the mission of the university. Even the dissemination of scholarly research in an appropriate academic context had to observe certain boundaries: "Even such strong advocates of freedom of speech as Milton and Locke placed blasphemy against God outside boundaries. This is the same for discussion regarding the national polity in Japan—I feel it, too, should be placed outside boundaries. But I think there should be no restrictions other than this limited exception."[25]

Ultimately Kawai recognized that the issue was one of authority to decide personnel matters:

> The Education Minister does not decide on the status of professors. The university president decides, and there has long been a recognition of a kind of unwritten law that the president depends on the decision of the faculty meeting in each department. In effect this means that the university has autonomy from the Education Ministry and that the department has autonomy from the university president.[26]

23. Kawai, "Takigawa jiken to daigaku jiyū no mondai," p. 210.
24. Ibid.
25. Ibid., p. 208.
26. Ibid., pp. 206–207. Kawai further stated that even if the decision was made by vote of the faculty meeting and the formal requirements to protect academic freedom were met, the result could be *formally* correct but *substantively* wrong if the faculty vote was based on "inappropriate reasons [*futō naru* riyū]."

The problem in the Takigawa case was the refusal of the education minister to accept the decision of the faculty meeting.

In postwar Japanese analyses of the political climate of the 1930s, the Takigawa affair has been called a major turning point by both liberal and Marxist commentators. Tōdai law professors Nanbara Shigeru, Rōyama Masamichi, and Yabe Teiji, all somewhere near the center of the postwar political spectrum, saw the 1933 case as pivotal because it was the first instance in which government suppression was turned against liberal, rather than Marxist, intellectuals. Ōuchi Hyōe, further to the Left in the political spectrum, came to view it as a major juncture because a critical opportunity to block the trend toward "fascism" was lost. This appraisal was shared by the postwar Marxist historian Tōyama Shigeki, who stressed that intellectuals from diverse camps did rally on this occasion to create associations such as the League for Freedom of the Arts and Sciences (Gakugei Jiyū Dōmei), but Tōyama called this "the last united front [in the prewar period] to protect liberalism."[27]

From the perspective of the politics of university autonomy, the 1933 confrontation was the first attempt at large-scale, overt faculty resistance since the Sawayanagi Affair of 1913–1914.[28] It also marked the last time the Education Ministry took the point in a frontal assault on the prerogatives of the presidency of an imperial university. Subsequent faculty losses were inflicted either through court proceedings or through the acts of fifth columnists within the university itself. This was true even of the Minobe affair of 1935.

The 1935 Minobe Affair

The Takigawa affair was directly linked to subsequent attacks on academic liberals, including the famous Minobe case that erupted in 1935. One of the key agitators in both of these cases was Minoda Muneki (1894–1946), who has been described as "an infamous denunciator."[29] Minoda, in addition to his numerous articles and

27. Nanbara et al., *Onozuka Kiheiji*, pp. 171–179; Ōuchi, *Keizaigaku*, p. 227; Tōyama et al., *Shōwashi*, p. 109.
28. Ienaga Saburō made the same point in *Daigaku no jiyū no rekishi*, p. 57.
29. Miller, *Minobe Tatsukichi*, pp. 203–206, 33n. The characters for Minoda's personal name are sometimes read as "Kyoki" or even as "Muneyoshi."

books reviling Marxists and liberals published through his Genri Nihon Sha (True Japan Society), was much given to visiting the Justice and Home ministries to lobby for censorship of offending works or even indictments against their authors. In 1935 he was involved in a concerted effort by a large number of right-wing nationalist groups, including some with close connections to Privy Councillor Hiranuma Kiichirō, to discredit liberal interpretations of the constitution. The ultimate targets included high-ranking civil servants and advisers to the throne, but the chief public focus of this attack was retired Tōdai professor Minobe Tatsukichi. Minobe was the chief author of the *tennō kikan*, or "emperor-as-organ-of-the state," theory that had long been dominant among Japanese scholars of constitutional law. As a result of the vehemence of this public campaign, Minobe eventually resigned his seat in the House of Peers and all other public posts.

But contrary to the impression left in some general histories of the period, the Minobe affair was not a good test of the will or strength of the universities to defend academic freedom and institutional autonomy. The famous professor had already reached retirement age and had left the Tōdai law faculty prior to these events. Although the public attacks on him did stimulate a full-scale Education Ministry investigation into the textbooks and syllabi on the constitution at the nation's universities, it would be erroneous to conclude the government was able thereby to dislodge academic dissenters from Tōdai. The affair did not directly involve the dismissal of any professors at Tōdai or Kyōdai. The affair's impact was perhaps best described by Professor Miyazawa Toshiyoshi, Minobe's closest academic heir:

It did not become a problem directly affecting the tenure of university professors. . . . Those of us at Tōdai at the time, myself included, just kept quiet, passively, and did nothing. The other professors had more or less the same idea, and so in the end nothing was done formally [*katachi no ue*]. We certainly felt the pressure, and there were corresponding effects from that pressure, but formally in the Tōdai Law Department there were absolutely no changes in, for instance, such things as the assignment of seminars, much less in the appointment or removal of professors. At other universities, however, there were some changes in such things as the assignment of seminars.[30]

30. Tanaka Kōtarō et al., *Daigaku no jiji*, p. 100. Miller's account of the efforts of the Education Ministry to "clarify the *kokutai*" summarized the records of the ministry's Shisō Kyoku. They included some references to Tōdai and Miyazawa in particular, but much more effort seemed to have been directed at other schools (pp. 359–360). Miller also quoted a source (p. 250) to the effect Miyazawa altered his lectures after 1935 to avoid trouble, something Miyazawa failed to mention in his reminiscences. Of course,

These pressures took several forms. Numerous law books were officially banned from publication, the right-wing press issued a continual stream of personal slander, and some individual professors were even physically harassed. Former Tōdai president Onozuka Kiheiji, himself a specialist in law, had his home placed under police guard after it was broken into by right-wing agitators. As Miyazawa suggested, the chilling effect these acts had on the academic atmosphere at the time was probably more significant than any official punitive measures against the faculty.

Kawai Eijirō and other liberals were again vocal in their reaction, but again they refused to challenge Minobe's critics on the issue of whether it was permissible to dissent from the traditional interpretations of the sacredness of the national polity:

Faith is the peculiarity of beliefs concerning the *kokutai;* legal studies possess the peculiarity of science. . . . If there is a violation in a legal theory, it is not a moral wrong; it is an error in reason. . . . It is not improper to oppose Dr. Minobe's theory, but the intention of eliminating that theory by violence and coercion is a sacrilege against learning. . . . To gag Dr. Minobe by threat of force . . . is a violation of the Imperial Rescript of the Meiji emperor, which enjoins us to respect the law and obey the constitution.[31]

The Renewed Attack on the Tōdai Left

The Japanese political atmosphere grew far more tense in mid-1937 as war clouds spread over the Asian mainland. The skirmishing between Japanese and Chinese troops at Marco Polo Bridge in July, despite initial efforts to localize it, escalated into full-scale Japanese military campaigns by the autumn. This China Emergency, as it was called (there was no official declaration of war), created new stresses on the already strained Tōdai campus, where reaction to the fighting was both mixed and heated.

Professor Hijikata Seibi, who earlier that year had become the economics chairman for a second time, threw his energies into organizing a mass march of students to the Meiji Shrine, the burial place of the now almost legendary emperor and a favorite memorial of right-wing

one might expect Miyazawa to understate—just as the ministry official reports probably overstated—the success of their efforts to silence academic dissent.

31. Kawai, "Minobe mondai no hihan," pp. 12–16.

patriots. Hijikata's stated purpose was to counter antimilitarism on campus and demonstrate the school's patriotic spirit to the public at large. There was heavy opposition to Hijikata's plan in the University Council and especially within the Economics Department, where leaders of the student club refused to cooperate in the pilgrimage.[32] Hijikata was undeterred and personally led the march, which had the desired effect of attracting considerable press coverage.

Afterward he sought revenge on some of those who had opposed his plan. He attempted to reorganize the student club to reorient it away from the left-wing influences he blamed on its former faculty adviser, Ōuchi Hyōe. Hijikata pressed his cause at the November 24, 1937, departmental meeting by formally raising the issue of support for the troops on the Asian mainland. He specifically condemned the attitude of Yanaihara Tadao, a Christian pacifist who was the department's leading expert on the results of previous Japanese imperialist ventures in Taiwan and Manchuria.[33] Even writing after the Pacific War, by which time Hijikata himself claimed to have always had doubts about the wisdom of the China War, he still maintained Yanaihara's appeal for peace was "improper in such times. . . . It did not help keep the situation under control to excite people's minds and damage the morale of troops in the front lines by writing an article in a mass circulation magazine that was cynically sarcastic about those in authority."[34] But Hijikata also denied later that he sought anything more than a departmental resolution condemning the articles.

Hijikata's true intentions aside, the eventuality was much more serious. Professors Honiden and Tanabe seized the opportunity to engage Yanaihara's defenders among the left wing of the department in heated debate. When Kawai Eijirō joined Yanaihara's side, the meeting ended in a deadlock.[35] Ōuchi Hyōe and Hijikata had managed previ-

32. According to Tanaka Kōtarō, Hijikata's promilitary enthusiasm had caused antagonism on the part of faculty leaders as early as 1933 (*Ikite kita michi*, pp. 84–85, 95).

33. See Fujita, "Yanaihara Tadao."

34. Hijikata, *Gakkai shunjūki*, p. 184. Hijikata argued that if his intention had been to oust Yanaihara, such a resolution, according to departmental rules, would have had to be circulated at least one week in advance. He denied any prior plotting with Honiden or Tanabe and somewhat disingenuously described his own behavior as "democratic" because he raised the issue for free and open discussion. Because Hijikata also pointed out it was probably the Yanaihara case as much as anything else that caused Hijikata to be placed on the U.S. Occupation purge list, it is not surprising that he devoted considerable space to the details in his memoirs (pp. 183–191).

35. Ōuchi, *Watakushi*, pp. 263–264. Ōuchi claimed he was quite surprised by this action by Kawai, whom he considered had been used by the Right as a tool against

ously in the year to reach a compromise on some departmental matters, and Ōuchi now approached his old foe in an effort to persuade him to drop the affair after the first inconclusive debate.[36] When Hijikata remained adamant, Ōuchi and Maide took their case to President Nagayo Matarō (1878–1941), previously head of the Medical School. President Nagayo was sympathetic but declined to intervene on the grounds it was a departmental matter. When two subsequent departmental meetings also failed to result in any consensus, Ōuchi sought the backing of ex-President Onozuka, who had the confidence of the Marxists in part because of his refusal to be stampeded by government attacks in 1928. Onozuka gave his support, and Ōuchi was then able to prevail upon President Nagayo to speak to Hijikata. Ōuchi claimed that at this point he actually believed Yanaihara's supporters had won and the matter could be settled within the faculty. He was soon to be convinced, however, that Yanaihara had been selected as a target in a concerted "plot to militarize the university in order to support the Japanese invasion of China."[37]

The affair was taken out of the confines of the university and into the public arena as government investigators became seriously interested in Yanaihara's criticism of the war. The professor had written another piece opposing the fighting in the November issue of a privately circulated newsletter (Tsūshin) intended primarily for other Christians. This attracted the attention of the police, who promptly confiscated the offending material and banned an earlier article for violation of censorship laws. Investigators also questioned members of the small audience

---

Marxism. But see Shakai Shisō Kenkyūkai, *Kawai Eijirō denki to tsuisō*, pp. 88–89; and Minobe, *Kumon suru demokurashī*.

36. Both Hijikata and Yamada Fumio (Kawai's friend and junior colleague) spoke of the détente that had taken place between Hijikata and Ōuchi during Kawai's term as chairman in 1936–1937. See Hijikata, *Gakkai shunjūki*, p. 173; and Yamada, "Tōdai keizaigakubu," pp. 71–80. Ōuchi remembered Kawai actually told him that both Ōuchi and Hijikata ought to resign (Ōshima, *Takano Iwasaburō den*, p. 357). A disagreement over the promotion of Associate Professor Sasaki had precipitated Kawai's stepping down as chairman after only a single year. In a noteworthy instance of harmony, Hijikata was voted chairman, with Ōuchi and Maide as representatives to the University Council; see also Sekiguchi, "Teikoku Daigaku no mondai," especially pp. 356–357.

37. Ōuchi, *Watakushi*, p. 264. Former economics professor Takano Iwasaburō is also said to have lobbied with his connections on campus on Yanaihara's behalf (Ōshima, *Takano Iwasaburō den*, pp. 355ff). Ōuchi's views of the Yanaihara case became part of the evidence introduced at the postwar trial of Japanese leaders—see Exhibit No. 130 and testimony under cross-examination on June 19, 1946; reproduced in Pritchard and Zaide, eds., *The Tokyo War Crimes Trial*, vol. 1, pp. 940–946, 950–954.

of Christians who had been present during a Yanaihara talk on the same theme.

Actually Yanaihara had not been unmindful of the possibility of running afoul of such censorship, which was being tightened after the outbreak of the fighting in China. Thus, he had been careful to couch his pacifist views in recondite biblical metaphors meaningful to his audiences but confusing to the police. Ironically, this effort had the opposite effect. In a printed version of a eulogy Yanaihara delivered at the funeral of a fellow Christian, the professor made reference to current national problems. His Christian terminology provoked hostility from Home Ministry officials and some members of the House of Peers, who professed to be outraged that an imperial university professor would even rhetorically refer to the need for contemporary Japan "to die" before it could be "reborn into a new life."[38]

Reacting to this right-wing offensive, Education Minister Kido Kōichi informed President Nagayo that, because the House of Peers was holding the ministry responsible, Yanaihara would have to be forced out of the university. On learning of these developments, Ōuchi and economics chairman Maide once again pressed ex-President Onozuka to use his influence on his successor. Although Onozuka is reported to have been angered at Nagayo's timorous response to the education minister, the former president is said to have eventually come to the conclusion that Yanaihara had to be sacrificed for the sake of the university.[39]

Abandoned by the university administration and repudiated by a significant element of his own department, Yanaihara took it on himself to resign on December 11, 1937, giving the following public explanation:

I have always been one who loved his country ardently, and I think it is regrettable that the problem of my articles ever arose. Because I recognize my continuing at the university would cause it difficulties, I have submitted my own resignation to the president today. . . . Although the ideal [risō no] university does have need of me, in the actual [genjitsu no] university my presence has come to be a disturbance.[40]

Almost before the news of Yanaihara's loss could begin to be digested, yet another alarm spread through the campus. A few days after

38. Yanaihara, Watakushi, pp. 45–49; Ōuchi, Watakushi, pp. 268–271; Ienaga, Daigaku no jiyū no rekishi, pp. 63–64; Sakisaka, Arashi, pp. 171–172.
39. Tanaka Kōtarō, Ikite kita michi, p. 97.
40. Yanaihara, Watakushi, pp. 101–102.

new year 1938 it was learned police were carrying out a fresh series of arrests aimed at destroying the Popular Front (Jinmin Sensen), an antifascist movement accused of following a communist strategy to undermine the military effort in China. Among the first of what eventually were to be some four hundred arrests was that of Ōmori Yoshitarō, the former economics associate professor who had been driven from Tōdai in 1928.

Professor Ōuchi and some of his colleagues in the Economics Department had particular cause for alarm because they had maintained close ties with Ōmori as well as with some of the others caught in the police roundup. Within weeks those fears proved justified as Ōuchi, Wakimura Yoshitarō, and Arisawa Hiromi from the Economics Department plus a number of Tōdai graduates teaching at other schools were jailed for questioning in what the press labeled the "Affair of the Professors' Group [Kyōju gurūpu jiken]."[41]

The Professors' Group consisted of a dozen or so academics headquartered in what they jokingly called the "Abe Business Office [Abe jimusho]," a rented room on the second story of a private medical building near the Tōdai campus—"a scholarly club," Ōuchi later wrote, "of men who had been or were about to be driven out of Tōdai." The group had begun meeting in 1931, originally in private homes, especially that of emeritus law professor Minobe Tatsukichi. Minobe's son Ryōkichi, a Tōdai graduate who taught at Hōsei University, was a participant. Meeting in people's homes proved unsatisfactory because, in Ōuchi's words, the members "were all young and vigorous and often talked through the night, causing great inconveniences to their households." The renting of space near the campus—the elder Minobe served as guarantor on the lease—also permitted the group to accumulate a small library of foreign newspapers, Japanese socialist literature, and other materials. These were used in the group members' collaboration in a monthly column for the monthly opinion magazine Chūōkōron as well as for a book of collected essays. Ōuchi maintained that, although the participants were as "close as brothers," "this research club [kenkyūkai] did not attempt to take any particular political stance, nor did it try to dictate our

41. For details in English on the Kyōju gurūpu, see Totten, The Social Democratic Movement in Prewar Japan, pp. 166–175, where it is referred to as the "Academicians' Group." Totten's discussion of the trial of Ōmori's Rōnōha should not be misunderstood, however, to refer to Ōuchi's case under discussion here.

individual [interpretation of] Marxism. On such matters each had complete freedom."[42]

The police, ever alert for signs of radical conspiracies, took note of the types of literature being collected. The frequent visits by such known radicals as Ōmori Yoshitarō and Sakisaka Itsurō probably also helped give officials the rationale they sought. Ōmori and Sakisaka had been among the organizers of the Japanese Proletarian Party (Nihon Musantō), a vehicle for the Popular Front. Ōuchi, Wakimura, and Arisawa claimed they were merely "academic Marxists and took no part in these political activities," but they, too, were taken into custody in February 1938.

Once again the Economics Department found itself divided in the face of an external attack on its faculty. Once again the Procurator's Office and the Education Ministry sought to have Ōuchi and his fellow offenders suspended from the university even before formal indictments had been secured. President Nagayo's health was failing, but he was pressured by the Law Department to call a meeting of the University Council. According to Professor Tanaka Kōtarō, writing in the postwar period when serving as chief justice of the Supreme Court, the strategy at the time was to use the University Council to formally reject the government's request. Instead, there was a heated debate in which economics chairman Hijikata Seibi and engineering chairman Hiraga Yuzuru spoke in favor of suspension while economics professor Maide Chōgorō and Law professor Tanaka spoke against.[43]

There was no reported formal vote in the University Council, but there was one taken in the Economics Department. There Professors Honiden and Tanabe, backed by Chairman Hijikata, pushed for suspension, arguing in part that the jailing of Ōuchi deprived the department of his services as representative on the University Council and that

42. Ōuchi, *Keizaigaku*, pp. 248–250. See also Ōuchi, *Watakushi*, pp. 286–287; and Minobe Ryōkichi, *Kumon suru demokurashī*, pp. 144–145. According to the younger Minobe, the group did tend to operate sub rosa and even published anonymously at times out of concern for Ōuchi's position at Tōdai. Minobe also placed greater stress on their cooperative efforts and exchange of mutual criticism than did Ōuchi and admitted that some of the group (but not Ōuchi or Wakimura) helped gather material for both Ōmori's monthly "World Report" in the magazine *Kaizō* and for the Marxist economic newsletter, *Keizai shiki jihō*. Nevertheless, Minobe vigorously denied, even writing in the postwar period, that either this group or Ōmori's Rōnōha could be defined as "associations seeking to alter the national polity" (pp. 149, 154). For more on the government's attempt at this time to censor such opinion magazines as *Kaizō* and *Chūōkōron*, see Kasza, *The State and Mass Media*, pp. 182–183.

43. Tanaka Kōtarō, *Ikite kita michi*, pp. 102–104.

the department was therefore forced to take some action.[44] Vigorous opposition was voiced by Professors Ueno and Maide and echoed by Kawai and Yamada Fumio. They insisted that suspension prior to formal indictment was contrary to university regulations. With the support of Kawai, the Marxists won the vote within the department, although this victory lost much of its significance once legal indictments were produced. The three indicted professors were all barred from the classroom under the automatic suspension provisions as their trial dragged through the courts for the next seven years.[45]

Ōuchi's account of his own case is especially valuable for its details about official procedures in such cases. The failure of the police initially sent to his home to bring an arrest warrant led to an almost farcical scene on the morning of February 1. Ōuchi first blocked the entrance with his dog until he could consult by telephone with his lawyer. He then invited the policemen into the house and served them all breakfast while awaiting the arrival of a proper arrest warrant. Only at this point was Ōuchi finally and politely transported to jail, the lone prisoner accompanied by a truck full of police. Formal interrogation did not begin until he had been jailed for almost two weeks, and in all he remained in custody for more than six months awaiting bail proceed-

44. Hijikata, *Gakkai shunjūki*, pp. 193–195. The specific problem of University Council representation was also given as a reason for not pressing on the Arisawa and Wakimura cases, but no mention was made of why, for example, a substitute was not an acceptable solution to the problem of representation. Ōuchi accused Hijikata of having triggered the arrests in the aftermath of their quarrel over the Yanaihara case, claiming Hijikata demanded Ōuchi resign during the December 1937 department meeting (*Watakushi*, pp. 283–284). Hijikata denied the allegation, saying it was not until he telephoned Ōuchi's home to inquire about the rumors of his arrest that Hijikata knew anything about the incident. Instead, Hijikata pointed the finger of suspicion at Professor Hashizume, who later emerged from the turmoil of 1938–1939 as wartime department chairman. The same suspicion was repeated by Minobe Ryōkichi (*Kumon suru demokurashi*, p. 154), but in the absence of hard evidence its main significance may be the further indication it gives of the poisoned atmosphere within the department.

45. Hijikata, *Gakkai shunjūki*, pp. 193–195; Shakai Shisō Kenkyūkai, eds., *Kawai Eijirō denki to tsuisō*, p. 91; Tōdai, *Keizaigakubu*, p. 35. The impact of the Yanaihara and Ōuchi cases on the department was nevertheless considerable. The working coalition between the Hijikata faction and Kawai Eijirō that had held from the mid-1920s was now completely destroyed, and as a result no faction had a clear majority. Hijikata himself stepped down as department chairman in recognition of his faction's defeat. The Marxist faction, however, had lost two full professors and two associate professors in a matter of months and was even more on the defensive. Somewhat surprisingly, Maide Chōgorō, who had long sided with Ōuchi, was named to succeed Hijikata as chairman; but the balance of power between Hijikata's supporters and those of Maide now rested with Kawai Eijirō.

ings. Throughout his imprisonment, however, Ōuchi emphasizes the respectful treatment he received from his warden, a former Tōdai law student who even took it on himself to pay a visit to Ōuchi's home to reassure his wife. Following release on bail in July 1938, Ōuchi spent three more years awaiting trial. During this whole time he actually continued to receive his salary from Tōdai—officially he had been suspended but not terminated from his appointment. Although largely free from police harassment, he was legally prohibited during these years from either lecturing or publishing while his case was before the courts.

The first trial of the Professors' Group resulted in an acquittal for all except Arisawa Hiromi and Abe Isamu, who were convicted for having contributed to the Marxist magazine *Rōnō*. Because Japanese law permitted appeals by the prosecution as well as the defense, Ōuchi and the other participants originally found innocent were retried two years later, again to be acquitted.[46] Hundreds of other Japanese charged with similar ideological crimes were not as fortunate as Ōuchi, but his autobiographical account illustrates both the deference a Tōdai professor could still command even in criminal proceedings and, at the same time, the effectiveness of drawn-out legal proceedings in silencing an intellectual by stripping him of his right to public expression while under indictment.

The chilling effect of these arrests in the Popular Front incident was felt throughout the Japanese academic community in the spring of 1938 as a new hail of allegations fell on "subversive" professors. In the House of Peers the Tōdai Economics and Law departments were characterized by one military peer as "the headquarters and command post of the Popular Front," while Kawai Eijirō and others who publicly defended Ōuchi were castigated as being themselves "only a hair's breadth away from communism." Agitated Tōdai students joined in harassing professors suspected of harboring Western liberal ideas or of lacking enthusiasm for Japan's mission in China.

46. Ōuchi, *Watakushi*, pp. 272–280. Minobe Ryōkichi remained in jail for more than nineteen months, and although he himself suffered no harsh treatment other than the close confinement and the incessant questioning, he gave reports of acquaintances who were treated brutally (*Kumon suru demokurashī*, pp. 171–173). The reversal on appeal of the group's original conviction was not all that rare. In another well-known court case, Waseda University professor Tsuda Sōkichi and publisher Iwanami Shigeo, convicted in 1940 for lèse-majesté in the contents of four books dealing with ancient Japanese history, had their jail sentences dismissed on retrial (*Kodansha Encyclopedia of Japan*, vol. 8, p. 112; vol. 3; p. 361. See also the Kawai case discussed later in this chapter.

The diary of Associate Professor Yabe Teiji of the Law Department affords an intimate glimpse of the impact of these attacks. Yabe, who had only recently returned from research leave in Europe, recorded his anxiety when he first learned Minoda Muneki's right-wing group was including his name in lists of subversive teachers. Yabe became especially alarmed when he heard rumors the police were probing whether he might be connected to the Popular Front. Repeatedly during this period Yabe confided his despair to his diary, fearing that his "life's work" as a scholar was at its end and that his family's future was in jeopardy. If he were not actually driven from the university itself, he feared he would at least be passed over for promotion by his department. Yabe's anxiety was further fueled by the appearance of "student spies" in his classes or at other campus talks where students frequently raised politically embarrassing questions. In one specific instance, right-wing students visited his office to demand he clarify his interpretation of the Japanese polity and explain why his course syllabi were heavily weighted toward Western works on political science. Yabe felt some relief only when he learned through a connection in a friendly publishing house that, if worse came to worst, he could count on a job there.[47]

Those affected by this oppressive atmosphere were not limited to the younger, less secure faculty. Law Department chairman Tanaka Kōtarō is quoted as remarking in private, "This is not a climate for scholarship. If you so much as show the top of your head, it gets shot at. What honor is there to stay on at such a university?"[48]

General Araki's Demands for University Reform

The climate took a turn for the worse as Education Minister Kido Kōichi, former chief secretary to the Lord Keeper of the Privy Seal and an increasingly influential bureaucrat, attempted to reassure right-wing critics within the House of Peers: "The universities are established, maintained, and administered under the supervision of the minister of education according to the university ordinances, the university civil service system, and other [government] regulations. University

47. Yabe, *Nikki*, vol. 1, pp. 74–81, 83–84, 92, 97, 142, 150.
48. Ibid., p. 89.

goals and the like cannot depart from those strictures, and so-called university self-governance [*daigaku no jiji*] cannot be sanctioned."[49]

Kido soon left the Education Ministry, but his successor, Baron General Araki Sadao, threatened to be a much more dangerous adversary. As principal of the Army War College in the late 1920s and then as chief of educational administration within the army, General Araki had become a hero to militant nationalists for his advocacy of the "imperial way" (*kōdō*) as an ideology to counter the threat of communism at home and abroad. He had served as army minister from 1931 to 1934 but was placed on the reserve list in 1936 because he was thought to have approved, at least tacitly, the mutiny and attempted coup of February 15. But Araki returned to government service in May 1938 when Prime Minister Konoe gave him the education portfolio to appease the political Right and show support for the Movement for Mobilizing the Popular Spirit behind the campaigns in China.[50] Araki was subsequently asked to remain in that post by the next prime minister, Hiranuma Kiichirō, and thus served a total of twenty-one months.

During General Araki's earlier tenure as army minister in 1933, the Tōdai administration had clashed with the military over the conditions under which commissioned officers were allowed to attend classes at the university.[51] The army's arrogant manner in making its demands had provoked a verbal show of solidarity among the faculty and the University Council. Shortly after taking office in 1938, the new minister of education made it clear he took a dim view of the considerable measure of independence that the imperial universities had won over the years and that he meant to take steps to reassert government control.

That summer the president of Kyoto University died in office, and in late July, as the Kyoto faculty prepared for the long-established routine of balloting to determine a successor, Araki summoned all the imperial university presidents to a meeting in Tokyo. There Araki made it clear he expected the schools to prepare reports on their standing procedures with an eye to reforms, especially practices that were not in keeping with a strict interpretation of the civil service regulations regarding imperial appointees. Specifically he had in mind the practice of ballot-

49. Horikawa, "Senji gakkai fūkei," p. 370.

50. See Berger's expert examination of the Konoe cabinet and the "mobilization" movement in *Parties Out of Power,* pp. 187–188.

51. See Tanaka Kōtarō, *Ikite kita michi,* pp. 83–86; and Tōdai, "Hyōgikai kirokushō" for July 21 and September 5, 1933.

ing for president, limited terms for department chairs, and faculty control in the recruitment of new professors.[52]

Araki thereby quickly convinced Tōdai faculty leaders that he was a serious threat to self-governance. The chairmen of the Economics and the Law departments, Tanaka Kōtarō and Maide Chōgorō, were particularly alarmed. In the hope of coordinating a successful defense strategy, the two undertook the long hot bus trip to Lake Yamaguchi where President Nagayo was vacationing. Nagayo, former head of the Medical School, seemed to them strangely indifferent to the potential danger but did agree to call a special meeting of the University Council. It met on August 1, and a university delegation then sought another meeting with General Araki himself.[53]

The discussion held at Minister Araki's official residence on August 12, 1938, was extraordinary in more ways than one. Not since the conferences on education reform held twenty years earlier had so many Tōdai academics and ministry officials sat down together with such an important agenda. In addition to General Araki, all the top-echelon officials responsible for higher education were present—the vice minister, the parliamentary vice minister, the ministerial counselor, the secretary of the ministry, two bureau chiefs, two section heads, and the chief of the ministerial secretariat. On the university side President Nagayo was accompanied by all seven of his department chairmen. The confidential minutes of the meeting provide a rare opportunity to observe the two sides in private debate.[54]

Araki spoke first and, after the obligatory words of welcome, stressed that the times demanded everyone—academics as well as military men and ordinary Japanese—to pool efforts. It was therefore especially deplorable that a cloud of suspicion hung over the nation's universities. He then lectured the assembled academics on the historical circumstances in which the Meiji emperor originally founded Tōdai, emphasizing the emperor's intention that the university's main purpose was to nurture talent to serve the needs of the state.

52. Tanaka Kōtarō, *Ikite kita michi*, pp. 85ff; Minobe Ryōkichi, *Kumon suru demokurashī*, pp. 223–224.

53. Tanaka et al., *Daigaku no jiji*, pp. 117–118. Tanaka Kōtarō, *Ikite kita michi*, pp. 86–87. Tanaka remembered that President Nagayo seemed to be avoiding discussion of the issue with the two despite the special trip they had made. Tanaka did not recall on whose initiative the meeting with Araki was finally arranged. The Tōdai Hyōgikai minutes for those years were not open to me when I used the archives in the 1980s.

54. The transcript of the meeting is reprinted in Tanaka et al., *Daigaku no jiji*, pp. 121–130; see also Tanaka Kōtarō, *Kyōiku to ken'i*, pp. 89–110.

Following a few more pointed references to the present need to "mobilize the spirit of the nation" through "self-discipline and self-reflection," General Araki got down to specifics: "Nothing is more urgently needed than the rectification of the basic practices of appointments and tenure in accordance with proper principles." In the ministry's view, he said, the present system of majority vote by the faculty violated the letter and spirit of the constitution by disregarding the sovereign prerogatives of the emperor to appoint and dismiss state officials. Moreover, those practices had given rise to various evils— which the minister did not bother to spell out in detail.[55]

President Nagayo replied briefly, saying that he was in agreement that there was a need for self-discipline and self-control in such times but that the faculty had its own viewpoint to present. He then left most of the presentation to his department heads.

Law chairman Tanaka Kōtarō spoke by far the longest, defending academic autonomy, or "self-government [*jiji*]," with considerable eloquence: "Self-government is the essence [*seimei*] of the university. The university bears the privileged responsibility [*kōei aru gimu*] to the state of sustaining and promoting the vitality of that life. Moreover, the state has entrusted higher education and research to the hands of the university." Touching only briefly on the West as a model for such academic autonomy, Tanaka then narrated his own version of recent Japanese history, beginning with the lessons of the confrontation over the Affair of the Seven Ph.D.s in 1905 and ending with the 1918 reforms in which former President Yamakawa Kenjirō—whom Tanaka called "a scientist, a patriot [*kokushi*], and an incarnation of the Japanese spirit"—had labored to establish the present system of self-government. Because, in Tanaka's view, the problem stemmed from the difficulty bureaucrats had in understanding such a system, he attempted to explain it in terms of analogies to the independence of the judicial branch of government. To serve the state properly, the university and the courts both had to transcend shifts in administration and stand aloof from political pressures.

At the same time, Tanaka expounded, the academic resembled the artist striving for creativity rather than the bureaucratic official operating under a hierarchical chain of command:

If you deprive the scholar of the freedom to research or the painter of the freedom to create, he cannot achieve satisfactory results. This is quite unlike

55. Tanaka et al., *Daigaku no jiji*, pp. 121–123.

[the case of] administrative officials. . . . The scholar's spirit of unfettered independence [*fuki dokuritsu*], the essence of a scholar, stems from a selfless attitude toward scholarship. . . . The virtues demanded of a profession are not all the same—for the administrative official, it is obedience; for the judicial official, it is justice; for the scholar and the artist, it is unfettered independence.

Tanaka went on to lecture the minister on the evil effects such a loss of freedom would cause, especially the resulting damage to the "spirit of familialism [*kazokushugi*]" that nurtured the university as an "independent society of colleagues":

The relationship between professors within the university differs from that of high and low in the ranks of the bureaucracy. It is one of elder and junior, teacher and pupil—of colleagues—rather than one of dominance and submission. It differs precisely because of this degree of intimacy. . . . If someone who does not fit into this school tradition [*gakufū*] is forced in, or if someone is forced out by external power, the life of this family becomes impossible.

Clearly the law professor was now struggling to defend the Tōdai system of internal governance against the implied charges it was dependent on acceptance of Western liberalism:

Self-government has developed on the basis of this familial spirit [*kazokuteki seishin*], and it is not in contradiction to the unique academic traditions of our country. To have it rejected as a concept of [Western] liberalism is extraordinarily shallow thinking. If open elections can be said to violate our national polity [*kokutai*], why, I wonder, would they be abolished only in the particular instance of university personnel matters?

In conclusion, Tanaka asserted that the present system required Araki's support because it had to be retained if the university was to perform its mission and thus serve the state.[56]

When it came to the turn of the economics chairman, Professor Maide Chōgorō spoke much more briefly but all the more bluntly. Despite an effort by President Nagayo to keep Maide off the topic, he launched into a detailed defense of his department against its recent attackers. The trouble, he asserted, was due to the external politics of the so-called Renovationist Movement, which had especially targeted Professor Ōuchi Hyōe. The department had voted against punitive

56. Ibid., pp. 124–127. For a treatment of the concept of familialism and its use as an ideological defense against charges of alien values or foreign patterns of organization, see Marshall, *Capitalism and Nationalism in Prewar Japan,* especially Chapters 5 and 6. For a caustic comment on Tanaka's defense of this form of paternalistic rule, see Ienaga, *Daigaku no jiyū no rekishi,* pp. 69–70.

measures prior to an official indictment of Ōuchi precisely because of the ordinances regulating the university and because of the belief that to be

devoted to the state was to keep its laws and defend reason. . . . In short, the problems within the Department of Economics do not originate in the faults of the present system but have developed because there are those who do not respect the present system. What is regrettable is that the Ministry of Education, by its attitude toward voting, actually invites support for those segments of the faculty that do not respect the present system.

At this point President Nagayo is said to have interrupted Maide with the abrupt comment "It won't do to bring up these things." The floor then passed to another of the chairman.[57]

At the very end of the meeting another noteworthy exchange occurred between Minister Araki and Chairman Tanaka. In summing up, Araki insisted on interpreting their conversation to mean the academic spokesmen recognized the need "to reform the university and clarify the attitudes of the Japanese nation." He also insisted on warning them again that changes would have to take place to ensure that the faculty "respected social morality." Tanaka then asked for the floor again, saying, "I think my [earlier] explanation was inadequate." He contended the issues in question were complex, involving constitutional law and administrative codes. The criticisms that had been made of the university in some quarters were not the type of public discussion that was needed if the true welfare of the state was to be served. He concluded by challenging Araki: "If elections [to administrative posts within the university] are illegal and cannot be justified, then I want the reasons made plain."

Araki's reply was couched in a somewhat more conciliatory, albeit no less direct, tone than previously:

I grant the point that an explanation must be given. It is not a problem of whether elections are held. Someone said earlier he did not believe they were harmful. I do see them as harmful in practice. The results of the faculty meetings appear in the newspapers, and the whole world is aware of them; thus it won't do if the minister of education takes steps regarding them. Doesn't that make him some kind of hired hand? Otherwise, he must fight a legal battle.

Despite further remarks by Tanaka and Nagayo, Araki was not moved. The minister made it plain he not only intended to have changes but

57. Tanaka Kōtarō, *Kyōiku to ken'i*, p. 128; see also Tanaka's comment on p. 119.

also expected the cooperation of the university administration in achieving them.[58]

The response of the Tōdai administration to the education minister's instructions was to appoint its department chairmen to a special committee to draft a set of revised regulations. This body met some twenty-two times in the following months. Contacts were also made with the other imperial universities, including two days of confidential discussion with delegates from Kyoto University. In early October 1938 a conference of representatives from each of these schools was held in an effort to establish a common front.[59]

The Education Ministry meanwhile continued to press for change. It indicated it was prepared to back off from a number of peripheral points if agreement could be achieved on the main issues: the procedures for selecting presidents, appointing department chairmen, hiring new faculty, and promoting present faculty. The Tōdai academics nonetheless persisted in their attempts to defend as many of the existing practices as possible.[60] On October 18, 1938, the University Council passed the final draft of a proposal for presentation to the ministry. As a formal statement of the representatives of the Tōdai faculty, who were in some sense speaking for the faculty of all the imperial universities, it is worth examining at some length.[61]

A. *Nomination of Candidates for President*
1. A nominee for president shall be determined by careful deliberation and after soliciting the opinions of all professors. The nomination shall then be made to the minister of education. . . .
2. In the responses of the professors, signed, written materials or other procedures shall be used to make responsibility clear. . . .

B. *Nomination of Candidates for Department Chairmen*
1. Candidates shall be nominated to the minister of education on the basis of the recommendation of the president.
2. A faculty meeting shall be consulted regarding the nomination of department chairman. . . .

---

58. Ibid., pp. 129–130.
59. Minobe Ryōkichi, *Kumon suru demokurashī*, p. 225.
60. See, for example, Nanbara, "Daigaku to jiji."
61. It is reprinted in Tanaka et al., *Daigaku no jiji*, pp. 133–134; I have added the numbering for the sake of clarity.

C. Nomination of Candidates for Professor and Associate Professor

1. The president shall nominate candidates on the basis of the recommendation of the department chairman.
2. A faculty meeting shall be consulted regarding the nomination of candidates for professor and associate professor.

Clearly the proposal retreated little from the established practices by which the faculty controlled the nomination of its chief administrators as well as the recruitment and promotion of its own members. In deference to the Education Ministry's concerns about "elections," no explicit mention of elections or voting was made, but there was a reference to "signed, written materials." The length of the terms of office for the chairmen and the president were also left unspecified.

Nevertheless, Minister Araki expressed his displeasure on the grounds that the method of selection of candidates might still be confused with voting in elections. Further wrangling over semantics ensued. The most serious objection was Araki's insistence that Clause 2 in Section A be included also under Sections B and C, thus stipulating the procedures for "consultation" in the appointment of chairmen and new faculty. This was discussed at length at the November 1, 1938, meeting of the Tōdai University Council. Law professor Wagatsuma Sakae is reported to have expressed his and others' suspicions that any further changes would constitute a surrender on the question of whether the process of consultation could, as in the past, take the form of balloting. President Nagayo and Professor Tanaka responded that present voting procedures were not actually prohibited by the language of the draft regulations and thus could indeed continue. On that interpretation the council passed the proposal with the clause specifying that the ballots be "signed, written materials" repeated in each section. Ultimately the university developed a voting system that preserved certain features of the secret ballot without violating the letter of the regulations. This entailed the use of a perforated ballot with the signed portion being detached and placed in a separate envelope, both portions bearing the same identification number.[62]

Thus, the confrontation between General Araki and the imperial universities ended in the reconfirmation of a tradition reaching back almost four decades. In 1913 the Sawayanagi Affair at Kyoto Univer-

---

62. Ibid., pp. 135–139. Apparently this satisfied all concerned for there is no mention of the ministry ever demanding to check the ballots or the faculty protesting such ballots were not sufficiently secret.

sity had demonstrated the de facto limitations on the power of the Education Ministry to appoint the top administrator at imperial universities. When President Sawayanagi had attempted to implement plans that had been rejected by faculty leaders, he and the Ministry of Education lost the battle. In the 1918 reforms the right of Tokyo and Kyoto imperial university faculties to nominate their presidents was established. Now in 1938 not even the militaristic atmosphere of 1938 could persuade faculty leaders to make more than a cosmetic adjustment. The faculty retained the power to choose, through formal ballot, its chief officer as well as department chairmen and members of the university Senate. Clearly the Tōdai leaders had not, in their view, given up any vital ground.

Yet within a matter of months the victory was to prove a Pyrrhic one. The factionalism that had cost the university so dearly in the preceding decade had continued to fester just below the surface, and the prolonged conflict with the government had placed further strain on faculty morale and solidarity.[63] Although General Araki's thrust directed at the heart of university autonomy was successfully parried, new blows to academic freedom were soon struck at points made more vulnerable by factional disunity.

President Hiraga's Purge

The immediate target was now Professor Kawai Eijirō. Long a major Japanese critic of Marxism and once an ally of the anti-Marxists in the running skirmishes with the Ōuchi-Maide faction within the Economics Department, Kawai had in recent years reassessed the threat to the liberalism he still ardently espoused. After the army's seizure of Manchuria in 1931 and his research trip to Germany and Italy in 1932, Kawai became increasingly concerned about the dangers of militarism. With the Minobe affair of 1935 and the young officers' mutiny against civilian rule in February 1936, Kawai began to concentrate his fire against "the evil of fascism [that] emerges from the military."[64] Outspoken in the defense of academic independence,

63. See the account by Ienaga, who blamed the Tōdai president and department chairmen for not rallying the faculty as a whole in the negotiations with Minister Araki (*Daigaku no jiyū no rekishi*, p. 70).

64. From "2.26 Jiken no hihan," published originally in the Tōdai campus newspa-

Kawai was identified as a leader of resistance to pressures aimed at "renovating" the university.[65] By 1938 it had become "an open secret" that the Education Ministry desired to rid itself of Kawai, and in October the Home Ministry initiated action on old complaints about the liberal excesses in Kawai's writings. It banned further sale of four of his books.[66] The Education Ministry then quickly ordered a board of inquiry to investigate Kawai's views in detail.

While this external investigation was in process, Kawai and his defenders were confronted with a change in school administration. President Nagayo had fallen fatally ill, and his successor, duly elected by faculty vote in December 1938, was engineering professor Hiraga Yuzuru. Hiraga had joined the Tōdai faculty in 1931 after a career as a leading naval architect with the rank of vice admiral. He had just finished serving as chairman of the Engineering Department, where he had made it known he favored government plans to enlarge the facilities to aid the war effort. During the Ōuchi case earlier in 1938, Hiraga had also spoken out in favor of suspending faculty members even before they were indicted lest the university be perceived as indifferent to the problem of unpatriotic academics.[67]

Although Hiraga's election was procedurally routine—not, as sometimes implied, the result of external action—once he became president he proposed to deal with the Kawai case in an unprecedented fashion.[68] After prior consultation with Law Department chairman Tanaka Kōtarō and others, a meeting of the University Council was held in December to secure agreement on the creation of an ad hoc university

---

per, *Teikoku Daigaku shinbun*, March 9, 1936; quoted in Hirai, "A Japanese Experiment in Individualism," p. 323. Even a cursory glance at the chronological list of Kawai's writings in these years is sufficient to reveal how prolific he became on these subjects in the mid-1930s (Egami, *Kawai*, pp. 318–322).

65. Horikawa, "Senji gakkai fūkei"; Sekiguchi, "Teikoku Daigaku no mondai," pp. 354–356; and Minobe Ryōkichi, *Kumon suru demokurashī*, pp. 206–223.

66. Nanbara et al., *Onozuka Kiheiji*, p. 286. The banned works included a collection of articles that had originally appeared in newspapers and magazines; see Shakai Shisō Kenkyūkai, *Kawai Eijirō denki to tsuisō*, pp. 93ff.

67. Tanaka Kōtarō, *Ikite kita michi*, p. 103.

68. Nanbara Shigeru stated that the faculty's first choice had been Yamada Saburō, the former Tōdai law professor and more recently president of Seoul Imperial University, but Yamada declined to return to Tōdai (*Onozuka Kiheiji*, p. 286). Tanaka Kōtarō recalled that there was then a three-way contest that forced a runoff in which Hiraga won by only "one or two ballots" (*Ikite kita michi*, p. 106). It is ultimately impossible to know now the underlying factors in such elections, but the fact remains that Hiraga received a majority of the votes cast and was thus the faculty's final nominee for appointment to the office.

committee to carry out an internal investigation of Kawai's writings.[69] The committee was drawn from the economics and law representatives on the University Council. It included Maide Chōgorō and Ueno Michisuke, both from the left wing of the Economics Department, as well as Professor Mori Shōsaburō. Tanaka Kōtarō and Wagatsuma Sakae, strong defenders of university self-government, represented the Law Department. The committee chairman, however, was law professor Kamikawa Hikomatsu, who some of Kawai's supporters later claimed was already convinced Kawai was guilty of subversive ideas.[70]

After three or four meetings, including one in which Kawai himself was interviewed, the ad hoc committee produced a somewhat equivocal report. While completely rejecting charges that Kawai's books were procommunist or otherwise subversive, the report nevertheless did concede that Kawai's manner of expressing himself was, on occasion at least, less than proper for an imperial university professor. President Hiraga seized on this single major negative finding as a cause for advising Kawai to resign his professorship to spare the university any further difficulties. Although the president was willing to promise efforts would be made to find the professor a nonteaching and less sensitive post within the university, Kawai refused any compromise. The economics professor pointed out that no indictment had been drawn by the Justice Ministry and that there had been no proper deliberations by his department.[71]

The government campaign against Kawai gathered momentum with the new year. The conservative ex-justice minister and longtime foe of leftist professors, Privy Councillor Hiranuma Kiichirō, had taken office as prime minister in early January 1939. Soon after, the Procurator's Office in the Justice Ministry began preliminary questioning of Kawai to determine probable cause for an indictment for violation of the publications laws. Hiraga then summoned Kawai once again, this time to inform the professor Hiraga was invoking his authority as president to suspend Kawai.

Hiraga's actions in January 1939 apparently aimed not only at ridding himself of the Kawai case but also at suppressing all factional

69. The original idea for the special committee may have been Tanaka Kōtarō's (*Ikite kita michi,* p. 107).

70. Minobe Ryōkichi charged that Mori also accused Kawai of being subversive (*Kumon suru demokurashī,* p. 229). Hijikata claimed neither Maide nor Ueno did anything to defend their colleague (*Gakkai shunjūki,* p. 201).

71. Shakai Shisō Kenkyūkai, eds., *Kawai Eijirō denki to tsuisō,* pp. 97–99.

disputes, for he suspended Professor Hijikata Seibi as well. Hiraga's formal explanation to the Education Ministry was that the liberal centrist Kawai and the conservative rightist Hijikata both shared responsibility for the internal turmoil that had for years disrupted the Economics Department.[72] It is not clear what Hiraga anticipated as a reaction, but the dual suspensions touched off an explosion within the department. No fewer than thirteen professors and staff tendered their resignations in protest at the failure of Hiraga to follow established consultative procedures.

The attack initiated from outside the university was now directed from within by President Hiraga. When faculty members in economics presented their joint resignations, Hiraga first consulted with the Education Ministry. He then in effect declared the department in receivership by the surprise move of making himself department chairman.[73] As department chairman as well as university president he accepted the resignations of five more faculty members, including Professor Honiden Yoshio and one graduate assistant. The others in the Economics Department allowed themselves to be persuaded to remain, but as this left Hiraga with only five full professors where there had been twelve a year earlier, the way was open for rebuilding the department. Hiraga directed this with the advice of Professor Emeritus Yamazaki Kakujirō, who was seventy-one and had been in retirement for ten years. They hired five new professors—all initially on joint appointments from other Tōdai departments or outside institutions. In the ensuing months Hiraga arranged the promotion of five associate professors and the appointment of six former graduate assistants to the staff.[74]

72. Ibid., pp. 99–100. Hijikata blamed Ueno and Maide for his own suspension. Attributing to them a revenge motive for the Yanaihara and Ōuchi incidents, Hijikata claimed that they attempted to have him censored in a June meeting of the University Council, and, when that failed, they tried again at an economics faculty meeting (*Gakkai shunjūki*, pp. 212–215).

73. The other three professors were Nakanishi Torao, Tanabe Chūshi, and Yamada Fumio; the graduate assistant was Kimura Takeyasu. Kimura Takeyasu named four of the thirteen as resigning because of Kawai: Professor Yamada Fumio, Lecturer Ōkōchi Kazuo, and graduate assistants Yasui Takuma and Kimura himself (Shakai Shisō Kenkyūkai, eds., *Kawai Eijirō denki to tsuisō*, pp. 104–105). The four had worked with Kawai and law professor Rōyama Masamichi in the Koten Kenkyūkai, a research group they formed in 1936 (Appendix, p. 6). Nine others were listed as objecting to the punishment of Hijikata. Tanaka Kōtarō's version of the sequence of events differed somewhat (*Ikite kita michi*, pp. 110ff).

74. Tōdai, *Gakujutsu taikan*, pp. 506–510. These included Ōkōchi Kazuo and Yasui Takuma, former Kawai partisans whose willingness to withdraw their resignations caused some bitterness within the Kawai camp (Shakai Shisō Kenkyūkai, eds., *Kawai Eijirō denki*

Reaction to the Hiraga Purge

Throughout what became known as the Hiraga Purge the Tōdai faculty outside the devastated Economics Department remained cautiously passive. Professor Rōyama Masamichi, a close friend and sometime collaborator with Kawai, was one of the few exceptions. Outraged at the failure of his colleagues to attempt to stop Hiraga, Rōyama resigned from the law faculty. In his condemnation of the purge he argued that neither the University Council nor the ad hoc university committee of inquiry had any legal authority to make judgments on a personnel matter internal to a department. Thus, the president had failed to consult with the appropriate faculty body.[75]

Individuals in Rōyama's own Law Department, judging from the daily entries in Professor Yabe Teiji's diary, were in informal consultation among themselves almost continuously during these weeks. Following Hiraga's suspension of Kawai a loud and acrimonious debate occurred during a departmental meeting that lasted more than five hours. Ultimately, amid the resurfacing of old animosities and new charges of conspiracy, the majority in the Law Department decided not to precipitate a full-scale institutional crisis by challenging President Hiraga's actions. Professor Tanaka Kōtarō, who had attempted to justify his participation in the ad hoc committee on the grounds the Economics Department was too polarized to deal with its own personnel matters, resigned as department chairman to atone for his role in advising the president. Tanaka nevertheless remained on the faculty.[76]

The personal motives of the law faculty members who individually and collectively made the decision not to challenge Hiraga cannot be easily reconstructed. But this willingness to sacrifice individuals to preserve the institution was in keeping with what law professor Nanbara

---

to tsuisō, pp. 105–106). In Ōuchi Hyōe's view, the firing of Hijikata and the resignations of Honiden and Tanabe merely amounted to replacing one "fascist" group with another. But Ōuchi also considered the retention of Maide, Ōkōchi, Ōtsuka Hisao, and Nanbada Haru as important in maintaining the traditions of scholarship within the department (*Keizaigaku gojūnen*, pp. 289, 294–304).

75. Rōyama, "Tōdai shukugaku mondai to watakushi no shinkyō"; see also Tamura, "Tōdai funjō uchimakubanashi."

76. Yabe, *Nikki*, pp. 177–201; Tanaka Kōtarō, *Ikite kita michi*, pp. 110–111. Even greater caution than usual should be exercised in using these sources because the relative paucity of other sources makes it much more difficult to substantiate the internal workings of the Law Department than those of the Economics Department.

Shigeru called, in a slightly different context, the "long tradition" by which senior Tōdai law professors "would put aside everything else to protect the autonomy of the university and the system as a whole."[77] As I have argued throughout this account, however, the "tradition" was actually much more complex. In 1905 at Tokyo Imperial University the law faculty, like that of other departments, had seen the protection of "the autonomy of the university and the system as a whole" as demanding continued confrontation to prevent the Education Ministry from firing a single professor. Even in 1920 the Tōdai administration and the Economics Department moved quickly to reinstate Ōuchi Hyōe as professor after he had served his probation for violating the press laws. But in 1928, 1930, 1933, 1937, and again in 1938, faculty leaders were willing to see individuals forced out rather than challenge the authority of the government and thereby run the risk of further interference in campus affairs. The collapse of the Kyoto Law Department resistance in 1933 and the internally directed purge of the Tōdai Economics Department in 1939 were simply the most dramatic examples of an obsession with blocking external interference in the internal management of the university. Thus, the principle of institutional autonomy from government intervention was upheld more frequently than not at the expense of the academic freedom of individual faculty members.

Evidence of the degree to which the faculty as a whole shared such a perspective is indicated by the votes in the two elections for university presidents held during these crises. In 1933 the majority of the Kyoto University faculty rejected the candidacy of Professor Sasaki Sōichi, a vigorous defender of Takigawa Yukitoki. In 1938 a majority vote of the Tōdai faculty elected Professor Hiraga Yuzuru, who had already clearly expressed his intolerance for academic dissent. To paraphrase Yanaihara Tadao's announcement of his resignation, although the "ideal university" might have need of academic dissenters, "in the actual university" their presence was too much of "a disturbance."

77. Nanbara et al., *Onozuka Iwasaburō den,* p. 281.

7

The Pacific War and
Its Aftermath

The history of Japan's imperial universities after 1941 and the emergence of a postwar academic elite during the U.S. Occupation belong properly to another book. Nevertheless, it may throw further light on the significance of the prewar events to take brief note here of what became of the major figures from these prewar struggles.

The War and Postwar Era

Kawai Eijirō fought the charges of subversion through four grueling years of police investigations and court hearings. He was actually acquitted at his first trial in October 1940, but the government procurators won a reversal in the Tokyo Court of Appeals in October 1941. Although Kawai had indeed criticized the 1931 invasion into Manchuria and had published numerous warnings about the dangers of fascism, after 1937 he had come to support the war in China and had not opposed opening new fronts against the United States or Great Britain if needed to win that war. He also had restated in court his faith in the sacredness of the Japanese *kokutai*. Nevertheless, he was convicted for espousing a foreign philosophy threatening to the public order and, more to the point here, for advocating freedom of speech for

Marxists who were intent on overthrowing the throne and destroying the *kokutai*.[1] Barred from teaching, his books banned, and his writing limited to his new interest in the history of Japanese Buddhism, Kawai used donations from his friends to pay the cost of taking the case to the Supreme Court. In June 1943 the Supreme Court upheld the convictions but limited Kawai's punishment to a small token fine of ¥300. Although there had been no jail sentence, Kawai's health was broken by the strain of the trials and wartime deprivations. In early 1944, at the age of fifty-three, he died of heart failure.[2] Despite Kawai's suspension and ultimate conviction, his family received the formal gift of silk from the emperor due an imperial official of his prior rank—just as Hiraga Yuzuru had when he died the previous year at the age of sixty-five.

Rōyama Masamichi, the Tōdai law professor who had resigned in protest over Kawai's ouster in 1939, had nonetheless continued to contribute to the braintrust of Prime Minister Konoe Fumimaro. Like Kawai, Rōyama supported the Pacific War, and for this he was purged by the U.S. Occupation. Depurged in 1950, Rōyama became president of Ochanomizu Women's College and eventually a director of the Nihon Shakai Shisō Kenkyūsha, a research institute in Tokyo that, among other activities in the 1960s, received U.S. subsidies to publish the *Journal of Social and Political Ideas*.[3]

The trials of Marxist Ōuchi Hyōe ended in a surprising, if much delayed, instance of wartime justice. In September 1944 the High Court reversed the earlier convictions of Ōuchi, Arisawa Hiromi, Wakimura Yoshitarō, and all but two others in the Professors' Group, clearing them of any wrongdoing in the 1938 Popular Front case. Of course, by this time their prosecutors had achieved the original intention of silencing antiwar critics, and the group had paid heavily in terms of professional careers. Two of the group had died by the time of their final acquittal. The activist Ōmori Yoshitarō, who had suffered for many years from intestinal tuberculosis, had become gravely ill with cancer shortly after his arrest. He died while free on bail in July 1940.[4]

1. See Hirai, *Individualism and Socialism*, pp. 195.
2. Shakai Shisō Kenkyūkai, eds., *Kawai Eijirō denki to tsiusō*, Appendix, p. 7; and Hirai, *Individualism and Socialism*, pp. 199–201. For a glimpse of Kawai's reaction to the long ordeal and the final verdict, see his speech to the banquet held by his supporters on June 27, 1943 (Kawai, *Kyōdan seikatsu nijūnen*, pp. 219–228). Suh's statement that Kawai was acquitted in 1943 is in error ("The Struggle for Academic Freedom," p. 200).
3. The journal was renamed in 1971 and published under new auspices. For a detailed account of the U.S. Occupation purges, see Baerwald, *The Purge of Japanese Leaders*.
4. The other death was that of Minami Kinji, a nephew of Minobe Tatsukichi who

Despite the legal vindication of the Tōdai faculty in this Professors' Group, the professors were not reinstated by the university during the war. After Ōuchi's acquittal President Uchida Yoshikazu, who refused to challenge opposition within the Economics Department and the government, told Ōuchi that the time was not yet ripe for reinstatement.[5] Ōuchi thus spent the war engaged in minor research projects.

Tōdai law professors Nanbara Shigeru and Tanaka Kōtarō had remained at their posts on campus throughout the war. Nanbara was elected Law Department chairman in March 1945, and in the last months of the war he and Tanaka, along with five other Tōdai professors, attempted to persuade their contacts among the navy and civilian elites to work toward an early peace.[6] As Christians with reputations as moderates, both men quickly won the confidence of U.S. officials in the postwar Occupation, and each became an important figure in postwar educational and legal reforms—Nanbara as Tokyo University president, 1945–1950; Tanaka first as chief of the Bureau of General Education and then as minister of education, 1946–1947.[7] Nanbara also served along with Minobe Tatsukichi as government adviser in the negotiations prior to the creation of the new constitution of 1947 and eventually became "a pillar of the moderate left establishment."[8] Tanaka was subsequently elected to the House of Councillors (the postwar replacement for the old House of Peers), and in 1950 he was appointed chief justice of the Supreme Court, a position he held for a decade before appointment to the bench of the International Court of Justice at the Hague.

As a result of the new regime, the Tōdai Economics Department was once again thoroughly reconstituted. This time the department's standing within the university was buttressed by the transfer to its purview of the disciplines of agricultural economics and sociology. Eight of the wartime faculty members soon departed the university, and Maide

---

had been on the faculty of Hōsei University. Minami's death in 1943 was attributed to the cruel conditions he suffered while in prison (Minobe Ryōkichi, *Kumon suru demokurashī*, pp. 171–173. For the fate of some of the others arrested in 1937–1938, see Totten, *The Social Democratic Movement in Prewar Japan*, pp. 167–171.

5. Ōuchi, *Watakushi*, pp. 292–305; Nanbara et al., *Onozuka Iwasaburō den*, p. 284.

6. The other five were Oka Yoshitake, Suenobu Sanji, Takagi Yasuka, Wagatsuma Sakae, and Suzuki Takeo: see Barshay, *State and Intellectuals*, Chapter 2.

7. R. Hall, *Education for a New Japan*, pp. 81–82.

8. Barshay, *State and the Intellectual in Imperial Japan*, pp. 120, 224–226; Miller, *Minobe, Tatsukichi*, pp. 256ff.

Chōgorō, the one member of the prewar Marxist faction who had served as department chairman, was renamed to that post. Ōuchi, Arisawa, and Wakimura were reinstated in November 1945, as were Yanaihara Tadao, Yamada Moritarō (one of the two surviving Tarōs), and Kimura Takeyoshi (the graduate assistant who had left in protest over the Kawai suspension).[9] Yamada Moritarō eventually served as chairman of the postwar Economics Department, and Yanaihara was later elected to the presidency of the new Tokyo University, which rediscovered its need for him. On retirement from Tōdai, Ōuchi became president of Hōsei University. He and his younger colleague Arisawa Hiromi played extremely important parts in the rebuilding of Japan: Arisawa as a major shaper of the conceptual framework for industrial policy; Ōuchi as an ideologue for the left wing of the Japanese Socialist Party.[10]

Kawakami Hajime, driven from Kyoto University in 1928, was subsequently convicted as a member of the illegal Japanese Communist Party and was jailed for four years between 1933 and 1937. He then spent the war years in seclusion and died at the age of seventy-seven just after the end of the war in 1946. His best-selling autobiography became celebrated as a tale of heroic martyrdom. His younger colleague, Takigawa Yukitoki, ousted from his professorship in 1933, returned to Kyoto University after the war, along with several other of his supporters. In 1953 he became its president. Sakisaka Itsurō, who had been ousted from Kyushu University in 1928 for his Marxist beliefs, was also reinstated. Sakisaka taught at Kyushu until 1960 while also serving, along with Ōuchi Hyōe, as an influential ideologue and a political activist in left-wing party and union movements.[11]

Tanaka Kōtarō's successor as postwar minister of education in 1947 was the original victim of attacks on academics in the 1920s, Morito Tatsuo. Elected to the House of Representatives, Morito served in the first postwar socialist cabinet of 1947–1948. He then accepted an appointment as president of the new Hiroshima University. Meanwhile Takano Iwasaburō, the mentor of Morito and Ōuchi, among other

9. Tōdai, *Keizaigakubu*, pp. 60–64.
10. On Arisawa's enormous postwar influence, see Johnson, *MITI and the Japanese Miracle*, pp. 160, 181, 216, 254.
11. A concise summary of the key role played by Sakisaka can be found in Curtis, *The Japanese Way of Politics*, pp. 133–144; see also L. Olsen, *Dimensions of Japan*, pp. 203–224.

radical economists, was named to head the Japan Public Broadcasting System (Nihon Hōsō Kyōkai).

Hijikata Seibi and Honiden Yoshio, the anti-Marxists who had spent the years 1939–1945 outside the university, were not invited back to Tōdai. They were among those included in the massive purges of rightists carried out under Occupation directives. Ultimately, both were depurged after 1950 and found teaching posts in major private colleges. Hijikata had continued to lecture at Chūō University even while suspended at Tōdai, and after the war he served there as chairman of first the Economics Department and then the School of Commerce until his retirement in 1958. Their colleague Tanabe Chūshi served as president of a lesser private institution.[12]

Among the other targets of the Occupation's retribution were some of the prewar academic elite's more formidable adversaries. Hiranuma Kiichirō, who through his influence in the Ministry of Justice had consistently used the government's legal machinery to suppress intellectual dissent, was tried as a class A war criminal for his role as prime minister during 1939. General Araki Sadao, the education minister who attempted to pressure Tōdai to reform in 1938, was likewise charged by the International Military Tribunal with a long list of chauvinistic activities, including his efforts to "militarize" Japanese education.[13] Also among the twenty-eight class A war criminals was another former education minister of the 1930s, Kido Kōichi, who had risen to the post of Privy Seal. All three were convicted of war crimes and sentenced to life in prison. Hiranuma died there in 1952, but both Araki and Kido were paroled and then pardoned in the late 1950s.

Hatoyama Ichirō, the education minister during the 1933 attack on the Kyoto law faculty, was among a number of prewar party politicians who made the Occupation blacklists. Hatoyama had been central in the revival of the Liberal Party and was on the verge of becoming prime minister in 1946 when purged as bearing partial responsibility for the evils of the 1930s. Much to the outrage of Japan's political Left, Hatoyama made a stunning comeback after the end of the Occupation, winning the prime ministership in 1954 and helping to found the Liberal Democratic Party that has continued to dominate Japanese

12. Hijikata, "Watakushi no ayunde kita michi." The only other Tōdai economists to be purged were Tsuchiya Takao and Miyamoto Susumu.

13. See Ōuchi's recollection of his testimony at Araki's trial in Tanaka et al., *Daigaku no jiji*, p. 131.

politics. Minoda Muneki, who had trumpeted the allegations against Professors Takigawa in 1933 and Minobe Tatsukichi in 1935, hung himself shortly after the war.

In addition to Ōuchi Hyōe and Sakisaka Itsurō, many other academic leftists of the 1930s resumed their roles in the now respectable left-wing opposition movements. The two surviving Tarōs, Hirano Yoshitarō and Yamada Moritarō, were both prominent postwar political activists. Minobe Ryōkichi, Tatsukichi's son who lost his Hōsei law professorship in the 1938 arrests, took a teaching position at Tokyo Metropolitan University of Education and wrote an award-winning popular history of the suppression of academic freedom. He left the university in 1967 to campaign for the governorship of Tokyo with the joint endorsement of the Socialist and Communist parties and served three terms as governor before winning a seat in the House of Councillors in 1979.

Among the many other indications of how much times had changed for academic Marxists in the postwar era was the one evidenced at the Imperial Palace when in 1968 Ōuchi Hyōe, having been appointed to the Japan Academy (Gakushiinkai), joined his fellow academicians at dinner with His Majesty the Shōwa Emperor.

Conclusion

As these and other Japanese academicians have reflected on the rival imperatives of scholarship and politics in prewar history, they have often disagreed on which lessons to draw from their painful experiences. Given the diverse roles they played in the prewar strife between the university and the state, this is not surprising. Nevertheless, most accounts of this conflict have focused on the transformations of the political climate in the 1930s to explain why academic intellectuals were not able to maintain the degree of autonomy for their institutions they had enjoyed in earlier decades. In such accounts, to borrow Nagai Michio's metaphor, the "takeoff" and "crash" of Japanese higher education have been explained as due primarily to turbulent weather exposing the design flaws in the original institutional structure. This book has given considerably more attention to the changes that occurred within the structure of higher education and within the academic elite that functioned inside those universities.

Between 1877 and 1905 relations between the Meiji government and the new academic elite had been on the whole harmonious. The Education Ministry in those decades was usually under the influence of men with close ties to Tōdai, and senior Meiji bureaucrats and leading faculty members demonstrated a remarkable consensus on ultimate goals as well as on the parameters of university autonomy. The imperial university can be said to have served then as an integral part of an evolving system aimed at the "political management" and "bureaucratization" of Japanese intellectual life.[14] Tensions between the state and the university in the years prior to 1905 arose primarily over how to formalize this relationship in legal administrative terms, but open conflict was prevented by compromises arranged through informal channels.

In 1905, however, those tensions erupted into the open in the Affair of the Seven Ph.D.s, a dramatic break with past patterns of conflict resolution and the first clear indication of the severe strains building within the mechanism of coordination and control of higher education. Nevertheless, the Affair of the Seven Ph.D.s differed from the conflict of later periods in several significant ways. In 1905 the main struggle was over the legitimate role of the academic intellectual within a bureaucratic system of politics. Despite the strains, the consensus between the bureaucratic and academic elites that had characterized the early Meiji was still largely intact. University spokesmen challenged the policies of the Katsura cabinet but not the concept of an administrative state, for Tomizu's supporters generally accepted the ideals of a nonpartisan bureaucratic elite.[15] If these academic civil servants sought greater autonomy for the university, it was, they claimed, to ensure independence from the partisan politics of cabinet governments and protection from parliamentary party interference. The chief argument set forth in their attempt to legitimize freedom of speech for the academic was an elitist justification that defined the scholar as an impartial, objective expert above the partisanship of political or social conflict.

Conflict between Japan's elite universities and government authorities took on a very different character during the 1910s and 1920s. A substantial minority of a new generation of faculty now accepted political partisanship as a legitimate means of taking part in the struggles of their times. This brought into sharper question the role of a univer-

14. Harootunian, "A Sense of Ending and the Problems of Taisho."
15. Silberman, "The Bureaucratic State in Japan."

sity as a government agency and exposed the inherent contradictions in the dual role of civil servant and academic intellectual. For the more radical academics the rejection of a university as an instrument of the state was no longer enough; increasingly they sought to transform the university so it might serve as their agency for bringing about a new social order. In this view the academic was to continue playing a leadership role, as had the Meiji academic elite; but that role was now to include leadership in popular movements that challenged the political and economic elites.

Underlying these shifts in the orientations of these faculties were two crucial developments within Japan's system of higher education. First, as the civil bureaucracy matured, acquiring an increasingly specialized expertise, the technocratic functions of the academic elite at the imperial universities eroded in importance. The professor's role within an administrative state was reduced proportionately. This development added to the pressures on those academic intellectuals who sought to influence political affairs as "public men" to find ways to do so outside the bureaucratic channels so much more open to them in the Meiji era.[16]

Second, the breakdown of coordination within the educational system led conservatives to try new measures aimed at asserting governmental authority over the elite universities. Thus, Education Ministry administrative procedures for mediating disputes began to be replaced by criminal proceedings instigated through the Justice Ministry. Such measures only further politicized the issues of university governance despite proving, until the war in China, largely ineffective in suppressing dissent on campus. Therefore, much of the breakdown of the Meiji patterns of political management of intellectual life can be traced to the inability of the state to accommodate the processes of rapid growth and structural change and to the decentralization of authority within the overall system of higher education.

Ultimately, it is impossible to assess with any precision the relative importance of external and internal variables here, but certainly the underlying causes of the vulnerability of Tōdai in the 1930s cannot be attributed wholly to flaws in either its formal institutional structure or its legal status within the state. As has been documented, there were important institutional bulwarks against government intervention cre-

16. I borrow the phrase from Barshay; for his definition see *State and the Intellectual in Imperial Japan*, especially pp. 16–19.

ated in the imperial universities during the years 1905–1918. True, in the 1920s the civil service status of imperial university professors was turned against academic dissidents in instances in which preliminary indictments were used to bring about suspensions from their posts long before convictions for any crime had occurred. But the fact remains that administrators and colleagues proved all too often willing to acquiesce in—or even to initiate—such suspensions, thereby underscoring the significance of the loss of consensus about the legitimate parameters of the academic role that took place during the bitter factional and ideological struggles of the 1920s.

Thus, it is very difficult to see how any legal arrangements, however rooted in constitutional guarantees, would have been sufficient to protect academic freedom and university self-governance in the 1930s unless at least two other prerequisites had also been met. First, a unity was needed of the sort displayed in the 1905 confrontation, when a great majority of Tōdai faculty members, supported by Japan's only other functioning university at Kyoto, were prepared to close their school rather than acquiesce in the loss of a single law professor, Tomizu Hiroto. Unfortunately for the cause of academic freedom, any display of such cohesiveness among imperial university faculty leaders in the 1930s was limited primarily to the defense of the principle of university self-governance. Hence the spirited response to Education Minister Araki in 1938, when they and their counterparts at the other imperial universities rallied to the defense of the institutional status quo.

But in the 1920s and 1930s, in contrast to the 1900s and 1910s, this principle of institutional autonomy was upheld more frequently than not at the expense of academic freedom itself. Again and again at Tōdai as well as at the other imperial universities, individual professors were sacrificed for "the sake of the university." Tōdai faculty leaders, including some prominent liberals, were willing to see individuals forced out rather than challenge the authority of the government. The support of an internally directed purge of the Tōdai Economics Department in 1939 was paradoxically the culmination of two decades of obsession with blocking external interference in the internal management of the university. Recognizing the vulnerability to outside attack of a university torn by internal factional strife, faculty leaders were willing to sacrifice the core of the Economics Department in the name of restoring harmony.

This is not to argue, however, that if somehow the cohesiveness shown in defending Professor Tomizu in 1905 could have been sustained it would have ipso facto discouraged the government. Clearly, by the 1930s Japanese political leaders no longer perceived the imperial universities as occupying an indispensable position within the central institutions of the state. The willingness of their predecessors to tolerate a considerable degree of university autonomy in the Meiji period had been in part a recognition that Tōdai faculty collectively possessed a disproportionately large share of the corpus of Western learning and modern technology deemed essential to solving the critical problems of the day and achieving the national goals of a society embarking on industrialization. By the 1930s, however, the political leaders of a much more developed industrial state were able to run the risk of a large-scale boycott by a later generation of academic elite at Tōdai and Kyōdai precisely because the valued knowledge and required techniques had become the common property not only of numerous other universities but also of rival elites outside of academe. The final irony to be noted here is that the majority of the latter—the higher civil servants, the corporate managers, and the political functionaries whose stock of expertise now permitted them to disregard dissenting professors—had themselves been trained in those imperial universities.

APPENDIX
Tōdai and the Production
of National Elites

The dominance of Tokyo University in the production of Japan's national elites is difficult to exaggerate, especially in the period prior to 1945. As the following compilation of data from various sources clearly indicates, no other school rivaled Tōdai in this respect.[1]

The Higher Civil Service

The upper echelons of the civil bureaucracy have formed one of the main components of Japan's political elite since the late nineteenth century. The regulations governing the civil service examination system and the laws restricting political appointees combined to make educational qualifications uppermost in determining entry into the prewar bureaucratic elite. Given that relatively few higher civil servants were removed in the postwar purges, the majority of the bureaucratic elite in the early decades after 1945 were also men who had received their education and were recruited under the old system (see Table A-1).[2]

1. Here, as elsewhere in the tables, unless otherwise indicated, Tōdai includes its predecessors—the Kaiseijo, Daigaku Nankō, and Kaisei Gakkō.
2. For a good summary of the importance of the prewar bureaucracy as an elite and the eventual centrality of examination men within it, see Spaulding, "The Bureaucracy as

Table A-1 *Education of the Higher Civil Service: Percentage Tōdai Alumni*

	1894–1901	1894–1926	1937	1945–1959	1960s	1975–1985
Passed administrative exams	60[a]					
Serving in office			74[b]	79[c]		80[d]
Vice ministers		92[e]				94[d]
Leadership in five ministries		71[f]				
Leadership in all ministries						62[d]
Bureau chiefs						83[d]
Bureau and section chiefs		71[e]			58–73[g]	

SOURCES: [a]Spaulding, Table 15, p. 131. [b]Inoki, "The Civil Bureaucracy: Japan," Table 1, p. 296. [c]From Kubota. [d]Kim, Table III-2, p. 147. [e]My calculations from lists of administrative vice ministers in Ijiri. [f]From lists in Ijiri for all administrative vice ministers and bureau chiefs in Ministries of Finance, Home, Justice, Commerce & Agriculture, and Foreign Affairs. [g]Shimizu, Table 11, p. 60; p. 175.

The modern court system, part of the higher civil service in the prewar years and only partially separated in the postwar, has also been dominated by Tōdai products (see Table A-2).[3]

Parliamentary Leadership

Tōdai alumni have also figured prominently among those elected to the Diet and/or appointed to the cabinet (see Table A-3).[4]

---

a Political Force." Titus documented the dominance of Tōdai men among the officials in the imperial household (*Palace and Politics,* p. 75; Table 6, p. 88). There is nothing quite as comprehensive as Spaulding, *Imperial Japan's Higher Civil Service Examinations,* for the postwar period, but the main outlines can be found in Inoki, "The Civil Bureaucracy"; Kim, *Japan's Civil Service System;* and Kubota, *Higher Civil Servants in Postwar Japan.* Other sources include Ijiri, *Rekidai kenkanroku;* and Shimizu, *Tōkyō Daigaku hōgakubu.* The most thorough English treatment of the political purges under the U.S. Occupation is still Baerwald, *The Purge of Japanese Leaders Under the Occupation.*

3. For a brief summary in English of the Japanese court system in comparative perspective, see Schubert, "Judges and Political Leadership"; in Japanese, see Ushiomi, *Hōritsuka.*

4. See Ahn, "The Japanese Cabinet Ministers"; Colbert, *The Left Wing in Japanese*

Table A-2 *Education of Judicial Officials: Percentage Tōdai Alumni*

	1937	1960s
Judicial officials	50[a]	—
Judges	—	43[b]
Higher courts	—	58[c]
Supreme Court	—	75[d]
Public procurators	—	30[b]

SOURCES: [a]Inoki, "The Civil Bureaucracy," Table 1, p. 296. [b]Ushiomi, *Hōritsuka*, p. 111. [c]Schubert, "Judges and Political Leadership," p. 243. [d]Itoh and Beer, eds., *The Constitutional Case Law of Japan*, Appendix, pp. 251ff.

Table A-3 *Education of Cabinet Ministers, 1918–1945 (%)*

	Prime Ministers[a] (N = 23)	All Ministers[b] (N = 480)
Tōdai	26	45
Kyōdai	4	6
Waseda or Keiō	4	8
Other Japanese universities	4	8
Foreign universities	4	3
Military cadet schools	52	11
None or unknown	5	20
Totals	100	100

SOURCES: [a]My calculations. [b]Ahn, "The Japanese Cabinet Ministers," Table 19, p. 110.

Almost half of the 480 individuals who served as cabinet members between 1918 and 1964 were Tōdai alumni. Because the positions of minister of army and minister of navy in prewar cabinets were always filled by professional military men and most of those were educated in military schools, the Tōdai share would be higher if we were considering only the other portfolios.

Japanese cabinets formed by the Liberal and Democrat parties in the postwar years were also dominated by men educated at Tōdai in the prewar years, including seven of the first nine postwar prime ministers (see Table A-4).

Twenty-seven percent of the total in both houses of the 1963 Diet

Politics; Passin, "Japan"; Scalapino and Masumi, *Parties and Politics in Contemporary Japan;* Wakata, "Japanese Diet Members"; and Yanaga, *Big Business in Japanese Politics.*

Table A-4   *Postwar Cabinet Ministers, 1940s and 1950s: College Attended (%)*

	1948	1949	1953	1954	1955	1956	1957	1958	1959
Tōdai	33	24	56	39	58	27	50	44	44
Kyōdai	27	18	—	6	5	20	6	11	17
Waseda	7	18	11	28	11	20	17	6	—
Other	13	24	33	17	11	27	11	28	33
NA	20	18	—	11	16	7	17	11	6

SOURCES: Calculated from Scalapino and Masumi, *Parties and Politics in Contemporary Japan,* p. 62; and Passin, "Japan," Table 6, p. 302; Table 7, p. 303.

NOTE: The number of cabinet members at any given time varied between fifteen and eighteen.

were Tōdai graduates for the most part educated prior to the end of World War II.[5] This percentage included a surprising number of those supported by the opposition parties. One list of 124 left-wing leaders in 1949 included 24 Tōdai men—almost 20 percent of all males with any college-level education (see Table A-5).

The Business World

College graduates were recruited into Japanese business from very early in the process of industrialization, and by the late 1920s the majority of prominent business executives had attended institutions of higher education.[6] Once again the prominence of Tōdai alumni in the world of industry and commerce is clear (see Table A-6). Studies of business leaders of the 1950s, a generation mostly, if not totally, educated in the prewar system, indicate Tōdai graduates made up between one-fifth and two-fifths. Alumni of Kyoto, Keiō, and Hitotsubashi lagged far behind, each with between 5 percent and 10 percent of the totals. Samples for the prewar era indicate that this pattern had been continuous since the 1920s.

5. Yanaga, *Big Business in Japanese Politics,* Table 3, p. 25.
6. See Aonuma, *Nihon no keieisō;* Azumi, *Higher Education and Business Recruitment in Japan;* Hirschmeier and Yui, *The Development of Japanese Business;* Yanaga, *Big Business in Japanese Politics;* Yamamura and Hanley, "Ichihime, ni Tarō"; and Yoshino, *Japan's Managerial System.*

Table A-5   *Postwar Left-Wing Leaders: School Attended (%)*

Males	
Tōdai	19
Kyōdai	3
Waseda	13
Keiō	2
Other colleges or higher schools	28
Females	3
Less than higher school or NA	32

SOURCE: Calculated from Colbert, *The Left Wing in Japanese Politics,* pp. 303–340.

Table A-6   *Business Executives, 1900–1965: College Attended*

	1900	1928	1944	1950	1954	1959	1962	1965
Number	1,000	1,000	1,000	1,000	133	3,000	1,000	9,743
Attended some college (%)	4.0	64	82	91	—	—	89	—
College attended (%)								
Tokyo	2.0	23	27	32	41	21	28	33
Kyoto	0.0	2	6	11	5	7	9	13
Hitotsubashi	0.2	10	9	11	10	6	9	6
Keiō	2.0	11	9	7	6	7	7	8
Waseda	0.0	2	3	4	3	4	5	10
Foreign	0.2	3	3	1	—	—	1	—

SOURCES: 1954 and 1959 from Yanaga, *Big Business in Japanese Politics,* Tables 1 and 2, p. 24; 1965 from Yamamura and Hanley, "Ichihime, ni Tarō," Table 4, p. 96; all other from Aonuma, *Nihon no keieisō,* Table 8, pp. 116–117.

Educational, Intellectual, and Literary Elites

The faculty of Tōdai was itself part of the intellectual elite of imperial Japan, and, as has been noted, Tōdai faculty members were usually themselves graduates of Tōdai. The hiring of one's own graduates was eventually to become the pattern at other major universities, but in the early stages of the development of the modern system of higher education Tōdai produced a large proportion of the academic staffs for other schools as well. More surprising, perhaps, is the role Tōdai continued to play even as that system matured. The data in Table

Table A-7   *Education of College Faculty by Department/Division (%)*

	Economics	Law	Letters	Medicine	Engineering	Science	Total
Tokyo	22	30	27	18	27	37	25
Kyoto	11	16	14	11	18	16	13
Tōhoku	3	2	3	6	9	8	6
Kyushu	6	4	3	8	3	5	5
Waseda	7	8	5	*	5	*	3
Keiō	5	9	3	4	*	*	2
Hitotsubashi	10	*	*	*	*	*	2
Foreign	*	*	10	*	*	5	2
Other	35	30	34	52	37	28	45

SOURCES: Shimbori, *Nihon no daigaku kyōju shijō*, Table 1, p. 49; Table 2, p. 53.
NOTE: $N = 31,934$.
*Not one of the top ten schools in this category.

A-7 on the faculty of 260 four-year colleges in 1962 clearly indicate the continued prominence of Tōdai's graduates in this sphere.[7]

Tōdai's role in providing imperial Japan with theoretical and applied scientists and technicians has been thoroughly explored by James Bartholomew.[8] In addition to specialists in the cognitive disciplines, Tōdai also produced far more influential and distinguished literary figures than any other university in imperial Japan. Any list used to quantify this generalization is certain to be more controversial than its counterpart in the political or business world. Nevertheless, general sources on literary and intellectual history can be used to at least give some indication of reputation (see Table A-8).

For example, a prestigious prewar publication selected sixty-eight novelists, playwrights, and poets active between 1902 and 1935 to be introduced to the English-speaking world. Of these, twenty-one (31 percent) had studied at least for some time at Tōdai, eleven (16 percent) had attended Waseda, six (9 percent) had been at Keiō, and seven (9 percent) had studied at other colleges.[9] The Tōdai alumni included such celebrated writers as Natsume Sōseki, Tanizaki Jun'ichirō, and Kukichi Kan, although the last two were among those who dropped out of college without graduating. In the postwar period an *Asahi jāneru* series listed sixty-seven of the most prominent thinkers in Japan since

7. Cummings, *Nihon no daigaku kyōju;* and Shimbori, *Nihon no daigaku kyōju shijō.*
8. See entries in List of Works Consulted.
9. Kokusai Bunka Shinkokai, *Introduction to Contemporary Japanese Literature.*

Table A-8   *Higher Education of Intellectuals*

	Writers[a]	Thinkers[b]
Tōdai	21 (31%)	24 (43%)
Kyoto	1 (1%)	2 (4%)
Waseda	11 (16%)	5 (9%)
Keiō	6 (9%)	1 (2%)
Other colleges	7 (9%)	12 (20%)
No college	22 (32%)	12 (21%)
Totals	68	56

SOURCES: [a]Kokusai Bunka Shinkokai, *Introduction to Contemporary Japanese Literature.* [b]Asahi Jānaru, eds., *Nihon no shisōka* (excluding those educated prior to the 1868 Restoration). Standard biographical dictionaries were also consulted.

1800. Eleven were educated in the Tokugawa period prior to the Restoration of 1868, but of the remaining fifty-six, twenty-four (43 percent) had studied at Tōdai, two (4 percent) at Kyoto, Waseda could claim only five (9 percent), and all other colleges could claim thirteen (22 percent).[10]

10. *Nihon no shisōka* originally appeared in the *Asahi jāneru* between March 1962 and June 1963; it was republished in three volumes in 1963.

Glossary and Biographical Notes

This list is intended as a brief guide to the most prominent of the actors and more important terms in this account. **Boldface** indicates cross-indexing to another entry.

AFFAIR OF THE SEVEN PH.D.s *Shichi hakase jiken* or *Tomizu jiken*; sometimes translated as the "Affair of the Seven Doctors." This term refers to the 1905 confrontation between faculty at the imperial universities and the Katsura cabinet (see chapters 1 and 2).

ARAKI SADAO (1877–1966, not to be confused with either Kyoto University president **Araki Torasaburō** or Tokyo University economics professor Araki Kōtarō): general and baron, education minister (May 1938–August 1939). A leader of the Kōdōha (Imperial Way Faction), Araki was viewed as a potential prime minister if the February 1936 mutiny had succeeded in overthrowing the government. As education minister in the cabinets of Konoe Fumimaro and **Hiranuma Kiichirō**, Araki attempted to abolish university autonomy. After the Pacific War he was convicted as a class A war criminal and was sentenced to life imprisonment; paroled in 1954 for health reasons, he was then pardoned in the late 1950s.

ARAKI TORASABURŌ (1866–1942, not to be confused with either General Baron **Araki Sadao** or Tokyo university economics professor Araki Kōtarō): professor and dean of medicine, president of Kyoto Imperial University, privy councillor. A graduate of Tokyo University, Araki held a doctorate in medicine and had served as dean of the Medical College for twelve years before being named president in 1915; he served in that position during the attacks on **Kawakami Hajime** and the early stages of the **Takigawa Affair.** In 1937 he was elevated to membership in the Privy Council.

ARISAWA HIROMI (b. 1896): Tokyo University economics assistant professor, postwar economics chairman, postwar president of Hōsei University. Jailed in 1938, Arisawa was subsequently convicted in the **Professors' Group Affair.** After the war he became a prominent economic adviser to several prime ministers and is credited as one of the chief architects of the postwar Japanese recovery.

ASSISTANT, ASSOCIATE PROFESSOR: the *jokyōju* academic rank. There were, and still are, usually only two professorial ranks in Japanese universities, and thus *jokyōju* is often translated as "assistant professor." I have chosen to render it herein as "associate professor" to clearly indicate the presumption that tenure was permanent, not probationary, as the English title implies in the U.S. academic context.

BANSHO SHIRABESHO: see **Institute for Western Studies.**

BUNGAKU: usually translated as "literature" or "literary studies." This traditionally included the belles lettres in general, and as a division in prewar Japanese universities it encompassed the study of history, religion, sociology, religion, and other departments often found in U.S. universities in a college of "letters."

CHŪŌKŌRON: *The Central Review.* This influential monthly magazine of opinion and general affairs supported social democracy and leftist causes in the 1920s and 1930s and was a major outlet for the views of academic intellectuals.

DAIGAKU HYŌGIKAI: the University Council or faculty Senate at Tokyo University.

DAIGAKU NANKŌ: The University's south campus. This division of Western studies in the first Meiji-era university was a predecessor to Tokyo University.

HAKUSHI: also read *hakase.* Until 1888 this was a professorial rank dating back to the Heian court period (794–1185); subsequently it was a prestigious degree awarded through the Education Ministry and was equivalent to something between the U.S. doctorate and the German *Habilitation* (see chapter 2).

HAMAO ARATA (1849–1925): longtime Tokyo University administrator and twice its president, chief of the Bureau of Professional Education, member of the House of Peers, privy councillor. Hamao was a compromise candidate for university president in the 1905 **Affair of the Seven Ph.D.s.**

HATOYAMA ICHIRŌ (1883–1959): chief cabinet secretary, education minister, postwar prime minister. Hatoyama was the son of the educator-politician **Hatoyama Kazuo** and a member of Seiyūkai Party cabinets in 1927–1929 and again in 1931–1934. As minister of education in 1933 he led the government's campaign against **Takigawa Yukitoki.** Following World War II, Hatoyama became head of the Liberal Party and was slated to become prime minister in 1946 but was purged by the U.S. Occupation. He was depurged and elected prime minister in 1954 and was one of the founding fathers of the Liberal Democrat Party, the dominant political party since 1955.

HATOYAMA KAZUO (1856–1911): Tokyo University law professor and dean, Waseda University president, Speaker of the House of Representatives. This influential educator and politician, who took a leading role in the conflict over the 1890 draft civil code (see chapter 3), was educated at Tokyo University in the 1870s and at Columbia and Yale in the United States. He subsequently served as president of **Waseda University.** He was also the father of two prominent sons, **Hatoyama Ichirō** and Tokyo University law professor Hatoyama Hideo (1884–1946).

HIJIKATA SEIBI (1890–1975): Tokyo University economics professor and department chairman. Hijikata, a specialist in public finance and a leader among anti-Marxists in the department, was a graduate of the economics section of Tokyo University Law Department, a son-in-law and adopted heir of Tokyo University law professor Hijikata Yasushi, and department chairman during the ouster of **Yanaihara Tadao.** Suspended from Tokyo University faculty in the **Hiraga Purge,** Hijikata subsequently taught at Chūō University and in the postwar period served as chairman of its Economics Department and then of its School of Commerce until his retirement in 1959.

HIRAGA PURGE: *Hiraga shukugaku.* This is a popular label for the events of 1939 in which President **Hiraga Yuzuru** temporarily assumed the chairmanship of the department and the majority of the economics faculty members at Tokyo Imperial University either were suspended or resigned.

HIRAGA YUZURU (1873–1943): vice admiral, Tokyo University professor of engineering, department chairman, university president. He joined the Tokyo faculty in 1931 after a career as a naval architect, served as the dean of engineering before being elected as president in 1938, and was a key figure in the **Hiraga Purge.**

HIRANO YOSHITARŌ (1897–1980): Tokyo University associate professor of economics. One of the **Three Tarōs** accused of communist ties, he resigned under duress in 1930. Hirano collaborated with **Yamada Moritarō** as a chief editor of a very influential 1932–1933 collection of essays by Marxists of the Kōza faction. After the war Hirano was appointed to a term on the prestigious, government-funded Science Council of Japan (Nihon Gakujutsu Kaigi) and remained active in a number of pacifist causes.

HIRANUMA KIICHIRŌ (1867–1952): procurator-general, chief of the Supreme Court, justice minister, member of the House of Peers, privy councillor, prime minister, home minister. A Tokyo University law graduate who was awarded a doctorate in law, Hiranuma was a central figure in a network of conservative political elite who attempted to suppress Marxist and social democratic ideas in the **Morito Case** and later incidents. He was sentenced to life imprisonment at the Tokyo War Crimes Trial and died in prison.

HŌGAKU: usually translated as "law" or "legal studies." This division in prewar Japanese universities encompassed the study of political systems, economics, and other fields in what today might be termed *public administration* or the *policy sciences;* only a relatively few graduates actually practiced as lawyers.

HOZUMI NOBUSHIGE (1856–1926): Tokyo University law professor and dean, law Ph.D., baron, privy councillor. A pioneer in legal studies educated first at Tokyo University in the 1870s and then at Middle Temple in London and the University of Berlin, Hozumi was an important participant in the conflict over the 1890 draft civil code. He was the elder brother of **Hozumi Yatsuka,** father of Hozumi Shigetō, and son-in-law of financier Shibusawa Eiichi.

HOZUMI YATSUKA (1860–1912): Tokyo University law professor and dean, member of the House of Peers. A specialist in constitutional law educated at Tokyo University and abroad, Hozumi was involved in the conflict over the 1890 draft civil code, engaged in important debates with Minobe Tatsukichi over the constitutional role of the emperor, and was a prominent nationalist who nevertheless defended university autonomy in the **Affair of the Seven Ph.D.s.** Hozumi was also the younger brother of **Hozumi Nobushige,** uncle of Tokyo University law professor Hozumi Shigetō, and son-in-law of industrialist Asano Sōichirō.

INSTITUTE FOR WESTERN STUDIES: known variously after 1850 as the Bansho Shirabesho, the Yōsho Shirabesho, the Yōgakusho, and the Kaiseijo. Created by the Tokugawa shogunate in 1855 to provide intelligence on the foreign policy issues faced after the visit of the U.S. squadron under Commodore Matthew Perry, the institute was a main progenitor of Tokyo University.

KAISEI GAKKŌ, KAISEI GAKUSHO, KAISEIJO: successor schools to the Institute for Western Studies and predecessors to Tokyo University in 1877.

KAIZŌ: *Reconstruction.* This monthly journal of opinion and analysis was influential especially in liberal and leftist intellectual circles and was a major outlet for debate over higher education and other related topics.

KANAI NOBURU (1865–1933): Tokyo University law professor and first economics chairman. He graduated from Tokyo University in 1885 and then spent three years as a student at various German universities plus a year in England before returning to a professorship in law. Kanai was involved in the **Affair of the Seven Ph.D.s,** a leading figure in the Social Policy Study Association, department chairman during the **Morito Case,** and father-in-law of **Kawai Eijirō.**

KAWAI EIJIRŌ (1891–1944): Tokyo University professor of economics. He was a leading spokesman for liberalism, a key figure in the **Hiraga Purge,** a Tokyo University law graduate, and the son-in-law of **Kanai Noburu.**

KAWAKAMI HAJIME (1879–1946): Kyoto University economics professor. He graduated from Tokyo University Law College in 1902 and then served on the faculty of Tokyo University School of Agriculture until appointed professor at Kyoto. His writings and personality were a great influence on radical students in the 1920s. He was forced to resign in 1928; subsequently convicted for political activities, he spent 1933–1937 in jail.

KEIŌ UNIVERSITY: with **Waseda University** one of the two leading private institutions of higher education in Japan. Founded in 1858 as Keiō Gijuku by famed educator and social critic Fukuzawa Yukichi, Keiō became a university in 1890.

KIKUCHI DAIROKU (1855–1917): Tokyo University science professor, dean, president, minister of education, president of Kyoto University, privy councillor. A son of Mitsukuri Shōhei, a teacher at the old shogunal **Institute for Western Studies,** Kikuchi studied there and became a pioneer in modern mathematics; he bridged the transition from Tokugawa to the twentieth century. Kikuchi was the father-in-law of Hatoyama Hideo and **Minobe Tatsukichi** (see figure of Mitsukuri family tree in chapter 2).

KONOE ATSUMARO (1863–1904, not to be confused with his son, Konoe Fumimaro, the prime minister in the late 1930s): prince, member of the House of Peers, privy councillor, president of Peers School (Gakushūin). This prominent spokesman for expanding Japanese interests on the Asian continent encouraged Tokyo University law professor **Tomizu Hiroto** and the others in the **Affair of the Seven Ph.D.s.**

KŌTŌ GAKKŌ: higher schools. These secondary schools, public and private, prior to 1945 were more analogous to the elite gymnasium or lycée of Europe than to the U.S. high school.

KYŌDAI: the common abbreviation for Kyōto Teikoku Daigaku (Kyoto Imperial University) or, since 1945, Kyōto Daigaku (University of Kyoto).

KYŌDAI JIKEN: the "Kyoto University Affair." This term refers to either of two confrontations between that school and the government: for 1933, see **Takigawa Yukitoki** and chapter 6; for 1913, see **Sawayanagi Affair** and chapter 3.

KYŌJU GURUPU JIKEN: see **Professors' Group Affair.**

LAW FACULTY: see **Hōgaku.**

LETTERS OR LITERATURE FACULTY: see **Bungaku.**

MARCH 15 INCIDENT: the March 15 *jiken* of 1928, when more than sixteen hundred suspected communist and other radicals were arrested. As many were students, the Education Ministry used the incident to press for the removal of leftist professors at Tokyo, Kyoto, and Kyushu Imperial universities (see chapter 5).

MINOBE AFFAIR: *Minobe jiken,* or *Tennō kikansetsu jiken.* This term refers to the events of 1935 in which **Minobe Tatsukichi** and a number of liberals in the field of constitutional law were subject to harassment and persecution. As a result, Minobe, who had already reached retirement at Tokyo University, resigned his seat in the House of Peers.

MINOBE RYŌKICHI (1904–1984): professor of politics at Hōsei University. This son of **Minobe Tatsukichi** was arrested as part of the **Professors' Group Affair.** Following the war he was appointed professor at Tokyo Education University and then served twelve years as governor of Tokyo before being elected to the House of Councillors in 1979.

MINOBE TATSUKICHI (1873–1948): Tokyo University law professor, department chairman, member of the House of Peers. This exponent of a liberal interpretation of the constitutional role of emperor was a central figure in the **Minobe Affair,** a son-in-law of **Kikuchi Dairoku,** and the father of **Minobe Ryōkichi.**

MINODA MUNEKI (Koki, Muneyoshi, 1894–1946): erstwhile Keiō University logic instructor and self-proclaimed disciple of **Uesugi Shinkichi.** Minoda founded Genri Nihonsha (Society for the True Japan) to publish attacks on such liberals and leftist faculty members as **Takigawa Yukitoki, Minobe Tatsukichi, Kawai Eijirō,** and **Nanbara Shigeru.**

MITSUKURI FAMILY: a veritable dynasty of scholars of Western studies reaching back to Mitsukuri Genpō (1789–1863), with at least eleven family members who served on the faculty of Tokyo University or its predecessor institutions, including Tokyo University president **Kikuchi Dairoku** (see figure of family tree in chapter 2).

MORITO CASE: **Morito jiken** of 1920. This term refers to events in which Tokyo University economics professors **Morito Tatsuo** and **Ōuchi Hyōe** were indicted for publishing an article on Russian anarchism (see chapters 4 and 5).

MORITO TATSUO (1888–1984): Tokyo University associate professor of economics, postwar education minister, Hiroshima University president. This central figure in the **Morito Case** thereafter became an influential writer as a staff member of the Ōhara Institute for Social Research. After World War II he was elected to the House of Representatives from the Socialist Party, served as education minister under the U.S Occupation, and then was elected president of Hiroshima University.

NANBARA SHIGERU (1889–1974): Tokyo University law professor, president of Tokyo University under the U.S. Occupation. He graduated from the First Higher School, where he was converted to Christianity, and then from Tokyo University Law College. He served seven years in the Home Ministry before being appointed to the Tokyo University Law Department in 1921.

ŌMORI YOSHITARŌ (Gentarō, 1898–1940): Tokyo University associate professor of economics. One of the **Three Tarōs** ousted from Tokyo University in the 1928–1930 crackdown on radical activities on campus, he continued as a political activist associated with the Rōnō faction of Marxists. Ōmori was arrested in the 1938 **Popular Front Incident** and was convicted of violations of the peace preservation law; he died while on bail in 1940.

ONOZUKA KIHEIJI (1871–1944): Tokyo University law professor, department chair, president, member of the House of Peers. One of the original members in the **Affair of the Seven Ph.D.s,** Onozuka was Tokyo University president during both the **March 15 Incident** and the **Takigawa Affair.** He was also a son-in-law of Privy Councillor Viscount General Ishiguro Tadanori and was related by marriage to Tokyo University law professors **Hozumi Nobushige, Hozumi Yatsuka,** and **Hozumi Shigetō.**

ŌUCHI HYŌE (1888–1980): Tokyo University economics professor, postwar president of Hōsei University. This codefendant in the **Morito Case** was a leader of leftists within the department until his suspension in 1938 following indictment in the **Professors' Group Affair.** After World War II he returned to Tokyo University until retirement in 1948 and then served as president of Hōsei University. With his former student **Sakisaka Itsurō,** Ōuchi was a major ideological influence on the left wing of the Japanese Socialist Party.

POPULAR FRONT INCIDENT: *Jinmin Senzen jiken.* This term refers to the arrests of some four hundred activists between December 1937 and February 1938 on charges that they were part of a Comintern-inspired conspiracy against the Japanese military action in China. Among those arrested were former imperial university faculty members **Ōmori Yoshitarō** and **Sakisaka Itsurō** (also see **Professors' Group Affair**).

PROFESSORS' GROUP AFFAIR: *Kyōju Gurupu jiken* or *Gakusha Gurupu jiken;* sometimes translated as "the Academicians' Group Incident." This popular label refers to the 1938 arrest of Tokyo University professors **Ōuchi Hyōe, Arisawa Hiromi, Wakimura Yoshitaro,** and **Minobe Ryōkichi** of Hōsei University in the aftermath of the **Popular Front Incident.**

RŌYAMA MASAMICHI (1895–1980): Tokyo University law professor. He resigned to protest the **Hiraga Purge,** served in the brain trust of Prime Minister Konoe Fumimaro, and hence was purged by the U.S. Occupation until 1950, after which he became president of Ochanomizu Women's College.

SAKISAKA ITSURŌ (b. 1897): Kyushu Imperial University associate professor. A 1921 graduate of the Tokyo University Economics Department, where he was close to Morito Tatsuo and Ōuchi Hyōe, Sakisaka was ousted from his post at Kyushu in the aftermath of the **March 15 Incident.** He became a journalist and political activist until indicted and sentenced to a two-year prison term in the **Popular Front Incident.** He was reinstated at Kyushu University in 1945 and appointed its president in 1946; he taught until 1960 while also serving, along with **Ōuchi Hyōe,** as a major ideologue for the left wings of the Japanese Socialist Party and labor union movements.

SASA HIROO (b. 1896): Kyushu Imperial University associate professor. He graduated from Tokyo University Law College in 1920, where he had been close to Morito Tatsuo and Ōuchi Hyōe. Sasa resigned under duress from Kyushu University in the 1928 **March 15 Incident.** He became a journalist and participant in the Shōwa Research Association in the late 1930s.

SASAKI SŌICHI (1878–1965): Kyoto University law professor. This political ally of Yoshino Sakuzō, defense attorney in the **Morito Case,** was runner-up for president in 1933 during the **Takigawa Affair** (he subsequently resigned). Sasaki taught briefly at Kobe University of Commerce but was suspended in 1935 in the aftermath of the **Minobe Affair.** After World War II Sasaki served briefly as adviser on constitutional reform, became president of Ritsumeikan University in 1945, and was awarded the Bunka Kunshō (Order of Culture) in 1952.

SAWAYANAGI AFFAIR: *Sawayanagi jiken* or *Kyōdai jiken* of 1913. This is the popular label for the events of 1913 when Kyoto University faculty forced the resignation of President **Sawayanagi Masatarō** after he attempted to remove a number of faculty members; the affair led to new provisions for faculty balloting to choose nominees for the university presidency.

SAWAYANAGI MASATARŌ (1865–1927): vice minister of education, president of Tōhoku and of Kyoto Imperial universities. As a bureaucrat appointed to the presidency of Kyoto University he became a central figure in the 1913 **Sawayanagi Affair.**

TAKANO IWASABURŌ (1871–1949): Tokyo University professor of law, founding member of Economics Department in 1919. A brother of a pioneer labor unionist and a central figure in the formation of a socialist circle among faculty and graduate students, he resigned after the **Morito Case** and served as head of the influential Ōhara Institute for Social Research in Osaka. After the war Takano was named head of Nihon Hōsō Kyōkai, Japan's public broadcasting system.

TAKIGAWA AFFAIR: *Takigawa jiken* or *Kyōdai jiken* of 1933. This is the popular label for the events of 1933 when Professor **Takigawa Yukitoki** was first suspended and then along with twenty others on the law faculty at Kyoto Imperial University resigned under duress (see chapter 6).

TAKIGAWA YUKITOKI (Takikawa, 1891–1962): Kyoto University law professor. He was a central figure in the **Takigawa Affair,** or second **Kyōdai Jiken** of 1933. After the war Takigawa was reinstated as professor and then elected president of the university in 1953.

TANAKA KŌTARŌ (1890–1974): Tokyo University law professor, department chairman (1939). He was an important spokesman for the university during the struggle with General **Araki Sadao.** Tanaka was postwar minister of education (1946–1947), was elected to the House of Councillors, and was appointed chief justice of the Supreme Court (1950–1960).

THREE TARŌS: *San Tarō.* This is a nickname for the trio **Ōmori Yoshitarō, Hirano Yoshitarō,** and **Yamada Moritarō,** all graduates at Tokyo University in the early 1920s who gained reputations for leftist political activities; they were forced to resign from their academic positions in the 1928–1930 crackdowns on campus Marxists.

TŌDAI: the common abbreviation for Tōkyō Teikoku Daigaku (Tokyo Imperial University) or, since 1945, Tōkyō Daigaku (University of Tokyo). The university is also referred to simply as Teidai (the Imperial U.), especially prior to the creation of the second imperial university at Kyoto.

TOMII MASAAKI (1858–1935): Tokyo University law professor. He was a leading figure in the drafting of the 1890 civil code as well as a participant in the **Affair of the Seven Ph.D.s.**

TOMIZU AFFAIR: *Tomizu jiken;* see the **Affair of the Seven Ph.D.s.**

TOMIZU HIROTO (Hirondo, 1861–1935): Tokyo University law professor. He was the central figure in the 1905 **Affair of the Seven Ph.D.s.** Tomizu studied at Middle Temple in London after his 1881 graduation from Tokyo University Law College. Although reinstated following the 1905 clash with the government, Tomizu eventually went into private law practice.

TOYAMA SHŌICHI (Masakazu, 1848–1900): dean of the Tokyo University College of Letters, Tokyo University president (1897–1898), Education Minister (1898). Trained in sociology at the University of Michigan, Toyama was also known as an influential literary critic.

UESUGI SHINKICHI (1878–1929): Tokyo University professor of constitutional law (1909–1929). He was the major intellectual adversary of **Minobe Tatsukichi**, and an important influence on right-wing students and journalists such as **Minoda Muneki** (see chapter 4).

UNIVERSITY COUNCIL: Daigaku Hyōgikai. This was the faculty Senate of elected representatives and department chairmen at Tokyo Imperial University (see chapter 3).

WASEDA UNIVERSITY: founded by prominent politician Ōkuma Shigenobu in 1882 as Tokyo Senmon Gakkō (Tokyo College), changed name to Waseda Daigaku in 1902. With Keiō University, it was one of the two leading private institutions of higher education in prewar Japan.

YAHAGI EIZŌ (1870–1933): Tokyo University professor of law and economics, economics chairman (1923–1931). He graduated from the law faculty in 1895 and served in that department from 1901 until he was transferred to the new Economics Department.

YAMADA MORITARŌ (1897–1980): Tokyo University associate professor of economics. A graduate from Tokyo University in economics (1923) who was appointed associate professor in 1925, he was one of the **Three Tarōs** who were forced to resign in the 1928–1930 crackdown on radical activities on campus (see chapter 5). He subsequently collaborated with **Hirano Yoshitaro** as one of the four chief editors for an influential collection of essays by members of the Kōza faction of Marxist scholars. After World War II he returned to Tokyo University to teach until 1957 while also serving as an influential ideologue for the postwar Marxist movement.

YAMAKAWA KENJIRŌ (Yamagawa, 1854–1931): Tokyo University science professor, dean, president. He served as president from 1901 to 1905 during the **Tomizu Affair** and again from 1913 to 1920 during the **Sawayanagi Affair** and the **Morito Case**. He was also president of Kyoto University and was influential in the university reforms of 1918.

YANAIHARA TADAO (Yanaibara, 1893–1961): Tokyo University economics professor, postwar Tokyo University president. A Christian pacifist who resigned in 1937 under attack for his opposition to the invasion of China, Yanaihara returned to the Tokyo University faculty in 1945 and served as its president between 1951 and 1957.

YŌGAKUSHO: see **Institute for Western Studies.**

YOSHINO SAKUZŌ (1878–1933): Tokyo University law professor, important political party activist in the 1910s and 1920s. He aided in the founding of Yūaikai (the Friendly Society), Japan's first viable trade union organization, and the youth association Shinjinkai (New Men Society). Yoshino resigned his professorship in 1924 to devote full-time attention to the social democratic party movement.

YŌSHO SHIRABESHO: see **Institute for Western Studies.**

List of Works Consulted

Abbreviations in Notes

Abe, *Teikoku Gikai*. See Abe Isoo, ed. *Teikoku Gikai giji kyōiku sōran*.
Danshaku Yamakawa. See Danshaku Yamakawa Sensei Kinenkai, eds. *Danshaku Yamakawa sensei den*.
Kawai zenshū. See Kawai Eijirō. *Kawai Eijirō zenshū*.
Monbushō, *Meiji ikō*. See Monbushō, Kyōikushi Hensankai, eds. *Meiji ikō kyōiku seido hattatsushi*.
Naikaku, *Tōkei nenkan*. See Naikaku Tōkei Kyoku. *Nihon teikoku tōkei nenkan*.
Tōdai, *Gakujutsu taikan*. See Tōkyō Teikoku Daigaku. *Tōkyō Teikoku Daigaku gakujutsu taikan*.
Tōdai, *Gojūnenshi*. See Tōkyō Teikoku Daigaku. *Tōkyō Teikoku Daigaku gojūnenshi*.
Tōdai, *Hyakunenshi*. See Tōkyō Daigaku Hyakunenshi Henshūiinkai, eds. *Tōkyō Daigaku hyakunenshi*.
Tōdai, "Hyōgikai kirokushō." See "Teikoku Daigaku Hyōgikai kirokushō."
Tōdai, *Keizaigakubu*. See Tōkyō Daigaku Keizaigakubu. *Tōkyō Daigaku Keizaigakubu gojūnenshi*.

Works Consulted

Abe Isoo, ed. *Teikoku Gikai gigi kyōiku sōran* (A digest of the proceedings of the Imperial Diet regarding education). 4 vols. Tokyo: Kōseikaku Shoten, 1932–1935.

Abosch, David. "Katō Hiroyuki and the Introduction of German Political Thought in Modern Japan, 1868–1883." Ph.D. diss., University of California, 1964.

Ahn, Choong-sik. "The Japanese Cabinet Ministers: Change and Continuity, 1885 through 1965." Ph.D. diss., Columbia University, 1973.

Akashi Hirotaka and Matsuura Sōzō. *Shōwa tōkō dan'atsushi I: Chishikijin ni taisuru dan'atsu, 1930–1945* (The history of suppression by the special higher police during the Shōwa period, I: Suppression of intellectuals, 1930–1945). Tokyo: Taihei Shuppansha, 1975.

Amano Ikuo. "Continuity and Change in the Structure of Japanese Higher Education." In *Changes in the Japanese University: A Comparative Perspective,* edited by William K. Cummings, Ikuo Amano, and Kazuyuki Kitagawa, 10–39. New York: Praeger, 1979.

———. *Kyūsei senmon gakkō: Kindaika no yakuwari o minaosu* (Professional schools in the old system: Reconsidering their role in modernization). Tokyo: Nihon Keizai Shinbunsha, 1978.

Anesaki Masaharu. "Daigaku kyōju no jiyū to sono seisai [The freedom of university professors and its restraint]." *Kokka Gakkai zasshi* 19, no. 10 (October 1905): 43–47.

Aono Hidekichi. "Daigaku kōba kara shakai ichiba e [From the university factory to society's marketplace]." *Kaizō* (April 1930): 118–124.

Aono Suekichi. "Tōkyō Teikoku Daigaku ron [A discussion of Tokyo Imperial University]." *Kaizō* (October 1929): 28–46.

Aonuma Yoshimatsu. *Nihon no keieisō: Sono shusshin to seikaku* (The managerial class in Japan: Its background and character). Tokyo: Nihon Keizai Shinbunsha, 1965.

Arima, Tatsuo. *The Failure of Freedom: A Portrait of Modern Japanese Intellectuals.* Cambridge, Mass.: Harvard University Press, 1969.

Arisawa Hiromi. *Gakumon to shisō to ningen to: Wasureenu hitobito o omoide* (Scholarship, thought, and human beings: Remembering unforgettable people). Tokyo: Mainichi Shinbunsha, 1957.

Asahi Jānaru, eds. *Nihon no shisōka* (Japanese thinkers). 3 vols. Tokyo: Asahi Shinbunsha, 1963.

Asō Makoto. *Daigaku to jinzai yōsei* (The university and the training of talent). Tokyo: Chūōkōronsha, 1970.

———. *Erīto to kyōiku* (Elites and education). Tokyo: Kamimura Shuppan, 1967.

———. "Meijiki ni okeru kōtō kyōiku no erīto keisei kinō ni kansuru kenkyū [A study of the elite formative function of higher education in the Meiji era]." *Kyōikugaku kenkyū* 36, no. 2 (1963): 109–124.

———. "Shidōsha yōsei [The training of leaders]." In *Nihon no kōtō kyōiku,* edited by Shimizu Yoshihirō, 47–100. Tokyo: Dalichi Hōki Shuppan Kaisha, 1968.

Austin, Lewis, ed. *Japan: The Paradox of Progress.* New Haven, Conn.: Yale University Press, 1976.

Azumi, Koya. *Higher Education and Business Recruitment in Japan.* New York: Teachers College, 1969.

Backus, Robert L. "The Kansei Prohibition of Heterodoxy and Its Effect on Education." *Harvard Journal of Asiatic Studies* 39 (1979): 55–106.

———. "The Motivation of Confucian Orthodoxy in Tokugawa Japan." *Harvard Journal of Asiatic Studies* 39 (1979): 275–338.

———. "The Relationship of Confucianism to the Tokugawa Bakufu as Revealed in the Kansei Educational Reform." *Harvard Journal of Asiatic Studies* 34 (1974): 97–162.

Baerwald, Hans. *The Purge of Japanese Leaders Under the Occupation.* Berkeley and Los Angeles: University of California Press, 1957.

Baldridge, J. Victor. *Power and Conflict in the University: Research in the Sociology of Complex Organizations.* New York: John Wiley and Sons, 1971.

Bamba, Nobuya. *Japanese Diplomacy in a Dilemma: New Light on Japan's Foreign Policy, 1924–1929.* Vancouver: University of British Columbia Press, 1972.

Bamba Nobuya and John F. Howes, eds. *Pacifism in Japan: The Christian and Socialist Tradition.* Vancouver: University of British Columbia Press, 1978.

Barshay, Andrew E. *State and the Intellectual in Imperial Japan: The Public Man in Crisis.* Berkeley and Los Angeles: University of California Press, 1988.

Bartholomew, James R. *The Formation of Science in Japan: Building a Research Tradition.* New Haven, Conn.: Yale University Press, 1989.

———. "Japanese Modernization and the Imperial Universities, 1876–1920." *Journal of Asian Studies* 37, no. 2 (February 1978): 251–271.

Beauchamp, Edward R. *An American Teacher in Early Meiji Japan.* Honolulu: University of Hawaii Press, 1976.

Beauchamp, Edward R., and Richard Rubinger. *Education in Japan: A Source Book.* New York: Garland, 1989.

Beckmann, George M., and Okubo Genji. *The Japanese Communist Party, 1922–1945.* Stanford, Calif.: Stanford University Press, 1969.

Bennett, John W., Herbert Passin, and Robert K. McKnight. *In Search of Identity: The Japanese Overseas Scholar in America and Japan.* Minneapolis: University of Minnesota Press, 1958.

Berger, Gordon Mark. *Parties Out of Power in Japan, 1931–1941.* Princeton, N.J.: Princeton University Press, 1977.

Bernstein, Gail. *Japanese Marxist: A Portrait of Kawakami Hajime, 1879–1946.* Cambridge, Mass.: Harvard University Press, 1976.

———. "Kawakami Hajime: A Japanese Marxist in Search of the Way." In *Japan in Crisis: Essays in Taishō Democracy,* edited by Bernard S. Silberman and H. D. Harootunian, 86–109. Princeton, N.J.: Princeton University Press, 1974.

Borg, Dorothy, and Shumpei Okamoto, eds. *Pearl Harbor as History.* New York: Columbia University Press, 1972.

Braisted, William Reynolds, trans. *Meiroku Zasshi: Journal of the Japanese Enlightenment.* Cambridge, Mass.: Harvard University Press, 1976.

Brown, Arlo Ayres, III. "The Great Tokyo Riot: The History and Historiography of the Hibiya Incendiary Incident of 1905." Ph.D. diss., Columbia University, 1986.

Clark, Terry N. *Prophets and Patrons: The French University and the Emergence of the Social Sciences.* Cambridge, Mass.: Harvard University Press, 1973.

Colbert, Evelyn S. *The Left Wing in Japanese Politics*. New York: Institute of Pacific Relations, 1952.

Cole, Allan B., George O. Totten, and Cecil H. Uyehara. *Socialist Parties in Postwar Japan*. New Haven, Conn.: Yale University Press, 1966.

Coleman, James S., ed. *Education and Political Development*. Princeton, N.J.: Princeton University Press, 1965.

Crowley, James B. "Intellectuals as Visionaries of the New Asian Order." In *Dilemmas of Growth in Prewar Japan*, edited by James William Morley, 319–373. Princeton, N.J.: Princeton University Press, 1971.

Cummings, William K. "The Conservatives Reform Higher Education." *The Japan Interpreter* 8, no. 4 (Winter 1974): 421–431.

———. *Nihon no daigaku kyōju* (The Japanese college professor). Tokyo: Shiseidō, 1972.

———. "The Problems and Prospects for Japanese Higher Education." In *Japan: The Paradox of Progress*, edited by Lewis Austin, 57–87. New Haven, Conn.: Yale University Press, 1976.

Cummings, William K., Ikuo Amano, and Kazuyuki Kitamura, eds. *Changes in the Japanese University: A Comparative Perspective*. New York: Praeger, 1979.

Curtis, Gerald L. *The Japanese Way of Politics*. New York: Columbia University Press, 1988.

"Daigaku kyōju no himen ni kansuru kōshō tenmatsu [An account of the negotiations concerning the dismissal of university professors]." *Kyōto Hōgakkai zasshi* 9, no. 1 (January 1914): 1–18.

"Daigaku kyōju no ninmen ni kansuru jigyō no keika oyobi kaiketsu [The development and resolution of the issues concerning the appointment and dismissal of university professors]." *Kyōto Hōgakkai zasshi* 9, no. 2 (February 1914): 1–5.

"Daigaku oyobi seifu no kokkakan ni tsuite [On the nationalist view of the government and the university]." *Kaizō* (July 1923): 1.

Daijinmei jiten (Biographical dictionary). 10 vols. Tokyo: Heibonsha, 1958.

Danshaku Yamakawa Sensei Kinenkai, eds. *Danshaku Yamakawa sensei den* (The biography of Baron Yamakawa). Tokyo: Iwanami Shoten, 1939.

Davis, Sandra T. W. *Intellectual Change and Political Development in Early Modern Japan: Ono Azusa, a Case Study*. Rutherford, N.J.: Associated University Presses, 1980.

Dore, R. P. *Education in Tokugawa Japan*. Berkeley and Los Angeles: University of California Press, 1965.

———. "Education: Japan." In *Modernization in Japan and Turkey*, edited by Robert E. Ward and Dankwart A. Rustow, 176–204. Princeton, N.J.: Princeton University Press, 1964.

———. "The Modernizer as a Special Case: Japanese Factory Legislation, 1882–1911." *Comparative Studies in Society and History* 2, no. 4 (October 1969): 433–450.

Dōshisha Daigaku Jinbunkagaku Kenkyūjo, eds. *Senjige teikōkenkyū: Kurisutosha, jiyūshugisha no baai* (Studies on wartime resistance: Cases of Christians and liberals). Tokyo: Misuzu Shobō, 1968.

Duke, Ben C. "The Struggle for Control of the Japanese University: The

Prospects for Continued University Autonomy." *Journal of Higher Education* 35, no. 1 (January 1964): 19–26.

Duus, Peter. "Liberal Intellectuals and Social Conflict in Taishō Japan." In *Conflict in Modern Japanese History,* edited by Tetsuo Najita and J. Victor Koschmann, 412–440. Princeton, N.J.: Princeton University Press, 1982.

———. "Yoshino Sakuzō: The Christian as Political Critic." *Journal of Japanese Studies* 4, no. 2 (Summer 1978): 301–326.

Edinger, Lewis J., ed. *Political Leadership in Industrialized Societies.* New York: Wiley, 1967.

Egami Teruhiko. *Kawai Eijirō den* (Biography of Kawai Eijirō). Tokyo: Shakai Shisōsha, 1971.

Epp, Robert. "The Challenge from Tradition: Attempts to Compile a Civil Code in Japan, 1866–1878." *Monumenta Nipponica* 22 (1967): 15–48.

———. "Threat to Tradition: The Reaction to Japan's 1890 Civil Code." Ph.D. diss., Harvard University, 1964.

Fisher, Jerry K. "The Meirokusha." Ph.D. diss., University of Virginia, 1974.

———. "The Meirokusha and the Building of a Strong and Prosperous Nation." In *Japan Examined: Perspectives on Modern Japanese History,* edited by Harry Wray and Hilary Conroy, 83–89. Honolulu: University of Hawaii Press, 1983.

Fogel, Joshua A. *Politics and Sinology: The Case of Naitō (1866–1934).* Cambridge, Mass.: Council on East Asian Studies, Harvard University, 1984.

Fridell, Wilbur M. "Government Ethics Textbooks in Late Meiji Japan." *Journal of Asian Studies* 29, no. 4 (August 1970): 823–833.

Fujii Akira. "Jiyūshugi no botsuraku [The failure of liberalism]." *Kokugakuin zasshi* (May 1937): 20–27.

———. "Kawai Kyōju no kokkashugi hihan ni tsuite [Concerning Professor Kawai's criticism of nationalism]." *Kokugakuin zasshi* (November 1934): 6–26.

Fujita, Wakao. "Yanaihara Tadao: Disciple of Uchimura Kanzō and Nitobe Inazō." In *Pacifism in Japan: The Christian and Socialist Tradition,* edited by Nobuya Bamba and John F. Howes, 199–219. Vancouver: University of British Columbia Press, 1978.

Fukumoto Kunio. *Gakubatsu, ningenbatsu, shihonbatsu* (School, personal, and capital cliques). Tokyo: Chiseisha, 1959.

Fukuzawa Yukichi. *Fukuzawa Yukichi zenshū* (The complete works of Fukuzawa Yukichi). Edited by Keiō Gijuku. Vol. 5. Tokyo: Iwanami Shoten, 1959.

Gakugei Jiyū Dōmei, ed. *Kyōdai mondai hihan* (A critique of the Kyoto University problem). Kyoto: Seikeisho, 1933.

Garon, Sheldon. *State and Labor in Modern Japan.* Berkeley and Los Angeles: University of California Press, 1987.

Gordon, Andrew. *Labor and Imperial Democracy in Japan.* Berkeley and Los Angeles: University of California Press, 1991.

Gotoda, Teruo. *The Local Politics of Kyoto.* Berkeley: Institute of East Asian Studies, University of California, 1985.

Griffis, William Elliott. *The Mikado's Empire.* 2d ed. New York: Harper and Brothers, 1877.

————. *Verbeck of Japan: A Citizen of No Country*. New York: Fleming H. Revell, 1900.

Groennings, Sven, F. W. Kelly, and Michael Leiserson, eds. *The Study of Coalition Behavior*. New York: Holt, Rinehart and Winston, 1970.

Hall, Ivan P. *Mori Arinori*. Cambridge, Mass.: Harvard University Press, 1973.

————. "Organizational Paralysis: The Case of Todai." In *Modern Japanese Organization and Decision-Making*, edited by Ezra F. Vogel, 304–330. Berkeley and Los Angeles: University of California Press, 1975.

Hall, John W. "The Confucian Teacher in Tokugawa Japan." In *Confucianism in Action*, edited by Davis S. Nivison and Arthur F. Wright, 286–301. Stanford, Calif.: Stanford University Press, 1959.

Hall, Robert King. *Education for a New Japan*. New Haven, Conn.: Yale University Press, 1949.

Hara Heizō. "Bansho Shirabesho no sōsetsu [The establishment of the Office for the Study of Barbarian Materials]." *Rekishigaku kenkyū*, no. 103 (1942): 1–42.

————. "Tokugawa bakufu no Eikoku ryūgakusei [Students sent to England by the Tokugawa shogunate]." *Rekishi chiri* 79, no. 5 (May 1942): 21–50.

————. "Wagakuni saisho no Rokoku ryūgakusei ni tsuite [Concerning our country's first students to study in Russia]." *Rekishigaku kenkyū* 10, no. 6 (June 1940): 74–92.

Hara Kei. *Hara Kei nikki* (The diary of Hara Kei). Edited by Hara Kei'ichirō. 9 vols. Tokyo: Gengensha, 1950–1951.

Hardacre, Helen. *Shintō and the State, 1868–1988*. Princeton, N.J.: Princeton University Press, 1989.

Harootunian, Harry D. "A Sense of Ending and the Problems of Taisho." In *Japan in Crisis: Essays in Taishō Democracy,* edited by Bernard S. Silberman and H. D. Harootunian. Princeton, N.J.: Princeton University Press, 1974.

————. *Things Seen and Unseen: Discourse and Ideology in Tokugawa Nativism*. Chicago: University of Chicago Press, 1988.

Hasegawa Nyozekan, "Daigaku = kokka no kikan? shakai no kikan? [The university—is it an organ of the state? of the society?]." *Kaizō* (September 1928): 22.

Hatoyama Haruko, ed. *Hatoyama no isshō* (The life of Hatoyama Kazuo). Tokyo: Hatoyama Haruko, 1939.

Havens, Thomas R. H. *Nishi Amane and Modern Japanese Thought*. Princeton, N.J.: Princeton University Press, 1970.

Hayashi Kentarō, ed. *Kaisō Tōkyō Daigaku hyakunen* (Memories of Tokyo University over a hundred years). Tokyo: Bideo Shuppan, 1969.

Higashikawa Tokuhara. *Hakushi Ume Kenjirō* (Doctor Ume Kenjirō). Tokyo: Hōsei Daigaku, 1917.

Hijikata Seibi. *Gakkai shunjūki: Marukushizumu to no kōsō nijūyonen* (A chronicle of academe: More than twenty years of resistance against Marxism). Tokyo: Chūō Keizaisha, 1960.

————. *Jiken wa tōku nari ni keri* (All that happened so long ago). Tokyo: Keizai Ōraisha, 1965.

————. "Watakushi no ayunde kita michi [The road by which I have come]." In *Hijikata Seibi hakase kijū kinen ronbun shū*, edited by Hijikata Seibi Hakase Kiju Kinen Ronbun Shū Kankōkai, 480–492. Tokyo: Kajima Kenkyū Shuppankai, 1967.

Hijikata Seibi Hakase Kiju Kinen Ronbun shū Kankōkai, eds. *Hijikata Seibi hakase kijū kinen ronbun shū* (Essays in honor of the seventy-seventh birthday of Dr. Hijikata Seibi). Tokyo: Kajima Kenkyū Shuppankai, 1967.

Hirai, Atsuko. *Individualism and Socialism: Kawai Eijirō's Life and Thought (1891–1944)*. Cambridge, Mass.: Council on East Asian Studies, Harvard University, 1986.

————. "A Japanese Experiment in Individualism: The Life and Thought of Kawai Eijirō (1891–1944)." Ph.D. diss., Harvard University, 1973.

Hirano Yoshitarō—Hito to Gakumon Henshuiinkai. *Hirano Yoshitarō—hito to gakumon* (Hirano Yoshitarō: The man and his scholarship). Tokyo: Ōtsuki Shoten, 1981.

Hiranuma Kiichirō. *Kaikoroku* (Memoirs). Tokyo: Hiranuma Kiichirō Kaikoroku Hensan Iinkai, 1955.

Hirschmeier, Johannes, and Yui Tsunehiko. *The Development of Japanese Business, 1600–1973*. Cambridge, Mass.: Harvard University Press, 1975.

Horikawa Naoyoshi. "Senji gakkai fūkei [The atmosphere of wartime academe]." *Chūōkōron* 53, no. 4 (April 1938): 370–379.

Hōsei Daigaku Bungakubu Shigaku Kenkyūshitsu, eds. *Nihon jinbutsu bunken mokuroku* (Bibliography of Japanese biographical materials). Tokyo: Heibonsha, 1974.

Hoshino Tōru. *Meiji minpō hensanshi kenkyū* (A study of the history of the compilation of the Meiji civil codes). Tokyo: Daiyamondosha, 1943.

Hoston, Germaine A. *Marxism and the Crisis of Development in Prewar Japan*. Princeton, N.J.: Princeton University Press, 1986.

Ide, Yoshinori, and Takeshi Ishida. "The Education and Recruitment of Governing Elites in Modern Japan." In *Governing Elites: Studies in Training and Selection*, edited by Rupert Wilkinson, 108–134. New York: Oxford University Press, 1969.

Ienaga Saburō. *Daigaku no jiyū no rekishi* (The history of freedom in the university). Tokyo: Hanawa Shobō, 1962.

Ijiri Tsunekichi, ed. *Rekidai kenkanroku* (Record of bureaucratic posts). Tokyo: Hara Shoten, 1967.

Ikazaki Akio. *Daigaku no jisei no rekishi* (A history of the autonomy of the university). Tokyo: Shin Nihon Shuppansha, 1965.

Imai Toshiki. "Daigaku jinji no mondai [The university personnel problem]." *Kaizō* (September 1938): 81–85.

Inoki, Masamichi. "The Civil Bureaucracy: Japan." In *Political Modernization in Japan and Turkey*, edited by Robert E. Ward and Dankwart Rustow, 283–300. Princeton, N.J.: Princeton University Press, 1964.

Inoue Tetsujirō. "Teikoku Daigaku ron [A discussion of the imperial university]." *Taiyō* 12, no. 1 (January 1906): 45–54.

Ishizuki Minoru. *Kindai Nihon no kaigai ryūgakushi* (Overseas study in modern Japanese history). Tokyo: Mineruba Shobō, 1973.

Itō Takashi. "Conflicts and Coalitions in Japan: Political Groups, 1930: The London Naval Disarmament Conference." In *The Study of Coalition Behavior,* edited by Sven Groennings, F. W. Kelly, and Michael Leiserson, 160–176. New York: Holt, Rinehart and Winston, 1970.

———. "The Role of Right-Wing Organizations in Japan." In *Pearl Harbor as History,* edited by Dorothy Borg and Shumpei Okamoto, 487–509. New York: Columbia University Press, 1972.

Itō Yoshio et al., eds. *Kindai Nihon shisōshi kōza* (Lectures on the history of modern Japanese thought). Vol. 5. Tokyo: Chikuma Shobō, 1952.

Itoh, Akira. "Senzenki Nihon ni okeru kōtōkyōiku to shūshokunan mondai [The problem of an excess of higher education graduates in prewar Japan]." *Daigaku Ronshu* 20 (1990): 149–167.

Itoh, Hiroshi, and Lawrence Ward Beer, eds. *The Constitutional Case Law of Japan.* Seattle: University of Washington Press, 1978.

Iwauchi Ryokichi, and William K. Cummings. "Decision-Making Structures in Japanese Universities." *Bulletin of the Tokyo Institute of Technology* 93 (1969): 45–70.

Izeki Kurō, ed. *Dai Nihon hakushi roku* (Japanese holders of the doctorate). 5 vols. Tokyo: Hattensha, 1921–1930.

Jansen, Marius B. *The Japanese and Sun Yat-sen.* Cambridge, Mass.: Harvard University Press, 1954.

———. "New Materials for the Study of the Intellectual History of Nineteenth Century Japan." *Harvard Journal of Asiatic Studies* 20 (1947): 567–597.

———, ed. *Changing Japanese Attitudes Toward Modernization.* Princeton, N.J.: Princeton University Press, 1965.

Jijin Kōshinjo. *Jinji kōshin roku* (A registry of information about people). Tokyo: Jinji Kōshinjo, annually from 1903 to 1939.

Johnson, Chalmers. *Conspiracy at Matsukawa.* Berkeley and Los Angeles: University of California Press, 1972.

———. *An Instance of Treason: Ozaki Hotsumi and the Sorge Spy Ring.* Stanford, Calif.: Stanford University Press, 1964.

———. *MITI and the Japanese Miracle: The Growth of Industrial Policy, 1925–1975.* Stanford, Calif.: Stanford University Press, 1982.

Jones, Hazel J. *Live Machines: Hired Foreigners and Meiji Japan.* Vancouver: University of British Columbia Press, 1980.

———. "The Meiji Government and Foreign Employees, 1868–1900." Ph.D. diss., University of Michigan, 1967.

Kada Tetsuji. "Kyōjukai no igi [The significance of the faculty meeting]." *Kaizō* (September 1938): 85–89.

Kadowaki Teiji. "Kangaku akademizumu no seiritsu [The establishment of government academicism]." In *Nihonshi gakushi* (History of Japanese historiography), edited by Rekishigaku Kenkyūkai and Nihonshi Kenkyūkai, 163–186. Tokyo: Tōkyō Daigaku Shuppankai, 1957.

Kahei Katsuhiko. "Gakusha no kokka ni okeru chii o ronzu [Discussing the place of the scholar in the state]." *Kokka Gakkai zasshi* 19, no. 10 (October 1905): 71–90; 19, no. 11 (November 1905): 72–116.

Kaigo Tokiomi, ed. *Inoue Kowashi no kyōiku seisaku* (The educational policies of Inoue Kowashi). Tokyo: Tōkyō Daigaku Shuppankai, 1968.

————. *Rinji Kyōiku Kaigi no kenkyū* (Research on the special conference on education). Tokyo: Tōkyō Daigaku Shuppankai, 1960.

Kaigo Tokiomi, and Terasaki Masao. "Daigaku no kyōiku [University education]." In *Sengo Nihon no kyōiku kaikaku* (Educational reforms in postwar Japan). Vol. 9. Tokyo: Tōkyō Daigaku Shuppankai, 1969.

Kakegawa Tomihiko, ed. *Shisō tōsei* (Thought control). Vol. 17 of *Gendai shiryō* (Materials on the modern era). Tokyo: Misuzu Shobō, 1962–1980.

Kanai Noboru. "Gakusha no genron ni appaku o kuwauru no fuka naru o toku [Why it is wrong to suppress the speech of scholars]." *Kokka Gakkai zasshi* 9, no. 10 (October 1905): 67–71.

Kanpō (Official gazette). Tokyo: Naikaku Insatsu Kyoku, daily from 1883.

Karasawa Tomitarō. *Gakusei no rekishi—gakusei seikatsu no shakaishiteki kōsatsu* (A history of students—an inquiry into the social history of student life). Tokyo: Sōbunsha, 1955.

————. *Kōshinsei—bakumatsu isshinki no erīto* (Tribute students—an elite of the Restoration in the last years of the shogunate). Tokyo: Gyōsai, 1974.

————. *Kyōkasho no rekishi* (A history of textbooks). Tokyo: Sōbunsha, 1956.

Kasza, Gregory J. *The State and Mass Media in Japan, 1918–1945*. Berkeley and Los Angeles: University of California Press, 1988.

Katō Hiroyuki. "Bansho Shirabesho ni tsuite [Concerning the Office for the Study of Barbarian Materials]." *Shigaku zasshi* 20, no. 7 (July 1909): 80–93.

Kato, Ichiro. "Japanese Universities: Student Revolts and Reform Plans." In *Universities in the Western World*, edited by Paul Seabury, 257–263. New York: Free Press, 1975.

Katō, Shūichi. "Japanese Writers and Modernization." In *Changing Japanese Attitudes Toward Modernization*, edited by Marius B. Jansen, 425–445. Princeton, N.J.: Princeton University Press, 1965.

Kawai Eijirō. "Daigaku gakuen ni okeru jiyūshugi no shimei to omou [Thinking about the mission of liberalism in academe]." *Kaizō* (June 1928): 2–21.

————. "Daigaku no jiyū to wa nani ka [What is academic freedom?]." *Chūōkōron* (November 1930); reprinted in *Kawai Eijirō zenshū*, by Kawai Eijirō, vol. 15, pp. 114–141. Tokyo: Shakai Shisōsha, 1969–1970.

————. "Daigaku no unmei to shimei: Futatabi Morito Tatsuo shi ni kotau [The fate and mission of the university: Responding again to Mr. Morito Tatsuo]." *Teikoku Daigaku shinbun*, February 24, 1930, p. 59; March 3, 1930, p. 65; March 10, 1930, p. 71; March 17, 1930, p. 77; reprinted in *Kawai Eijirō zenshū*, by Kawai Eijirō, vol. 15, pp. 83, 66, 82. Tokyo: Shakai Shisōsha, 1969–1970.

————. "Daigaku no unmei to shimei: Morito Tatsuo shi ni kotau [The fate and mission of the university: Responding to Mr. Morito Tatsuo]." *Teikoku Daigaku shinbun*, December 9, 1929, pp. 549, 557; reprinted in *Kawai Eijirō zenshū*, by Kawai Eijirō, vol. 15, pp. 66–82. Tokyo: Shakai Shisōsha, 1969–1970.

————. *Daigaku seikatsu no hansei* (Reflections on a life in the university). Tokyo: Nihon Hyōronsha, 1931.

————. *Kanai Noboru no shōgai to gakuseki* (The life and scholarly achievements of Kanai Noboru). Tokyo: Nihon Hyōronsha, 1939.

————. *Kawai Eijirō zenshū* (The complete works of Kawai Eijirō). 24 vols. Tokyo: Shakai Shisōsha, 1969–1970.

————. "Ken'o subeki gakkai no ichi keikō [One trend in the academic world we should abhor]." *Kaizō* (October 1929); 37–43.

————. "Kokka, daigaku, daigakurei [The state, the university and the university ordinance]." *Keizai ōrai* (July 1933); reprinted in *Kawai Eijirō zenshū*, by Kawai Eijirō, vol. 11, pp. 217–232. Tokyo: Shakai Shisōsha, 1969–1970.

————. *Kyōdan seikatsu nijūnen* (Twenty years of life at the lectern). Tokyo: Onitaka Shobō, 1948; reprinted from *Nihon hyōron* (April and May 1939).

————. *Meiji shisōshi no ichi danmen—Kanai Noboru o chūshin to shite* (One aspect of Meiji intellectual history—centering on Kanai Noboru). Tokyo: Nihon Hyōronsha, 1941.

————. "Minobe mondai no hihan [A critique of the Minobe question]." *Teikoku Daigaku shinbun*, April 15, 1935; reprinted in *Kawai Eijirō zenshū*, by Kawai Eijirō, Vol. 12, pp. 11–17. Tokyo: Shakai Shisōsha, 1969–1970.

————. *Nikki* (Diary). Vols. 22 and 23 of *Kawai Eijirō zenshū*.

————. "Niniroku jiken no hihan [A criticism of the February 26 incident]." *Teikoku Daigaku shinbun*, January 19, 1931; reprinted in *Kawai Eijirō zenshū*, by Kawai Eijirō, Vol. 12, pp. 45–50. Tokyo: Shakai Shisōsha, 1969–1970.

————. "Shūshokunan to daigaku kyōiku [The employment problem and university education]." *Teikoku Daigaku shinbun*, January 19, 1931.

————. "Takigawa jiken to daigaku jiyū no mondai [The Takigawa affair and the question of the freedom of the university]." *Teikoku Daigaku shinbun*, May 29, 1933, p. 187; reprinted in *Kawai Eijirō zenshū*, by Kawai Eijirō, Vol. 11, pp. 205–215. Tokyo: Shakai Shisōsha, 1969–1970.

Kawai Eijirō and Rōyama Masamichi. *Gakusei shisō mondai* (The student thought problem). Tokyo: Iwanami Shoten, 1932.

Kawakami Hajime. *Jijoden* (Autobiography). Tokyo: Iwanami Shoten, 1962.

Kazahaya Yasoji. *Nihon shakai seisakushi* (A history of social policy in Japan). 2d ed. Tokyo: Nihon Hyōronsha, 1947.

Keiō Gijuku, eds. *Keiō Gijuku gojūnenshi* (Fifty years of Keiō Gijuku). Tokyo: Keiō Gijuku, 1907.

————. *Keiō Gijuku hyakunenshi* (One hundred years of Keiō Gijuku). 6 vols. Tokyo: Keiō Gijuku, 1969.

Keller, Suzanne. *Beyond the Ruling Class: Strategic Elites in Modern Societies.* New York: Random House, 1963.

Kim, Paul S. *Japan's Civil Service System: Its Structure, Personnel, and Politics.* Westport, Conn.: Greenwood Press, 1988.

Kindai Nihon Kyōiku Seido Shiryō Hensankai, eds. *Kindai Nihon kyōiku seido shiryō* (Historical materials on the modern Japanese education system). 35 vols. Tokyo: Dai Nihon Yūbenkai Kōdansha Kaisha, 1956–1969.

Kinzley, W. Dean. *Industrial Harmony in Modern Japan: The Invention of a Tradition*. London: Routledge, 1991.

Kishimoto Eitarō. *Nihon zettaishugi no shakai seisakushi* (A history of social policies of Japanese absolutism). Tokyo: Yūhikaku, 1955.

Kitamura, Kazuyuki, and William K. Cummings. "The 'Big Bang' Theory and Japanese University Reform." *Comparative Educational Review* 16, no. 2 (June 1972): 303–324.

Kōdansha Encyclopedia of Japan. 9 vols. Tokyo: Kōdansha, 1983.

Kokuritsu Kyōiku Kenkyūjo Daiichi Kenkyūbu. *Rinji kyōiku kaigi monjo mokuroku* (Index to documents concerning the special conferences on education). Tokyo: Kokuritsu Kyōiku Kenkyūjo, 1977.

Kokusai Bunka Shinkokai. *Introduction to Contemporary Japanese Literature*. Tokyo: Kokusai Bunka Shinkokai, 1939.

"Kubi kirareta daigaku kyōju retsuden [Biographical sketches of fired professors]." *Chūōkōron* 48, no. 7 (July 1933): 234–243.

Kublin, Hyman. *Meiji rōdō undōshi no issetsu: Takano Fusatarō shōgai to shisō* (One aspect of the Meiji labor movement: The life and thought of Takano Fusatarō). Tokyo: Yūhikaku, 1959.

Kubota, Akira. *Higher Civil Servants in Postwar Japan: Their Social Origins, Educational Backgrounds, and Career Patterns*. Princeton, N.J.: Princeton University Press, 1969.

Kure Shuzō. *Mitsukuri Genpō* (Mitsukuri Genpō). Tokyo: Dai Nihon Tosho, 1914.

Kuwahara Takeo, ed. *Nihon no meicho: Kindai no shisō* (Masterpieces of Japan: Modern thought). Tokyo: Chūkō Shinsho, 1962.

Kyōchōkai, ed. *Saikin no shakai undō* (Recent social movements). Tokyo: Kyōchōkai, 1929.

Kyōto Daigaku Shichijūnenshi Henshū Iinkai, eds. *Kyōto Daigaku shichijūnenshi* (The seventy-year history of Kyoto University). Kyoto: Kyōto Daigaku Shichijūnenshi Henshū Iinkai, 1967.

"Kyōto Teikoku Daigaku hōgakubu shukuin sōjishoku ni kansuru seimei [Statement of the staff of the Kyoto Imperial University Law Department regarding their joint resignation]." *Hōgaku ronsō* 29, no. 6 (June 1933): 1–9.

Large, Stephen S. *The Yūaikai, 1912–1919: The Rise of Labor in Japan*. Tokyo: Sophia University, 1972.

Maeda Tatsuo. "Nihon shihonshugi to daigaku: Hōgakubu [Japanese capitalism and the university: The Law Department]." In *Daigaku mondai no hōshakaigakuteki kenkyū*, edited by Nihon Hōshakai Gakki. Tokyo: Yōhikaku, 1970.

Maki Tetsu. "Sayoku kyōju jishoku no rimen [The inside story of the resignation of the leftist professors]." *Chūōkōron* 45, no. 9 (September 1930): 190–202.

Mannari, Hiroshi. *The Japanese Business Leaders*. Tokyo: Tokyo University Press, 1974.

Marshall, Byron K. "Academic Factionalism in Japan: The Case of the Tōdai

Economics Department, 1919–1939," *Modern Asian Studies* 12, no. 4 (1978): 529–551.

―――. *Capitalism and Nationalism in Prewar Japan: The Ideology of the Business Elite, 1868–1941*. Stanford, Calif.: Stanford University Press, 1967.

―――. "Growth and Conflict in Japanese Higher Education, 1905–1930." In *Conflict in Modern Japanese History: The Neglected Tradition*, edited by Tetsuo Najita and J. Victor Koschmann, 276–294. Princeton, N.J.: Princeton University Press, 1982.

―――. "Professors and Politics: The Meiji Academic Elite." *Journal of Japanese Studies* 3, no. 1 (Winter 1977): 71–97.

―――. "The Tradition of Conflict in the Governance of Japan's Imperial Universities." *History of Education Quarterly* 17, no. 4 (Winter 1977): 385–406.

―――. "Universal Social Dilemmas and Japanese Educational History: The Writings of R. P. Dore." *History of Education Quarterly* 12, no. 1 (Spring 1972): 97–106.

Marsland, Stephen E. *The Birth of the Japanese Labor Union Movement: Takano Fusatarō and the Rōdō Kumiai Kiseikai*. Honolulu: University of Hawaii Press, 1989.

Matsunari Yoshie, Izumtani Hajime, Tanuma Hajime, and Noda Masao. *Nihon no sarariiman* (The Japanese salaryman). Tokyo: Aoki Shōten, 1957.

McMullen, I. J. "Non-Agnatic Adoption: A Confucian Controversy in Seventeenth- and Eighteenth-Century Japan." *Harvard Journal of Asiatic Studies* 40 (1980): 133–189.

Meiji Bunka Shiryō Sōsho Kankōkai, eds. *Meiji bunka shiryō sōsho: Dai hakkan kyōiku hen* (Collection of materials on Meiji culture: Volume 8, education). Tokyo: Kazama Shobō, 1961.

Metzger, Walter P. *Academic Freedom in the Age of the University*. New York: Columbia University Press, 1955.

Metzger, Walter P., Sanford H. Kadish, Arthur DeBardeleben, and Edward J. Bloustein. *Dimensions of Academic Freedom*. Urbana: University of Illinois Press, 1969.

Miller, Frank O. *Minobe Tatsukichi: Interpreter of Constitutionalism in Japan*. Berkeley and Los Angeles: University of California Press, 1965.

Minear, Richard. *Japanese Tradition and Western Law: Emperor, State, and Law in the Thought of Hozumi Yatsuka*. Cambridge, Mass.: Harvard University Press, 1970.

Ministry of Education. *Higher Education in Postwar Japan: The Ministry of Education's 1964 White Paper*. Edited and translated by John E. Blewett. Tokyo: Sophia University Press, 1965.

Ministry of Education. *Japan's Growth and Education: Educational Development in Relation to Socio-Economic Growth*. Tokyo: Ministry of Education, 1963.

Ministry of Education, Research Bureau. *Demand and Supply for University Graduates—Japan: 1958*. Tokyo: Ministry of Education, 1958.

Minobe Ryōkichi. *Kumon suru demokurashī* (Democracy in agony). Tokyo: Bungei Shunjusha, 1959.

Minobe Tatsukichi. "Kenryoku no ran'yo to kore ni taisuru hankō [The misuse of power and resistance to it]." *Kokka Gakkai zasshi* 19, no. 10 (October 1905): 67–71.

Mitchell, Richard H. *Censorship in Imperial Japan.* Princeton, N.J.: Princeton University Press, 1983.

———. "Japan's Peace Preservation Law of 1925: Its Origins and Significance." *Monumenta Nipponica* 28 (1973): 317–345.

———. *Thought Control in Prewar Japan.* Ithaca, N.Y.: Cornell University Press, 1976.

Miyaji Masato. "Morito jiken: Gakumon no jiyū no hajime no shiren [The Morito case: The first test of academic freedom]." In *Nihon seiji saiban shiroku: Taishō,* edited by Wagatsuma Sakae et al., 228–272. Tokyo: Daiichi Hōki Kaisha, 1969.

Miyamoto Hideo. "Kyōdai mondai no shinsō o katari." *Chūōkōron* (July 1933); reprinted in *Kyōdai jiken,* edited by Sasaki Sōichi et al., 309–339. Tokyo: Iwanami Shoten, 1933.

Miyazawa Toshiyoshi. *Tennō kikansetsu jiken: Shiryō wa kataru* (The emperor-as-organ theory affair: A discussion of the source materials). 2 vols. Tokyo: Yūhikaku, 1970.

Monbushō. *Gakusei hachijūnenshi* (The school system over the past eighty years). Tokyo: Monbushō, 1954.

———. *Gakusei hyakunenshi* (The school system over the past hundred years). 2 vols. Tokyo: Teikoku Chihō Gyōseikai, 1972.

———. *Gakusei kyūjūnenshi* (The school system over the past ninety years). Tokyo: Ōkurashō Insatsu Kyoku, 1964.

———. *Monbushō nenpō* (Annual report of the Education Ministry). Tokyo: Monbushō, annually from 1875.

———. *Nihon kyōikushi shiryō* (Materials on the history of Japanese education). 21 vols. Tokyo: Monbushō Daijin Kanpō Hōkokuka, 1892.

———. *Wagakuni no kōtō kyōiku: Sengo ni okeru kōtō kyōiku no ayumi* (Higher education in our country: Progress of higher education after the war). Tokyo: Monbushō, 1964.

———. *Wagakuni no shiritsu gakkō* (Private schools in our country). Tokyo: Monbushō, 1968.

Monbushō, Chōsa Fukyūkoku Chōsaka. *Daigaku kankei hōrei no enkaku* (The development of laws relating to universities). 4 vols. Tokyo: Monbushō, 1949–1950.

Monbushō, Chōsakyoku. *Nihon no seichō to kyōiku: Kyōiku no hatten to keizai no hattatsu* (Growth and education in Japan: Educational development and economic progress). Tokyo: Teikoku Chihō Gyōsei Gakkai, 1962.

Monbushō, Daigakuka. *Nihon hakushi roku* (A registry of Japanese doctorate degree holders). Tokyo: Kyōiku Gyōsei Kenkyūjo, 1956.

Monbushō, Kyōikushi Hensankai. *Meiji ikō kyōiku seido hattatsushi* (The history of the development of the education system from the beginning of Meiji). 12 vols. Tokyo: Ryūginsha, 1938–1939; revised edition, 1964–1965.

Monbushō, Senmon Gakumu Kyoku. *Gakui roku* (Registry of degrees). 14 vols. Tokyo: Monbushō, 1922–1936.

Monbushō, Shisō Kyoku. "Shisō chōsa shiryō: Daiichi—sanjūsanshū [Materials from survey on thought: Volumes 1–33]." Unpublished ms. stamped "secret," March 1936.

———. *Shisō kyoku yōkō* (Thought Bureau digest). Tokyo: Monbushō, 1934.

Monbushō, Shisōmondai Kenkyūkai, eds. *Shisō mondai no tenbō to hihan* (Critiques and observations on the thought problem). Tokyo: Shakai Kyōikukai, 1933.

"Monshō haiseki undō [Movement to oust minister of education]." *Kyōiku Jiron* 998 (January 5, 1913): 43–44.

Mori Arinori. *Mori Arinori zenshū* (The complete works of Mori Arinori). Tokyo: Senbundō, 1972.

Morito Tatsuo. "Daigaku no saikyō [The restoring of the university: Replying to Professor Kawai]." *Teikoku Daigaku shinbun,* January 27, 1930, p. 3; February 3, 1930, p. 2; February 10, 1930, p. 3; February 17, 1930, p. 3.

———. "Daigaku no tenraku [The fall of the university]." *Kaizō* (September 1929): 2–22.

Morley, James William, ed. *Dilemmas of Growth in Prewar Japan.* Princeton, N.J.: Princeton University Press, 1971.

Nagai Michio. "The Development of Intellectuals in the Meiji and Taisho Periods." *Journal of Social and Political Ideas in Japan* 2, no. 1 (April 1964): 28–32.

———. *Higher Education in Japan: Its Takeoff and Crash.* Translated by Jerry Dusenbury. Tokyo: University of Tokyo Press, 1971.

———. *Nihon no daigaku: Sangyō shakai ni hatasu yakuwari* (The Japanese university: Its role in industrial society). Tokyo: Chūōkōronsha, 1965.

Nagai Michio, ed. *Nihon no kyōiku shisō* (Educational thought in Japan). Tokyo: Tokuma Shoten, 1967.

Naikaku Tōkei Kyoku. *Nihon teikoku tōkei nenkan* (Statistical annual of the Japanese empire). Tokyo: Naikaku Tōkei Kyoku, annually.

Naimushō Keihōkyoku. *Shakai undō no jōkyō: Shōwa 2–17* (Conditions in the social movements: 1927–1942). 14 vols. Tokyo: San'ichi Shobō, 1971–1972.

Najita, Tetsuo. *Hara Kei in the Politics of Compromise, 1905–1915.* Cambridge, Mass.: Harvard University Press, 1967.

———. "Some Reflections on Idealism in the Political Thought of Yoshino Sakuzō." In *Japan in Crisis: Essays in Taishō Democracy,* edited by Bernard S. Silberman and H. D. Harootunian. Princeton, N.J.: Princeton University Press, 1974.

Najita, Tetsuo, and J. Victor Koschmann, eds. *Conflict in Modern Japanese History: The Neglected Tradition.* Princeton, N.J.: Princeton University Press, 1982.

Nakamura Yūjirō. *Kindai Nihon ni okeru seido to shisō: Meiji hōshisōshi kenkyū josetsu* (System and thought in modern Japan: An introductory study in the history of Meiji legal thought). Tokyo: Miraisha, 1967.

Nakano Reishirō. *Kume hakase kyūjūnen kaikoroku* (Ninety years of memories of Dr. Kume Kunitake). 2 vols. Tokyo: Waseda Daigaku Shuppanbu, 1934.

Nakayama Shigeru. *Teikoku daigaku no tanjō: Kokusai hikaku no naka de no*

Tōdai (The birth of the imperial university: Tōdai in international comparison). Tokyo: Chūōkōronsha, 1978.

Nanbara Shigeru. "Daigaku to jiji [The university and self-government]." *Teikoku Daigaku shinbun,* September 5, 1938; reprinted in *Nanbara Shigeru chosakushū,* by Nanbara Shigeru, vol. 6, 10–15. Tokyo: Iwanami Shoten, 1972.

————. *Nanbara Shigeru chosakushū* (The works of Nanbara Shigeru). 10 vols. Tokyo: Iwanami Shoten, 1972.

Nanbara Shigeru, Rōyama Masamichi, and Yabe Teiji. *Onozuka Kiheiji* (Onozuka Kiheiji). Tokyo: Iwanami Shoten, 1963.

Niho Kamematsu. "Shisō mondai oyobi Morito jiken to Uesugi kyōju no ronsetsu ni tsuite [Regarding the thought problem, the Morito Affair, and Professor Uesugi's opinions]." *Hōgaku ronsō* 3, no. 3 (March 1920); 315–341.

Nihon Gakushiin, eds. *Nihon Gakushiin hachijūnenshi* (The eighty-year history of the Japan Academy). 5 vols. Tokyo: Nihon Gakushiin, 1961–1963.

Nihon Hōshakai Gakkai, eds. *Daigaku mondai no hōshakaigakuteki kenkyū* (Studies of the university problem from the point of view of the sociology of law). Tokyo: Yūhikaku, 1970.

Nihon Hyōronsha, eds. *Nihon no hōgaku* (The Study of law in Japan). Tokyo: Nihon Hyōronsha, 1950.

Nish, Ian. *The Origins of the Russo-Japanese War.* London: Longman, 1985.

Nivison, David S., and Arthur F. Wright, eds. *Confucianism in Action.* Stanford, Calif.: Stanford University Press, 1959.

Notehelfer, Fred. "Ebina Danjō: A Christian Samurai of the Meiji Period." *Papers on Japan.* Vol. 2. Cambridge, Mass.: Harvard Univ., 1963.

Numada Inejirō. "Rōdōhō" [Labor law]." In *Nihon kindai hō hattatsushi* (A history of the development of modern Japanese law), edited by Ukai Nobushige et al., vol. 5, 207–290. Tokyo: Keisō Shobō, 1958.

Ogata Hiroyasu. "Kōkan ryōgakujo no jittai [The actual conditions in the two schools, the Kōgakujo and the Kangakujo]." *Shakai kagaku tōkyū* 1, no. 2 (June 1956): 89–146.

————. "Meiji shoki Kō Kan Yō sangakuha no kōsō [The struggles in the early Meiji period among the three academic factions: Native, Chinese, and Western]." *Shakai kagaku tōkyū* 1, no. 1 (January 1956): 141–181.

————. *Seiyō kyōiku inyū no hōhō* (The process of importing Western education). Tokyo: Kōdansha, 1961.

Ogata, Sadako. "The Role of Liberal Non-governmental Organizations in Japan." In *Pearl Harbor as History,* edited by Dorothy Borg and Shumpei Okamoto, 459–486. New York: Columbia University Press, 1972.

Okada Asatarō. "Bungei no kaishaku to kyōju no genron [The interpretation of the personnel regulations and the speech of professors]." *Kokka Gakkai zasshi* 19, no. 10 (October 1905). 13–24.

Okamoto, Shumpei. "The Emperor and the Crowd: The Historical Significance of the Hibiya Riots." In *Conflict in Modern Japanese History: The Neglected Tradition,* edited by Tetsuo Najita and J. Victor Koschmann, 258–275. Princeton, N.J.: Princeton University Press, 1982.

———. *The Japanese Oligarchy and the Russo-Japanese War.* New York: Columbia University Press, 1970.

Ōkōchi Kazuo. *Shakai seisaku yonjūnen: Tsuioku to iken* (Forty years of social policy: Reminiscences and opinions). Tokyo: Tōkyō Daigaku Shuppankai, 1970.

Ōkubo Toshiaki. "The Birth of the Modern University in Japan." *Cahiers d'histoire mondiale* 10, no. 4 (1967): 763–779.

———. "Meiji shonen no gakkō mondai to Kōgakujo [The Kogakujo and the school problem in the early years of Meiji]." *Rekishi chiri* 69, no. 1 (January 1937): 37–57; 69, no. 2 (February 1937): 29–54; 69, no. 3 (March 1937): 53–58.

———. "Meiji shonen no gakushinmatsuri ni tsuite [Concerning academic rituals in the early years of Meiji]." *Kokugakuin zasshi* (January 1939): 60–65; 45, no. 2 (February 1939): 33–48.

———. *Nihon no daigaku* (The university in Japan). Tokyo: Sōgensha, 1945.

Olsen, Lawrence. *Dimensions of Japan.* New York: American Universities Field Staff, 1963.

Olsen, Marvin E., ed. *Power in Societies.* New York: Macmillan, 1970.

Ōmori Gitarō. "Materiarisumusu—miritansu [Materialism and militantism]." *Kaizō* (December 1927): 17–32.

Ōmori Yoshitarō. "Gakkō sōdō uraomote [Behind the strife in the schools]." *Chūōkōron* 45, no. 8 (August 1930): 213–220.

———. "Kawai kyōju no denmei o hanbaku suru [In refutation of Professor Kawai's explanation)." *Nihon hyōron* (December 1935): 33–55.

Ooms, Herman. *Tokugawa Ideology.* Princeton, N.J.: Princeton University Press, 1985.

Ōshima Kiyoshi. *Takano Iwasaburō den* (The biography of Takano Iwasaburō). Tokyo: Iwanami Shoten, 1968.

Ōtsuki Fumihiko. *Mitsukuri Rinshō kun den* (The biography of Mitsukuri Rinshō). Tokyo: Maruzen, 1907.

Ōuchi Hyōe. *Keizaigaku gojūnen* (Fifty years in the study of economics). 2 vols. Tokyo: Tōkyō Daigaku Shuppankai, 1959.

———. "Tōdai gakusei seikatsu no ichidanmen— 'Tōkyō Daigaku daigakusei seikatsu chōsa hōkoku' o yomu [One aspect of the life of today's students—on reading 'The Tokyo Imperial University report on the survey on the lives of students']." *Kaizō* (August 1935): 1–17.

———. *Watakushi no rirekisho* (My curriculum vitae). Tokyo: Kawade Shobō, 1956.

Ōuchi Hyōe and Tsuchiya Takao, eds. *Meiji zenki keizai shiryō shū* (Collected materials on the economy and finances of the early Meiji period). 21 vols. Tokyo: Ōkurashō, 1961.

Packard, George R., III. *Protest in Tokyo: The Security Treaty Crisis of 1960.* Princeton, N.J.: Princeton University Press, 1966.

Parsons, Talcott, and Gerald D. Platt. *The American University.* Cambridge, Mass.: Harvard University Press, 1973.

Passin, Herbert. "Japan." In *Education and Political Development,* edited by

James S. Coleman, 272–312. Princeton, N.J.: Princeton University Press, 1965.

———. *Japanese Education: A Bibliography of Materials in the English Language.* New York: Teachers College, 1970.

———. "Modernization and the Japanese Intellectual: Some Comparative Observations." In *Changing Japanese Attitudes Toward Modernization,* edited by Marius B. Jensen, 447–487. Princeton, N.J.: Princeton University Press, 1965.

———. *Society and Education in Japan.* New York: Teachers College, 1965.

———. "Writer and Journalist in the Transitional Society." In *Communications and Political Development,* edited by Lucien W. Pye, 82–123. Princeton, N.J.: Princeton University Press, 1963.

Pempel, T. J. *Patterns of Japanese Decision-Making: Experiences from Higher Education.* Boulder, Colo.: Westview Press, 1978.

Pritchard, R. John, and Sonia Magbanua Zaide, eds. *The Tokyo War Crimes Trials: The Complete Transcripts of the Proceedings of the International Military Tribunal for the Far East.* 22 vols. New York: Garland, 1981.

Pye, Lucien W., ed. *Communications and Political Development.* Princeton, N.J.: Princeton University Press, 1963.

Pyle, Kenneth B. "Advantages of Followership: German Economics and Japanese Bureaucrats, 1890–1915," *Journal of Japanese Studies* 1, no. 1 (Autumn 1974): 127–164.

———. "The Technology of Japanese Nationalism: The Local Improvement Movement, 1900–1918." *Journal of Asian Studies* 23, no. 1 (November 1973): 51–65.

Rieff, Philip, ed. *On Intellectuals: Theoretical Studies, Case Studies.* New York: Doubleday, 1969.

Roden, Donald T. *Schooldays in Imperial Japan: A Study in the Culture of a Student Elite.* Berkeley and Los Angeles: University of California Press, 1980.

Rōyama Masamichi. "Kyōdai gakusei ni atauru no gaki [A letter to the students of Kyoto University]." *Chūōkōron* 48, no. 10 (October 1933): 43–52.

———. "Tōdai shukugaku mondai to watakushi no shinkyō [The Tōdai purge problem and my state of mind]." *Bungei shunjū* (May 1939): 139–144.

Rubinger, Richard. *Private Academies of Tokugawa Japan.* Princeton, N.J.: Princeton University Press, 1982.

Sakisaka Itsurō. *Arashi no naka no hyakunen: Gakumon dan'atsu shoshi* (A century amidst the storm: A short history of the suppression of scholarship). Tokyo: Keisō Shobō, 1952.

———. "Ishihama, Ōmori, Arisawa, Yamada, Hirano [Ishihama, Ōmori, Arisawa, Yamada, and Hirano]." *Chūōkōron* 46, no. 9 (September 1931): 156–169.

———. *Nagare ni kōshite: Aru shakaishugisha no jigazō* (Against the current: A self-portrait of a socialist). Tokyo: Kōdansha, 1964.

Sakurai Jōji. *Omoide no kazukazu: Danshaku Sakurai Jōji ikō* (Memories of many things: The unpublished writings of Baron Sakurai Jōji). Tokyo: Herado, 1940.

Sanders, Jane. *Cold War on Campus*. Seattle: University of Washington Press, 1979.

Sasa Hiroo. "Daigaku sōchō ron [Discussions of university presidents]." *Kaizō* (September 1933): 176–192; reprinted in Sasa Hiroo. *Jinbutsu shunjū* (Biographical annals). Tokyo: Kaizōsha, 1933.

Sasaki Kyohei. "A Western Influence on Japanese Economic Thought: The Marxian–Non-Marxian Controversies in the 1920s and Their Significance for Today." Ph.D. diss., Columbia University, 1957.

Sasaki Sōichi. "Daigaku kyōju no kenkyū no genkai [Limitations on the research of university professors]." *Hōgaku ronsō* 3, no. 3 (March 1920): 18–41.

———. *Sorin* (Sparse woods). Kyoto: Kōbunsha, 1947.

Sasaki Sōichi et al. *Kyōdai jiken* (The Kyoto University affair). Tokyo: Iwanami Shoten, 1933.

Sawayanagi Masatarō. *Sawayanagi zenshū* (The works of Sawayanagi Masatarō). 6 vols. Tokyo: Sawayanagi Zenshū Kankōkai, 1925–1926.

Scalapino, Robert A., and Junnosuke Masumi. *Parties and Politics in Contemporary Japan*. Berkeley and Los Angeles: University of California Press, 1967.

Scheiner, Irwin. *Christian Converts and Social Protest in Meiji Japan*. Berkeley and Los Angeles: University of California Press, 1970.

Schrecker, Ellen W. *No Ivory Tower: McCarthyism and the Universities*. New York: Oxford University Press, 1986.

Schubert, Glendon. "Judges and Political Leadership." In *Political Leadership in Industrialized Societies,* edited by Lewis J. Edinger, 220–265. New York: Wiley, 1967.

Seabury, Paul, ed. *Universities in the Western World*. New York: Free Press, 1975.

Searing, Donald D. "Models and Images of Man and Society in Leadership Theory." *Journal of Politics* 30, no. 1 (February 1969): 3–31.

Sekiguchi Tai. "Teikoku Daigaku no mondai [The Imperial University problem]." *Chūōkōron* 53, no. 4 (April 1938): 354–361.

Shakai Seisaku Gakkaishi Kōiinkai, eds. "Shakai Seisaku Gakkai nenpu [Chronology of the Social Policy Study Association]." *Shakai Seisaku Gakkai nenpō* 8 (1960) (Special issue).

Shakai Shisō Kenkyūkai, eds. *Kawai Eijirō denki to tsuisō* (A biography and reminiscences of Kawai Eijirō). Tokyo: Shakai Shisō Kenkyūkai Shuppanbu, 1948.

Shida Kotarō. "Teikoku Daigaku kyōju no chii [The status of imperial university professors]." *Kokka Gakkai zasshi* 9, no. 10 (October 1905): 60–62.

Shigehisa Tokutarō. "Goyatoi gaijin Eigo kyōshi" [Foreign employees as English teachers]." In *Nihon no Eigaku hyakunen: Meiji hen* (One hundred years of English studies in Japan: Meiji period), edited by Nihon no Eigaku Hyakunen Henshūbu, 404–440. Tokyo: Kenkyūsha, 1960.

———. *Oyatoi gaikokujin, 5: Kyōiku, shukyō* (Foreign employees, 5: Education and religion). Tokyo: Noma Kenkyūjo Shuppankai, 1968.

Shillony, Ben-ami. "Universities and Students in Wartime Japan." *Journal of Asian Studies* 45, no. 4 (August 1986): 769–787.

Shils, Edward A. "Toward a Modern Intellectual Community in the New States." In *Education and Political Development,* edited by James S. Coleman, 498–518. Princeton, N.J.: Princeton University Press, 1965.

Shimizu Hideo. "Tōkyō Daigaku hōgakubu [The Tokyo University Law Department)." *Tenpo* 76 (April 1965): 110–129.

———. *Tōkyō Daigaku hōgakubu: Nihon erīto no manmosu kichi* (The Tokyo University Law Department: The mammoth base of Japan's elite). Tokyo: Kōdansha, 1965.

Shimizu Hiroo, ed. *Kōtō kyōiku no taishūka* (The shift toward mass higher education). Tokyo: Daiichi Hōki Shuppansha, 1968.

Shimizu Yoshihiro, ed. *Nihon no kōtō kyōiku* (Higher education in Japan). Tokyo: Daiichi Hōki Shuppan Kaisha, 1968.

"Shin Teikoku Daigaku sōchō [New presidents for the imperial universities]." *Kyōiku Jiron* 1011 (May 1913): 26.

Shinbori Michiya. *Nihon no daigaku kyōju shijō: Gakubatsu no kenkyū* [The marketplace for Japanese college professors: A study of academic factions). Tokyo: Tōyōkan, 1965.

Shinbori Michiya, ed. *Gakubatsu* (School factions). Tokyo: Fukumura Shuppan Kaisha, 1974.

Shokuin roku (Register of government employees). Tokyo: Ōkurashō Insatsu Kyoku, annually from 1886.

Shūgiin Sangiin. *Gikai seido shichijūnenshi: Kizoku Sangiin giin meiroku* [Seventy-year history of the Diet system: Rosters of the House of Peers and the House of Councillors). Tokyo: Ōkurashō Insatsu Kyoku, 1950.

Silberman, Bernard S. "Bureaucratic Development and the Structure of Decision-Making in Japan, 1868–1925." *Journal of Asian Studies* 29, no. 2 (February 1970): 347–362.

———. "The Bureaucratic State in Japan: The Problem of Authority and Legitimacy." In *Conflict in Modern Japanese History: The Neglected Tradition,* edited by Tetsuo Najita and J. Victor Koschmann, 226–257. Princeton, N.J.: Princeton University Press, 1982.

———. "The Democracy Movement in Japan." Ph.D. diss., University of Michigan, 1956.

———. "Elite Transformation in the Meiji Restoration: The Upper Civil Service, 1868–1873." In *Modern Japanese Leadership: Tradition and Change,* edited by Bernard S. Silberman and H. D. Harootunian, 233–259. Tucson: University of Arizona Press, 1966.

———. *Ministers of Modernization: Elite Mobility in the Meiji Restoration.* Tucson: University of Arizona Press, 1964.

Silberman, Bernard S., and H. D. Harootunian, eds. *Japan in Crisis: Essays in Taishō Democracy.* Princeton, N.J.: Princeton University Press, 1974.

———. *Modern Japanese Leadership: Tradition and Change.* Tucson: University of Arizona Press, 1966.

Smelser, Neil J. "Epilogue: Social-Structural Dimensions of Higher Education." In *The American University,* edited by Talcott Parsons and Gerald D. Platt, 389–422. Cambridge, Mass.: Harvard University Press, 1973.

———. "Growth, Structural Change and Conflict in California Public Higher Education, 1950–1970." In *Public Higher Education in California,* edited by Neil J. Smelser and Gabriel Almond, 9–141. Berkeley and Los Angeles: University of California Press, 1974.

Smelser, Neil J., and Gabriel Almond, eds. *Public Higher Education in California.* Berkeley and Los Angeles: University of California Press, 1974.

Smethurst, Richard J. "The Military Reserve Association and the Minobe Crisis of 1935." In *Crisis Politics in Prewar Japan: Institutional and Ideological Problems of the 1930s,* edited by George M. Wilson, 1–23. Tokyo: Sophia University Press, 1970.

Smith, Henry D., II. *Japan's First Student Radicals.* Cambridge, Mass.: Harvard University Press, 1972.

Spaulding, Robert M., Jr. "The Bureaucracy as a Political Force, 1920–1945." In *Dilemmas of Growth in Prewar Japan,* edited by James William Morley, 33–80. Princeton, N.J.: Princeton University Press, 1971.

———. *Imperial Japan's Higher Civil Service Examinations.* Princeton, N.J.: Princeton University Press, 1967.

Steinhoff, Patricia G. "Tenkō: Ideology and Societal Integration in Prewar Japan." Ph.D. diss., Harvard University, 1969.

Suehiro Izutarō. *Dancho zengo—ikō to nikki* (Before and after the heartbreak—unpublished writings and diary). Tokyo: Hitotsubusha, 1962.

Suh, Doo Soo. "The Struggle for Academic Freedom in Japanese Universities before 1945." Ph.D. diss., Columbia University, 1953.

Sumiya Etsuji. "Kyōdai hōgakubu Konjaku monogatari [Tales of time past in the Kyoto Law Department]." *Chūōkōron* 48, no. 7 (July 1933): 273–288.

Sumiya Mikio. "Shakai undō no hassei to shakai shisō [Social thought and the birth of the social movement]." In *Iwanami Koza Nihon no rekishi* (Iwanami Series on Japanese history), edited by Ienaga Saburō et al., vol. 18, 153–196. Tokyo: Iwanami Shoten, 1963.

Sumiya, Mikio, and Koji Taira, eds. *An Outline of Japanese Economic History, 1603–1940: Major Works and Research Findings.* Tokyo: University of Tokyo Press, 1979.

Suzuki Bunji. *Rōdō undō nijūnen* (Twenty years in the labor movement). Tokyo: Ichigensha, 1931.

Suzuki Kōichirō. *Ichizu no hito—Tōdai no keizaigakushatachi* [Earnest men—Tōdai's economists]. Tokyo: Shin Hyōron, 1978.

Tabata Shinobu. *Katō Hiroyuki* (Katō Hiroyuki). Tokyo: Yoshikawa Kobunkan, 1959.

Tachi Akira. "Taishō sannen no Teikoku Daigakurei kaiseian to Tōkyō Teikoku Daigaku [Tokyo Imperial University and the 1914 bill for amending the imperial university ordinance]." *Tōkyō Daigakushi kiyō* 1 (February 1978): 38–62.

Taira, Koji. "Factory Legislation and Management Modernization During Japan's Industrialization, 1886–1916." *Business History Review* 45, no. 1 (Spring 1970): 84–109.

Takahashi Sakue. "Kokusai hōgakusha no genron [The speech of scholars of international law]." *Kokka Gakkai zasshi* 19, no. 10 (October 1905): 91–92.

Takane Gijin. *Daigaku seido kanken* (An opinion on the university system). Tokyo: Hōbunkan, 1902.

Takane Masa'aki. "Factors Influencing the Mobility of the Japanese Political Elite: 1860–1920." Ph.D. diss., University of California, 1972.

Takano Iwasaburō. *Kappa no he: Ikōshū* (Kappa Flatus: A posthumous collection). Edited by Suzuki Kōichirō. Tokyo: Hōsei Daigaku Shuppan Kyoku, 1961.

Takayanagi, Kenzo. "A Century of Innovation: The Development of Japanese Law, 1868–1961." In *Law in Japan: The Legal Order in a Changing Society,* edited by Arthur Taylor von Mehren, 5–40. Cambridge, Mass.: Harvard University Press, 1963.

Takigawa Yukitoki. *Gekiryū—Shōwa rejisutansu no danmen* (Raging current: An instance of resistance in the Shōwa period). Tokyo: Kawade Shobō Shinsha, 1963.

———. *Kenkyū no jiyū* (Freedom of research). Tokyo: Seikatsusha, 1947.

Takimoto Eikichi. "Tōdai hōgakubu to Kyōdai hōgakubu [The Tōdai Law Department and the Kyōdai Law Department]." *Kaizō* (August 1933): 161–167.

Tamura Ichio, "Tōdai funjō uchimakubanashi [Tales from behind the scenes of the commotion at Tōdai]." *Chūōkōron* 55, no. 3 (March 1940): 206–210.

Tanaka Kōtarō. *Ikite kita michi* (The road by which I have come)." 2nd edition. Tokyo: Kawade Shobō Shinsha, 1963.

———. *Kyōiku to ken'i* (Education and authority). Tokyo: Keisō Shobō, 1949.

Tanaka Kōtarō, Suekawa Hiroshi, Wagatsuma Sakae, Ōuchi Hyōe, and Miyazawa Toshiyoshi. *Daigaku no jiji* (University self-government). Tokyo: Asahi Shinbunsha, 1963.

Tanaka Sōgorō. *Yoshino Sakuzō: Nihonteki demokurashī shito* (Yoshino Sakuzō: An apostle of Japanese democracy). Tokyo: Miraisha, 1958.

"Teikoku Daigaku hyōgikai kirokushō [The summary minutes of the University Council, Imperial University of Tokyo, 1886–1930]." In the University Archives, University of Tokyo.

Terao Tōru. "Gakusetsu to seiron [Scholarly theory and political discourse]." *Kokka Gakkai zasshi* 19, no. 10 (October 1905): 7–12.

Terasaki Masao. "Daigakushi bunken mokuroku [Bibliography for the history of universities]." *Kyōikugaku kenkyū* 32, nos. 2–3 (1965): 62–109.

———. "Kōtō kyōiku [Higher education]." In *Inoue Kowashi no kyōiku seisaku* (The educational policies of Inoue Kowashi), edited by Kaigo Tokiomi, 299–464. Tokyo: Tōkyō Daigaku Shuppankai, 1968.

———. "Nihon no daigaku ni okeru jijiteki kankō no keisei [The formation of the tradition of academic autonomy in modern universities in Japan]." *Kyōikugaku kenkyū* 32, nos. 1–2 (1965): 134–147.

———. "Teikoku Daigaku keiseiki no daigakukan [Views of the university in the formative period of the imperial university]." In *Gakkōkan no shiteki kenkyū,* edited by Teresaki Masao et al., 183–265. Tokyo: Noma Kyōiku Kenkyūjo, 1972.

Terasaki Masao et al. *Gakkōkan no shiteki kenkyū* (Historical research on views of schools). Tokyo: Noma Kyōiku Kenkyūjo, 1972.

Tipton, Elise K. "The Civil Police in the Suppression of the Prewar Japanese Left." Ph.D. diss., Indiana University, 1977.

Titus, David Anson. *Palace and Politics in Prewar Japan.* New York: Columbia University Press, 1974.

Tōkyō Daigaku Hyakunenshi Henshūiinkai, eds. *Tōkyō Daigaku hyakunenshi* (The hundred-year history of Tokyo University). 9 vols. Tokyo: Tōkyō Daigaku, 1984–1985.

Tōkyō Daigaku Keizaigakubu. *Tōkyō Daigaku keizaigakubu gojūnenshi* (The fifty-year history of the Tokyo University Economics Department). Tokyo: Tōkyō Daigaku Shuppankai, 1976.

Tōkyō Teikoku Daigaku. *Tōkyō Teikoku Daigaku gakujutsu taikan* (An overview of scholarship at Tokyo Imperial University). 5 vols. Tokyo: Tōkyō Teikoku Daigaku, 1942–1944.

———. *Tōkyō Teikoku Daigaku gojūnenshi* (Fifty years of Tokyo Imperial University). 2 vols. Tokyo: Tōkyō Teikoku Daigaku, 1932.

———. *Teikoku Daigaku ichiran* (Imperial university catalog). Tokyo: Teikoku Daigaku, 1889 and 1891.

Tomizu Hiroto. *Kaikoroku* (Memoirs). Tokyo: Author, 1904.

———. *Zoku kaikoroku* (Memoirs continued). Tokyo: Yūhikaku Shobō, 1906.

Totten, George O., III. *The Social Democratic Movement in Prewar Japan.* New Haven, Conn.: Yale University Press, 1966.

Tōyama Shigeki. "Ishin no henkaku to kindaiteki chishikijin no tanjō [Restoration reforms and the birth of the modern intellectual]." In *Kindai Nihon shisōshi kōza,* edited by Itō Yoshio et al., vol. 4, 155–195. Tokyo: Chikuma Shobō, 1952.

Tōyama Shigeki, Imai Seiichi, and Fujiwara Akira. *Shōwashi* (A history of the Shōwa period). Tokyo: Iwanami Shoten, 1974.

Tsurumi Shunsuke et al. *Tenkō* (Conversion). 3 vols. Tokyo: Heibonsha, 1960–1962.

Ukai Nobushige et al., eds. *Nihon kindai hō hattatsushi* (A history of the development of modern Japanese law). 10 vols. Tokyo: Keisō Shobō, 1958.

Umetani Noboru. *Oyatoi gaikokujin, I: Gaisetsu* (Foreign employees, I: Overview). Tokyo: Noma Kenkyūjo Shuppankai, 1968.

———. *Oyatoi gaikokujin: Meiji Nihon no wakiyakutachi* (Foreign employees: Supporting players in Meiji Japan). Tokyo: Nihon Keizai Shinpōsha, 1965.

———. *The Role of Foreign Employees in the Meiji Era in Japan,* Tokyo: Institute of Developing Economies, 1971.

"University and Society." *Journal of Social and Political Ideas in Japan* 5, nos. 2–3 (December 1967) (Special issue).

"University Reform." *Journal of Social and Political Ideas in Japan* 1, no. 2 (August 1963) (Special issue).

Ushiomi Toshitaka. *Hōritsuka* (Men of the law). Tokyo: Iwanami Shoten, 1970.

Ushiomi Toshitaka and Toshitani Nobuyoshi, eds. *Nihon no hōgakusha* (Legal scholars of Japan). Tokyo: Nihon Hyōronsha, 1975.

Vogel, Ezra F., ed. *Modern Japanese Organization and Decision-Making*. Berkeley and Los Angeles: University of California Press, 1975.

Von Mehren, Arthur Taylor, ed. *Law in Japan: The Legal Order in a Changing Society*. Cambridge, Mass.: Harvard University Press, 1963.

Wagatsuma Sakae. "Teikoku Daigaku dokuritsu anshiko: Daigaku [A private plan for the independence of the imperial university]." *Jurisuto* 259 (October 1962): 25.

Wagatsuma Sakae et al., eds. *Nihon seiji saiban shiroku* (Historical record of political trials in Japan). 5 vols. Tokyo: Daiichi Hōki Kaisha, 1969–1970.

Wakata, Kyoji. "Japanese Diet Members: Social Background, General Values, and Role Perception." Ph.D. diss., Rice University, 1977.

Ward, Robert E, and Dankwart A. Rustow, eds. *Modernization in Japan and Turkey*. Princeton, N.J.: Princeton University Press, 1964.

Waseda Daigaku. *Hanseki no Waseda* (A half-century of Waseda University). Tokyo: Waseda Daigaku Shuppanbu, 1932.

———. *Kindai Nihon no shakai kagaku to Waseda Daigaku* (Waseda University and the social sciences in modern Japan). Tokyo: Waseda Daigaku, 1957.

Waseda Daigaku Daigakushi Shiryō Shitsu, eds. *Waseda Daigaku hachijūnenshi* (A history of Waseda University over eighty years). Tokyo: Waseda Daigaku, 1962.

Waseda Daigaku Shichijūnen Kinen Shuppaniinkai, eds. *Nihon no kindai bungei to Waseda Daigaku* (Waseda University and the modern arts in Japan). Tokyo: Waseda Daigaku, 1957.

Watanabe, Shinichi, comp. *A Select List of Books on the History of Education in Japan and a Selected List of Periodicals on Education*. Ann Arbor: Asia Library and the Center for Japanese Studies, University of Michigan, 1976.

Watanabe Shūjirō. "Bakumatsu jidai oyobi Meiji shonen no yōkō ryūgakusei [Overseas students at the end of the shogunate and the early years of Meiji]." *Meiji bunka kenkyū* 3, no. 4 (April 1927): 2–12.

Wheeler, John K. "Rōyama Masamichi and the Search for a Middle Ground, 1932–1940." *Papers on Japan*, vol. 6, 70–101. Cambridge, Mass.: East Asian Research Center, Harvard University, 1963.

Wilkinson, Rupert, ed. *Governing Elites: Studies in Training and Selection*. New York: Oxford University Press, 1969.

Wilson, George M., ed. *Crisis Politics in Prewar Japan: Institutional and Ideological Problems of the 1930s*. Tokyo: Sophia University Press, 1970.

Wray, Harry, and Hilary Conroy, eds. *Japan Examined: Perspectives on Modern Japanese History*. Honolulu: University of Hawaii Press, 1983.

Yabe Teiji. *Yabe Teiji nikki* (The diary of Yabe Teiji). Tokyo: Yomiuru Shinbun, 1974.

Yamada Fumio. "Tōdai keizaigakubu mondai no shinsō [The facts about the problem in the Tokyo University Economics Department]." *Kaizō* (March 1939): 71–80.

Yamada Saburō. *Kaikoroku* (Memoirs). Tokyo: Yamada Saburō Sensei Beiju Shukaga, 1957.

Yamamura Kozo, and Susan B. Hanley, "Ichihime, ni Tarō: Educational Aspirations and the Decline in Fertility in Postwar Japan." *Journal of Japanese Studies* 2, no. 1 (Autumn 1975): 83–125.

Yamanaka Einosuke. "Meijiki Nihon no seiōhō keiju ni kansuru kenkyū [Research on Japan's adoption of Western European law during the Meiji period]." *Hōseishi kenkyū* 22 (1973): 161–171.

Yamanouchi, Tarō. "Daigaku to Senmon gakkō [Universities and colleges]." In *Rinji Kyōiku Kaigi no kenkyū* (Research on the special conference on education), edited by Kaigo Tokiomi, 465–550. Tokyo: Tōkyō Daigaku Shuppankai, 1968.

Yanaga, Chitoshi. *Big Business in Japanese Politics.* New Haven, Conn.: Yale University Press, 1968.

Yanaihara Tadao. *Watakushi no ayunde kita michi* (The road by which I have come). Tokyo: Tōkyō Daigaku Shuppankai, 1958.

Yasko, Richard. "Hiranuma Kiichiro and Conservative Politics in Prewar Japan." Ph.D. diss., University of Chicago, 1973.

Yasuba Yasukichi. "Anatomy of the Debate on Japanese Capitalism." *Journal of Japanese Studies* 2, no. 1 (Autumn 1975): 63–82.

Yoshino, M. Y. *Japan's Managerial System: Tradition and Innovation.* Boston: MIT Press, 1968.

Yoshino Sakuzō. "Daigaku ni taisuru shisō dan'atsu [The suppression of thought in the university]." *Chūōkōron* 43, no. 6 (June 1928): 57–62.

———. "Kyōju to seitōin to no ryōritsu furyōritsu [Professor and political party member: Compatible or incompatible?]." *Chūōkōron* 42, no. 3 (March 1927): 176–181.

Index

Compositor: Braun-Brumfield, Inc.
Text: 10/13 Galliard
Display: Galliard
Printer: Braun-Brumfield, Inc.
Binder: Braun-Brumfield, Inc.